VANISHED HOUSES
OF
CORNWALL

Rosemary Lauder

Published by North Devon Books, North Devon

ISBN 978-0-9528645-1-6

Printed by Short Run Press Ltd, Exeter, Devon

Contents

Stowe

'But, whilst we flatter ourselves with ideas of permanence, we must not forget **Nanswhiden** – we must remember **Stowe**. The superb edifices which have perished the splendid families which have been extinguished, call forth the most effecting sentiments of melancholy. And we contemplate with a sigh, and "not without a fear" the fleetingness of mortal prosperity – the awful uncertainty of human grandeur. Under such dispensations of mysterious wisdom, we learn important lessons; They humble our pride, and instruct our reason.'

The History of Cornwall, Vol 3. Richard Polwhele 1803

Author's Note & Acknowledgements

This is the story of a number of houses, once well known and full of life, now vanished from the scene. When I embarked on this project – beginning with Stowe because I live within a few miles of that intriguing site – I had no idea how many lost houses I would find. A few I knew of , but my research through almost every book that has been written on the history of Cornwall revealed a long list. My choice was determined by those of which some record remained and whose owners had been important and interesting.

I have not set out to write a definitive work; rather this is an attempt to trace the history of the houses and their owners, and set it down before much of it is lost. After many decades of lack of interest, it is heartening to see a surge, a reawakening, in the past and a desire to set it in the context of the present. Hopefully, this book is a step in that direction. Many long years have gone into its research and I have striven for accuracy – but there are bound to be errors which I hope will be forgiven.

Along the way I have met with great kindness and patience. The list of those who have helped me is a long one and research was not helped by the fact only one of the owners – the Sneyds at Coldrenick – retain any link with their former properties. In many cases the trail had grown very cold. The book could not have been written without the tireless help of the staff at the Cornwall Record Office, then situated in the grounds of the former County Hall. Invaluable, too, were the librarian and staff at the Courtney Library, Royal Institution of Cornwall, and at The Cornish Studies Library. I received help from many individuals, providing me with old press cuttings, snippets of information here, memories there, and was fortunate to be given great help, support and encouragement from many people, in particular from one scholarly gentleman to whom I am deeply indebted, otherwise the book would never have been finished. Research on this sort of project never is completely finished – always one more source, one more memory. I have also tried to find the owners of the various illustrations used but in some cases, unsuccessfully, for which I apologize.

I am very indebted to Dr. Jo Mattingley who edited the manuscript for me, and encouraged me.

It has been hugely enjoyable and I have discovered many unknown corners of the county – I hope you enjoy the result.

Bibliography

Cornwall is rich in the number of books on its history, some very old, some not so, and some written recently. I have delved into most of them and gleaned fragments in all sorts of places – far too numerous to list. Given below are the principal sources, common to most books about the county. Specific sources are listed at the end of each chapter.

An Historical Survey of Cornwall (1817–20) C. S. Gilbert
A Parochial History of Cornwall (1838) Davies Gilbert
Mansions of England and Wales; County of Cornwall (1846) Edward Twycross
Observations on the Antiquities Historical and Monumental, of the County of Cornwall (1754) William Borlase
Natural History of Cornwall (1758) William Borlase
The Parks and Gardens of Cornwall (1998) Douglas Ellory Pett
The Buildings of England (1970) Nikolaus Pevsner
The Book of the House of Spoure (1694)
Magna Britannia (1814) Daniel Lysons

Introduction

If Cornwall has lost fewer great houses than some other counties, one reason is because there were less to lose in the first place. Cornwall has always been at the end of a long road from the capital, and before that road was properly surfaced, the distance was prohibitive. And when travelling did become easier, the traffic tended to flow out of the county rather than in. For anyone involved in politics or the law, with long months spent in the capital, a London house was a necessity rather than a luxury. Their Cornish estates were largely left in the hands of relatives or agents.

What the county was rich in, when Cornish squires were content to stay put, were a large number of small or medium-sized manor houses, some little more than glorified farmhouses. The seventeenth century *Book of the House of Spoure* illustrates many such and the county's many history books record some of them.

This is the Draught of Crockadon the Mansion house of Peter Trevila Esq.

Some had been major estates;

'Cardinham Castle, once an important seat of the mighty Dinham family, comprising 71 knight's fees, is now a crumbling ruin …'

In the very early years of the sixteenth century the male line died out, and the Cardinham estate was divided amongst the daughters of the last Lord Dinham.

The long history of Trematon Castle, Saltash, overlooking the Hamoaze, dates back to at least the time of William the Conqueror. It passed from the Valletorts to the Duchy of Cornwall, but was

Crocadon from The Book of the House of Spoure
(Courtesy Lady Rennell)

recorded as being ruinous by the time of Elizabeth I. Nothing remains of the original domestic buildings, replaced in 1807 with a Georgian house, built for the agent of the Duchy lands.

Gone, too, is all trace of the summer residence of the Bishop's of Exeter in the quiet fields of Lawhitton, near Lauceston.

The original home of the Trelawny family was in the upland parish of Altarnun – the barton of Tre-lawn-y – the oak grove town – '… but now there is not left standing any house or trees' wrote Jonathan Couch in 1867. He continues that some of the inhabitants of the parish told him that 'tradition saith the greatest of the stones that built the present church and tower of Altarnun were provided from the dilapidated walls of Trelawny and much of the oak timber that roofs the same was also cut and carried from the barton.' There is in the north of the parish a farm called Trelawne, supposedly the site. Gilbert states that this was the property of the Trelawnys before the Norman conquest, and the manor was purchased from them by the Vyvyans in 1791. The mansion, with a deer park, was the home of Sir John Trelawny, a 'distinguished military gentleman in the time of Henry V', whose eldest son died without issue, and the property was divided between his daughters. 'The house fell into ruins and is now utterly destroyed.'

Also owned by the Trelawnys was the house at Pool in Menheniot parish. This was where they lived for several generations before moving to Trelawny House in Pelynt,

Pool

around 1600, and was described as 'being in decay, with a large gothic opening on to a quadrangle of mean buildings which are divided into sixteen dwellings.' It had become the parish poorhouse, but all this was replaced by a 'neat villa'. Pool was once renowned for its extensive deer park, of which only traces of the wall remain. Inside the church are several memorials to the Trelawnys, all that remains of their presence in the parish.

In the same parish, Trenant was recorded as 'charmingly situated on an eminence overlooking the winding vale, richly wooded and watered by the river Seaton.' The Honey family had been the owners in the time of Charles II, and was the property of the Revd. John Honey of Liskeard when it burnt down around 1790.

On the banks of the Lynher river as it makes its way south from Altarnun were Upton and Trebartha. Upton, once the home of John Upton, Viscount Templedown and described as a 'most ancient and honourable house' passed through several hands before becoming the property of Col. Rodd of Trebartha, who decided to demolish it and build a farmhouse on the site. The same fate befell several once venerable family seats – including nearby Manaton House. Here a 'plain dwelling erected on the site' but features of antiquity could be found in the stables and other remaining buildings, including a date stone of 1687 with the initials F.M., and some old fishponds below the house.

At Trefrys (Linkinhorne), the map marks an ancient well, which could be all that survives of the 'ruins of a very large house, including an oven nine feet in diameter, once the seat of Lord Trefry, with, at one time, its own chapel.' Lysons mentions the ruins of a great hall with large windows and a chapel a quarter of a mile from the house but 'work was discontinued and no proof and no trace remains.'

Close to the border in the north of the county is Hornacott, now described as 'Barton' but once the home of illustrious families, including the Fitz, Courtenays, Howards, d'Arcy and latterly the Grenvilles, the last of whom died without issue. Perhaps its decay was gradual, and by 1820 it was recorded as 'long since been destroyed' and although the chapel survived, it served 'as a shelter for cattle'.

The Grenville family were also owners of Swannacott in neighbouring Whitestone parish, now a substantial and ancient farmhouse. Whitestone itself was once anciently the property of the Cobham family and passed through several hands before being described as 'approaching to a state of gentle decay.'

The 'large, brick building' at Tremeer, St. Tudy, once the property of the Courtenays was described as partly ruinous. So was Halwin House at St. Issey, once the home of the Hamleys and the Champernownes. Dr. Borlase commented on the ruins of extensive buildings on both sides of the creek, including what had been a private chapel.

A house with a long pedigree that has all but vanished was Inceworth House on the Rame peninsula. Its illustrious neighbours – Mount Edgecumbe, Antony, Port Eliot, and Ince, have all survived, but only the chapel and a few walls remains of Inceworth (in Maker). Henry I granted the manor to Reginald, his natural son, which passed to the Champernowne family. Sir Richard Champernowne was granted licence to erect a chapel there in 1331. At some stage the manor was acquired by the Rolles, and when Lake was writing in 1870, it was owned by Lord Clinton. Gilbert (1820), refers to 'one of the most venerable piles of antiquity known in the neighbourhood, probably built by the Champernownes in the fourteenth century. 'Many of its gothic arches remained and several of its gloomy apartments were inhabited until about 20 years ago, when the whole were taken down except the gothic chapel which is now used as a granary.' Surviving remnants include 100 foot of thick walling with an archway and windows, blocked doors and a fireplace.

A similar fate befell the house known as Golden, or Wolvedon in Probus, the remains of which were demolished around 1800 – parts used as barns. Lysons records a 'magnificent mansion built by the Tregians, or Tregyons, who acquired the estate in 1512 after the last male Wulvedon had died. It was visited by John Leland in 1534–43, who commented that it was 'richly begun but not ended.' The family were Catholic and Francis, in 1577 aged 28, was imprisoned for 20 years as a recusant. Apparently his wife lived with him in prison and of their 18 children, 11 survived.

Wootton House, in Landrake, an estate of some 300 acres, passed through the Woottons, Courtenays and Rouse families but by the end of the eighteenth century had sunk to farmhouse status, and later became ruinous.

Pentillie Castle, so beautifully sited overlooking the river Tamar, was dramatically enlarged in 1810 to the designs of William Wilkins with gothic wing – and reduced back again in 1967.

Pentillie Castle

Old families have a habit of dwindling and dying out, and Cornwall was no exception. Lord de Dunstanville (Francis Basset) expanded on this theme to his visitor Joseph Farington in 1810;

Lord de Dunstanville said that when Carew wrote his account of this county towards the end of the reign of Elizabeth there were then 20 families existing in Cornwall whose ancestors came into England at the Conquest, of which only three or four now remain, Sir John St. Aubyn's & his Lordship's families are included in this number. Lord Falmouth's family is comparatively of modern date; & Sir William Lemon's grandfather was a miner without a shilling, but by industry and good luck acquired £200,000.

And that sums up the change in fortune that occurred with the mining boom. Cornwall was never a wealthy county. Estates based on agricultural returns bumped along. There had always been some tin mining on a small scale and returns began to creep up in the early days of the eighteenth century when the Hanoverian accession brought an end to civil unrest in the country. They continued to rise until the slump of the 1760s. Then from the 1790s for almost a hundred years the returns from copper dramatically changed the fortunes and the face of Cornwall. Suddenly Cornish gentry had incomes to match those in more prosperous counties – and they spent accordingly, although to most of them, their great houses were only occasionally used. Then came the twentieth century with all its woes. Most of the mines had closed by then leaving landowners struggling with large houses and diminished incomes. By the end of the previous century, agriculture had suffered a severe slump, with tenants finding it increasingly difficult to pay their rent which, in turn, meant their landlords had problems meeting their own obligations, such as mortgages and annuities. The Great War dealt a fatal blow, hammered home by successive increases in death duty, which had been around since the end of the eighteenth century, but in a very minor way. In 1894 Death Duty was introduced and in 1909 Lloyd George introduced a tax on land. Asquith in 1914 – as if there weren't enough problems – took estate duty seriously, and with the loss of so many owners and their heirs, this had a deadly impact.

No great names in the world of state or politics came from Cornwall – no Pitt or Walpole, no Marlborough or Wellington, no Churchill or Lloyd George; just a large number of worthy Cornish men content to play their part in a modest way. And when the income from the mines dried up, life in Cornwall sank back to what it had been and the glory days departed.

I have attempted to recapture some of that lost grandeur and the lives of those who built, lived in and worked on the those estates, before their decline.

The end for most of the houses in this book was ignominious – for many a slow decline, ending in the wrecking ball. Only six suffered disastrous fires, causing complete destruction in the case of Trehane, Carclew and Nanswhyden. Clowance and Newton Ferrers were rebuilt, and Thanckes is a rarity – a house that moved. Of the rest, little remains, the building stone plundered, leaving in some cases so little trace that it is difficult to imagine a great house ever existed. In others the stable block and outhouses, usually converted, lodges, park walls – and intriguing humps and bumps are all that is left.

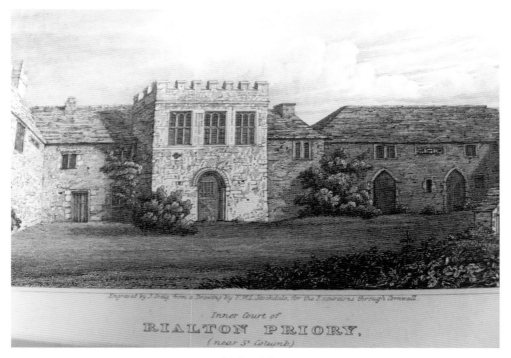

Engraved by J.Dray from a Drawing by F.W.L.Stockdale, for the Excursions through Cornwall.

Inner Court of

RIALTON PRIORY,

(near S.t Columb)

Rialton Manor

History has departed from this tranquil backwater, just a stone's throw from the bustle of Newquay and few now have heard of Rialton. The old buildings have been converted into holiday accommodation and the neighbouring Barton contains all that is left of the once great Priory. Rialton was a Domesday manor and early on was given by the Earl of Cornwall to the Prior of Bodmin. And until Henry VIII's infamous Dissolution of the monasteries came into effect in the mid sixteenth century, so it remained. From what is left, it would seem to have been of considerable size. The last but one Prior, Thomas Vyvyan, is said to have largely rebuilt and extended the main dwelling and it was said to have been a favourite residence; he did not live to see the destruction of both Bodmin and Rialton. Under the last prior, Thomas Wansworth, the manor was leased to John Monday, William Monday and Elizabeth Prideaux for a term of 99 years. This was in 1537, when Henry VIII was beginning his destruction of the monasteries, and the smaller ones were the first to be sold off. In 1599 the lease was surrendered and the manors were granted to John Monday for 31 years at a rent of £60 per annum. 'Royalton, the house of John Myntaye' is marked on Norden's map of 1584.

The Parliamentary Survey of 1649 records Rialton as having an Imp. value of £919 7s 7¼d, with Antony Monday in possession. The same survey gives a description of 'Rialton and Reterth manors in possession of the late King Charles I and Henrietta Maria but now settled on trust for the use of the Commonwealth.'

The said house consisted of one faire Hall and a room adjoining for the servants to dine in, one kitchen, one larder, one brewhouse and a room for cooling the worte, one dairy chamber with a lodging chamber for the servants over it and one buttery: these below stairs. Over the said lower rooms there is one faire dining room with diverse other rooms thereto adjoining viz; kitchen chamber, the upper chamber, the Priors chamber, the chapel chamber, the inner chamber, the maids chamber and chamber at head of the stairs, all of which are in reasonably good repair, the said house be built of stone and the windows barred with iron barres. The outhouses belonging to the said house are as follows, viz; one water corn mill, two stables each of them consisting of three bays of building, one wayne house, one cart house, two barns consisting of eight bays of building, and one oxe house.

The site of the house consisting of one square close in the midst whereof there is a well of fresh water. On the one side of the house there is one outer court, two gardens, two orchards and diverse parcels of waste land near unto the said house and two groves of trees adjoining. Of which site contains six acres of land.

The survey continued with a list of the arable land, all of which, including the house and land, totalled 244½ acres, valued at £203 19s per annum with a separate value of £80 for the trees.

The Prior's dwelling was separated from the other monastic buildings by a courtyard, and when it was owned by Sir Samuel Caseworth in the 1660's was recorded as having 13 hearths, which made it a substantial house. Shortly after this, Rialton became the property of the Godolphin family, and when Sydney Godolphin, (b 1664), was created Baron Godolphin in 1684, he chose Rialton as his title. In 1706 he became Viscount Rialton and Earl of Godolphin, with his son and heir known as Lord Rialton in his father's lifetime.

Pevsner in his *Buildings of England*, described the farmhouse as being of great charm inside and out, with substantial remains from Prior Vyvyan's time, including his study and bedchamber on the first floor. An extra floor had been inserted into the Great Hall but the decorated wagon-roof and great three light windows were untouched. All historians mention the inscribed stone in the farmyard wall, dating back to the fifth or sixth centuries and with a Roman inscription – but its origins are not recorded.

The manor passed out of Godolphin ownership when a Deed of Covenant of the Manor of Rialton, dated 11th November, 1800 was drawn up between John Rowe, Thomas Rawlings and 13 others, naming the property of the late Prior of Bodmin and Convent of the late Priory, the Manor of Rialton.

The manor is listed in the inventory of Thomas Rawlings' property as being held under lease from the Crown, due to expire in October 1841, at £745.14s 1d, granted by George III in December, 1813.

WEARDE HOUSE in Saltash survived until a fire in 1903. It was a quirky house of no great architectural merit, with two small pavilions, built about 1740 for John Harrison, son of Admiral Harrison of Port Damerel, Plymouth. It replaced an older house, which

in 1905 could still be seen hidden away in a valley. Miss Margaret Porter, an overseer of the poor, was recorded as living there in 1690. The grand replacement on the hill had a 40 foot ballroom, an observatory and fine ceilings with bas relief representing the four seasons surrounded with flowers, cupids etc. Over the window was Neptune driving over the sea in his chariot.

Mr Harrison was High Sherriff for Cornwall in 1758 and was succeeded by his son, the Revd. Henry Harrison of Exeter College, Oxford, although a series of tenants were recorded. In 1852, Wearde House 'a capital freehold mansion house, grounds and sundry valuable farms formerly the property of Major Harrison' were offered for sale.

In his book *Around and About Saltash (1905)*, Phillip Porter states that a Mr. Couch 'got possession of the property 60 years ago and opened the quarry with subterranean passages down to the Quay where he had workshops etc, but a lawsuit resulted in his expulsion.' He tells us that the estate now belongs to Sir Richard Pole Carew, but Lady Harrison still owns a 'good many acres at one part of it.'

C R O
GHW/7/2/14/7
FS/3/1215

DUPORTH HOUSE, Charlestown was built in the late 1700s by Charles Rashleigh (d. 1823). He was the developer of the port of Charlestown, who subsequently lost a great deal of money and the property had to be sold, changing hands several times. George Freeth was living at Duporth in 1891 and the next year Walter Sessions paid £8,000 for it and later turned it into a hotel. The next owners made it into a seaside holiday camp with chalets in the grounds. Guests could stay in the house which had the only available bath. During the war Duporth was requisitioned and the Indian army, complete with mules, took over the house for the officers and the soldiers occupied the chalets. One wing was gutted by fire. After the war, the same family, the Rankins, resumed their holiday camp business but on 8th June, 1961 fire swept through the house, leaving it a ruin which was finally demolished in 1989. The Rankins sold out to Butlins in 1976.

Duporth House

NEWTON FERRERS, *St. Mellion*

Fortunately, Newton Ferrers is not lost, but it was a close thing. A disastrous fire in April, 1940 destroyed two thirds of the house, leaving the older domestic wing reduced to rubble and apart from the east wing, little more than a roofless gutted shell. The easiest solution, given the problems of building materials after the war, would have been to walk away from it. Instead it was 'patched up' with a flat concrete roof over the central portion, kitchens created in the basement and the west wing left as an open shell. Pevsner described it as the earliest classical Cornish mansion without Tudor remnants.

Newton Ferrers had been an early possession of the de Ferrers family. In the 13th century the heiress married a Coryton and the manor remained with this family until 1834.

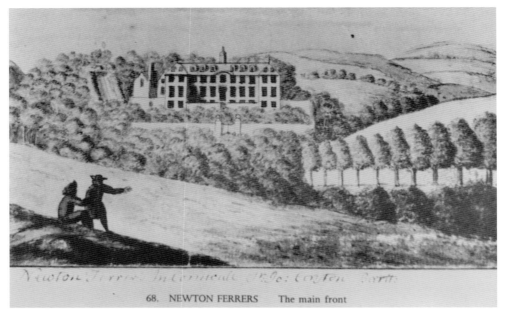

68. NEWTON FERRERS   The main front

Newton Ferrers – Edmund Prideaux, 1727   (courtesy Peter Prideaux Brune)

The existing house was built around 1685 for Sir William Coryton, whose father had been a staunch Royalist rewarded with a baronetcy in 1661. Sir William, who died in 1711, married three times and his third wife was an elderly widow of a wealthy London goldsmith and banker. He built what has been described as the earliest Renaissance house in the Duchy, predating Antony by some twenty years. The earliest drawing is one of Edmund Prideaux's series of houses, dated around 1735. This shows an earlier building alongside, believed to have been the original manor house. The garden front as built had a central bay and pediment, and there was a line of dormers in the roof. There also appears to be a clock tower to the rear. What was, and still is, truly remarkable about Newton House as it was called, was the terracing, balustrading and flights of stone steps. It is fortunate that they have survived, possibly because of the steep nature of the site and possibly because the estate never 'had to be sold'. They are important enough to be Grade I listed, as are the gate piers by the house, which have been broken up and reset since the fire, with the date stone of 1695 taken from the house set in walling now blocking the former entrance.

Sir William's only son, John, died childless and the estate passed to his widow Rachel Helyer. The Helyers, of Croker Court in Somerset, sold Newton Ferrers in 1834 to Edward Collins, whose son Digby, re-roofed the house and probably modernised the interior. *Country Life* visited in 1904, although it is largely the terraces and exterior that was featured. The property remained in the hands of the Collins until 1934 when it was purchased by Sir Robert Abdy.

It is distressing how prone redecorated and finely furnished Georgian houses seem to be to devastating fire. Sir Robert Abdy's exquisite home in Cornwall closely follows the destruction of Buxted which it had rivalled in the value and beauty of its contents. Sir Robert is on active service and Lady Diana was alone with her baby. Happily there was no loss of life in the fire which broke out early in the morning. A good deal of its contents is reported to have been saved including the library – Sir Robert specialises in valuable bindings and fine illustrated books.'

CALLINGTON MANSION DESTROYED BY FIRE.

After the fire

This was the entry that appeared in *Country Life* in April, 1940. Sir Robert had purchased Newton Ferrers just four years earlier and in two years had transformed the interiors with the contents of his former French home including a fine art collection, his library and a large quantity of drapes and swags – all recorded in a well illustrated article in *Country Life* in 1938.

As stated, Sir Robert was away at the time of the fire, and, Lady Abdy set about the reconstruction using whatever materials came to hand, and showing great ingenuity, recreated some of the interiors by painting fake panelling, and replacing those fabulous drapes with curtains made of parachute silk lined with dust sheets, hung on gilded drain pipes!

The east wing was little damaged and retained its panelled interiors.

Newton Ferrers was sold in 1994, and the new owners set about an ambitious restoration programme on the roofless west wing, so that today, from the exterior, Newton Ferrers looks as it always has done.

CRO
AD 1909/38
CY/5041
County Life 17.12.1938, 9.1.1904

Cleave House   (courtesy of R.M. Heard)

CLEAVE HOUSE, *Morwenstow*

Described in 1820 as a neat house surrounded by beautiful open grounds and fine walks – all has been totally obliterated by the coastal headquarters of GCHQ known as Cleave Camp. Coombe valley, deeply wooded and secretive, runs down from Kilkhampton to the sea at Duck Pool. On the southern height is all that remains of 'the Great House of Stowe', and on the northern are the ultra modern dishes of a radar tracking system, fundamental to the security of this country and heavily guarded with high fences and barbed wire. At one time these extended almost to the cliff edge, but latterly more land has been released so that the remains of the war time defences can be seen.

Cleave was originally part of Eastaway Manor, one of the many possessions of the Priory of St. Stephens at Launceston. This passed to the Duchy of Cornwall at the dissolution in the 16th century. In the eighteenth century Dennis Waddon (1697–1764), steward and land agent of the Grenville/Carteret estates in north Cornwall was described as 'of Cleave'.

The 1842 tithe apportionment gives the tenant as Richard Harris, Cleave farm comprising 200 acres with a value of £16 18s 3d. He had six children and three female and four male servants, so lived in some style.

Duchy lands could only be sold with Parliament's permission and accordingly, in 1844, the Prince of Wales was enabled to sell or exchange lands and possessions of the Duchy of Cornwall to purchase other lands and for other purposes. A similar Act was passed in 1863 and Cleave was let to a succession of tenant farmers until it passed to the War Office in January 1939. It had been in use as an airfield for some time previously and now found favour because of the 'excellent field of fire and because few ships passed through the range'. Cleave farmhouse became the officers' mess and gun emplacements – still evident – built on the cliff edge. Tents were followed by Nissen huts and barrack blocks and RAF Cleave was operational. They departed in 1945 and activity ceased on the windswept cliff tops – still owned by the MoD. In 1969 the importance of the site, first recognised all those years before, led to the setting up of CSOS Morwenstow and the first satellite interceptors were installed. This later became known as GCHQ and a third huge silent tracking dish was installed. When a sea mist rolls in over the cliffs, the station takes on a surreal air.

But of Cleave itself, nothing remains except a few ruined farm buildings, a substantial hedge bank surrounding a large field and a footpath running down to Duck Pool from the original house.

PENHALLAM, *Jacobstow*

Deep in a wooded combe, the ruins of the ancient house of the Cardinhams, lay undisturbed for around six centuries. Penhallam is one of Cornwall's most ancient settlements, deserted in the fourteenth century and forgotten ever since. Until the 1960's, when forestry operations uncovered the remains, and someone called in the archeologists.

What was gradually uncovered was the remains of an extensive early settlement, dating from around the twelfth or early thirteenth centuries, with the possibility of even earlier earthworks. Penhallam has survived so well because of its massive stonework foundations and stone walls. Only strong defensive castles were built of stone at that

Penhallam

xix

time; domestic buildings were of wood, and have long since vanished. Why Penhallam was so constructed is a mystery. The site is secluded, even today, reached down a long valley, built at the confluence of two streams and overlooked by hillsides, one of which is topped by Astbury, an ancient hill fort.

The settlement that gradually appeared from the undergrowth of centuries was remarkably complete. Surrounded by a small moat, the archeologists have identified the foundations of a sophisticated household with a great hall, service rooms, buttery, a chapel, and a camera, or private apartments, 41ft by 20ft raised above an undercroft. The moat was crossed by a counter-balanced drawbridge with a gate house. The moat is neither wide enough nor deep enough to be defensive, and is more likely to have been a fish larder and a deterrent against chance attack.

The earliest known Cardinham was Turold who, in 1035, went Crusading. It is surmised that the builder of this delightful complex was Robert, the first known to be called 'de Cardinham' and possessor of Cardinham Castle. The manors passed to the Champernownes when the Cardinham male line failed in around 1260. Penhallam was abandoned in the fourteenth century.

Since then the site lay forgotten and undisturbed, except by plunderers of the stone walls, until all was covered in a mantle of bramble – a sleeping beauty in the true sense of the word, with the unlikely hero being the Forestry Commission!

One theory is that Penhallam was built, or at least used, as a kind of summer hunting lodge, a retreat from Cardinham Castle. Somewhere in the surrounding woods the remains of a deer park may yet be found.

The site has been thoroughly explored and a detailed interpretation board provided explaining the remains which are surprisingly extensive. Penhallam lies a short woodland walk away from a narrow north Cornish lane, provided with a small car park, and it makes a very pleasant short expedition – an unsung gem, an early part of Cornwall's history.

Harewood in decay   (Courtesy Brian Stanbury)

Harewood House, Calstock

Few houses have had a more intriguing history than Harewood House. Its heyday was in the nineteenth century with the ownership of Sir William Trelawny and his wife Patience, a story steeped in romance from their marriage when she was just 16, to their deaths within a few months of each other almost fifty years later. It was as well they died when they did, for they would have hated to see the desecration of their once-beautiful valley.

Harewood is shown on Benjamin Donn's *Map of Devon*, 1765, owned by Foote, Esq., and it is known that a substantial house existed there from Jacobean times. The Georgian house that replaced the older property was abandoned at the end of the nineteenth century, stripped of its fittings and left a roofless ruin. None of the usual reasons applied to Harewood. There was no fire; there was no shortage of money; the family did not die out. It was abandoned for the most unusual of causes – a slow death by arsenical poisoning.

Harewood passed to the Duchy of Cornwall when it was created in the fourteenth century, having previously been a royal possession, but there is no record of any house or dwelling. Its history begins with Richard Connock (d. 1620), who was auditor for the Duchy from 1603, and amongst the various properties he rented from them was the Harewood estate. His nephew John was his heir, inheriting the lease of Harewood and the sum of '£200 to erect a building of a conventual little house for himself upon the conventual place of Harewood'. Richard also left his nephew the furniture from a property in Calstock, and all his household goods in the Parsonage in Calstock to furnish his new home.

John Connock carried out his uncle's wishes, for a Parliamentary survey of 1649 recorded that 'one John Connocke hath lately built a faire dwelling house with barns and stables called Harewood.' The house had 'one faire hall, one buttery, one kitchen and one pantrie below stairs and four rooms above stairs, and to the backside of the house adjoynes a washhouse and brewhouse.' A stone with the date 1631 was still in evidence at the end of the twentieth century, and the Hearth Tax returns record 15 for Harewood.

Over a century and a half later, Harewood was described as an E-shaped mansion with a large central block and wings to north and south. An avenue of trees led from the central door westward to Calstock church and to the south were the stables. As was customary for the time, the walled garden was a little distance off and had a summerhouse built into the north wall overlooking the river. This has survived, albeit ruinous.

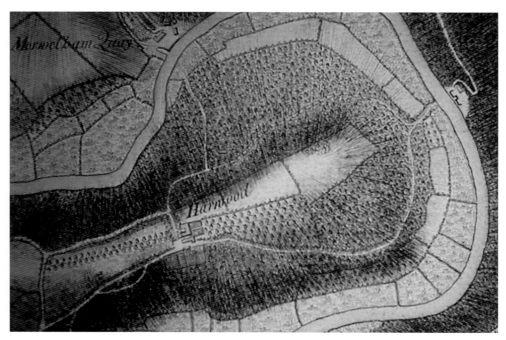

Wm Gardner 1784 - detail   (BL K Top 11.80.a.8)
The house has two projecting wings and formal gardens, and an avenue leading to the road

The estate passed through a number of families, and in 1733 John Foote, a London merchant, became the owner, and it was this house which was home to the Foote family for 60 years. When John Pearson Foote purchased the freehold from the Duchy in 1798, this kind of house would have seemed very old-fashioned indeed, even in such a remote part of the country. According to some sources John Foote demolished the entire house and built himself a new one at a cost of £27,000. Canon Running, in the *Journal of the Friends of Morwellham*, states that he pulled down the central portion and the south wing, leaving just the north wing, which was altered or rebuilt to appear as a neat Georgian house, with a central doorway facing Morwellham to the north. This would mean that the original house was three times the size of the remaining wing – a very large and imposing mansion, – and it seems strange that no records exist of such a house, occupied by the same family from the 1640's until 1798.

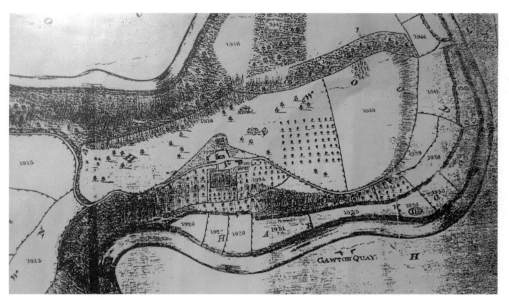

An early map of the Harewood estate, dated 1815   (Calstock Parish archive)
The shape of the house has changed, the avenue and formal gardens have gone

How much, if anything, of the old house survived is not known, although the Canon records a stone dated 1631 in his notes of 1989. John Foote, it was said, overspent himself to such an extent on his lavish new house, that in 1806 he was forced to sell, and it changed hands twice before being bought by William Salusbury Trelawny in 1814, when it was described as being the 'finest house in one of the prettiest places in the county.'

A good description of the house built by John Foote comes from Gilbert's *Historical Survey of Cornwall (1820)*;

... the elegant seat of Salusbury Trelawny, esq. is a modern mansion, built of freestone, with three regular fronts, and has a background of full grown plantations, by which the numerous offices on either side, are nearly concealed. A flight of steps ascends to a vestibule in the centre, on the right of which is the drawing room, thirty feet by twenty, and sixteen high: on the left is the dining-room of the same dimensions. Farther on is an inner hall, and stair-case, on the right of which is a library, twenty-four feet by twenty, and sixteen high, and on the left is a breakfast room, twenty foot square. An elegant stair-case, with skylights, ascends to the upper floor, upon which, in the centre is a gallery, opening separately into elegant bedchambers, and dressing rooms. The buildings are nearly surrounded by a delightful lawn, skirted with a sunk fence, over-hung with a rich variety of full grown trees. The whole is situated on a tongue of land, washed on three sides by the River Tamar, and from this beautiful seat, the waters are seen winding amidst the most diversified and enchanting scenery.

This perfectly describes the typical Georgian house of a small landowner, set in its own acres and content in its rural existence. From this description, it seems unlikely that the earlier house was adapted. The size of the rooms, and their considerable height, does not really fit in with a house built well over a century earlier.

William Salusbury Trelawny was born in 1781, the eldest son of Harry Trelawny, head of the ancient Cornish family, with estates near Looe. Sir Harry converted to Catholicism; his son did not, so Trelawny House was left to his sisters for their lifetime and William was effectively disinherited. When he fell in love with Patience Carpenter from Mount Tavy, she was just 16, and it was thought too young for marriage – or perhaps it was his father's actions that caused her father's disapproval. One account mentions a proposed elopement, but in the event the young lovers were married in Tavistock church in 1807. Patience was the daughter of John Carpenter and Elizabeth Stribling; her grandmother, Christian Phillips, was said to have inherited property from her brother, Sir Jonathon Phillips, including Mount Tavy, the family home on the outskirts of Tavistock. The Carpenters were an old-established family around Launceston and Tavistock – and Patience, so it was rumoured, brought to her husband a considerable dowry. William had added Salusbury to his name in 1802 on inheriting estates in Wales from a kinsman, Owen Salusbury Brereton. The couple's first child was born in 1808, and their last, a boy who lived less than a month, in 1831. Patience and William raised a family of eleven – five sons and six daughters.

When Harewood House was offered for sale in 1814, it seemed the ideal home for his growing family, and it was to this 'finest house in one of the prettiest places in the county' that William Trelawny brought them all.

It would seem that William was an energetic landowner. He drained the riverside marshes and built the embankment opposite Morwellham and was responsible for the planting of many of the trees around the estate. His horsemanship was renowned and he both bred and raced horses, and continued hunting into his seventies. He served both as an MP and as JP, and was Lord Lieutenant of Cornwall from 1839 until his death.

A member of the family kept a record of those halcyon days at Harewood during the Trelawny's ownership. The estate, it would seem, was almost self-sufficient. The

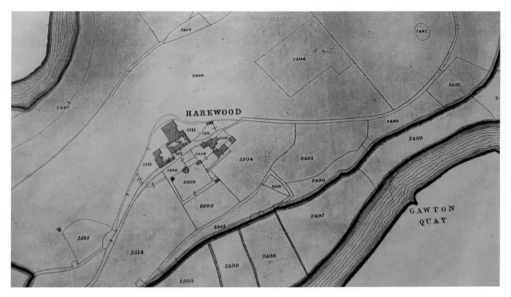

Map dated 1840 showing the extent of the outbuildings   (Calstock Parish Archive)

house was surrounded by apple and cherry orchards and they made their own cider. Sufficient butter and honey was produced for there to be a surplus that was then sold, and the wheat harvest was stored in the attics until needed – the account does not make clear which attics. The 300 acre estate had its own limekilns and its own quays. At Christmas, open house was kept and meat and cider distributed to the needy. At one stage they ventured into turkey farming and successfully reared a flock of 55 birds. Lady Trelawny would appear to have been a remarkable woman; she, too, was a fearless rider and sufficiently well educated to teach her daughters Greek, Latin and Hebrew. In their turn, they taught in the local schools, and three of them married local parsons. Lady Trelawny would often travel downstream to Plymouth to attend concerts and lectures, and as well as attending the local church, she would also support the Baptist, Methodist and Wesleyan chapels. She died in 1857, never having left her bed since Sir William's death the year before. He was 75, and was buried in Calstock church; the grave is marked by a tall granite Celtic cross, close to the churchyard boundary, overlooking his own land and under the shade of his own trees as he had wished, and she lies close by.

One of their granddaughters, Alice Cann, recorded her memories of her grandfather, and of Harewood 'I can only remember a fine, outstanding old man in a well-worn hunting kit, very kindly in his manner to his little grandchildren. The house was reached via the lodge, but there was another gate and shrubs, and at the top of the lawn were pillars and another gate where we used to get out and run over the grass instead of driving round – and tradition said that grandfather used to come that way, on horseback, jumping the gate.'

Then she gives an account of the house;

The entrance was on the river side of the house, a pillared portico; glass doors shut off an entrance out of which opened a mysterious unfinished room to the right and the dining room to the left. My grandfather had a great dislike of having servants prowling around the room at meals, when they were alone the man waited outside the door until he was wanted, I do not know how Grannie liked this arrangement; things were more orderly and stately at Mount Tavy. The glass door opened into the hall which had pillars and a gallery running over half of its staircase and a branch of stairs leading to the nurseries half way up shut off by a baize door. Here were smaller and probably older rooms; and from the nursery stairs led off down to the kitchen regions. Here reigned kind Lizzie, the cook of my days, who used to give me yellow cake and cream. The kitchen passage ran from the hall, shut off by baize doors, to the back entrance which was in itself a kind of hall, flagged with granite and with two entrances, one from the stables and one from the piggeries and gardens. Here was a great pair of scales and heavy weights … A little court led to the stables and in it were doors to the laundry etc. and one little space was a sort of tinsmith' shop, where Sarrel the butler used to employ his idle hours for he had been a tradesman in Launceston, and Mother got him the place. Then I can remember the laundry up a few steps, and the 'three Tammies' at work – Tamsin Branch, Tamsin Heale and another, and the little flat iron they used to keep for us children to play at ironing with.

The drawing room and library opened on the hall; the former not an interesting room having little view from the windows. The library was much frequented … the doors were of mahogany and when the house was dismantled, Lewis Batchelor secured some for Langston in Brentor which was being restored at the time.

Sloping away were gardens and orchards of apples and cherries. It was very productive … at the top of the garden was a walk leading from wall to wall and in the middle was a sort of half greenhouse, half summerhouse of two stories – plants in the under part and a room sacred to Mother above, where she had her sofa and table and where she read and wrote.

The eldest son of William and Patience, Owen, had died aged 22. John, born 1816, was heir to the Trelawny estates and was able to move into his inheritance when the last aunt had finally died. Harewood House passed to the next son, Reginald, (b.1826), who was an army man. It was he who, in 1867, made the decision to sell Harewood and move his family to the healthier air of Poltair, near Penzance.

The Tamar valley had long been known for its beauty and for its gentle climate. The river itself was an important highway, reaching many miles inland, and along its banks grew up small communities, and industries. The fertile banks were heavily cultivated, providing Plymouth, and the navy, with fresh fruit and vegetables – and its strawberries were famous. Pleasure boats, as well as barges, sailed up and down and the valley was a place of peace and plenty. Development had been controlled by the two great landowners, the Bedford Estates on the Devon side and the Mount Edgecumbe estate on the Cornish. Harewood House was situated in a particularly lovely setting, on a tongue of level, fertile land in a great loop of the river opposite the steeply wooded banks of the Devon side. Although silver had been mined in a small way since the thirteenth century, there was no indication of the wealth that was to be wrenched from the valley in the middle years of the nineteenth century, or of the desecration that this would cause. Copper mining had been carried on around Tavistock for some time and with increasing demand, the Tavistock canal was built, reaching the Tamar by means of an incline down to Morwellham, where the level of activity was dramatically increasing with barges loading and unloading, wagons descending and ascending, and the constant bustle of sailors, workmen and miners. The opening of the Devon Great Consuls mine at Blanchdown in the 1840's had a major impact. The Tamar valley became the most important producer of copper in this country, copper of an exceptional quality and by 1859 had reached a maximum of 209,000 tons, of which 29,000 came from the Devon Great Consuls mine. All this activity lead to a huge rise in population requiring new housing, roads, schools etc.

The Trelawnys had no part in this wealth – far from it for it was destroying their home, and when the arsenic mines at Gawton, on the opposite bank, and at Okel mine adjacent to the Harewood estate, were opened, life in the valley became impossible. By 1865 it was reckoned that at least seventeen mines were working within five miles of Calstock, and all of them used Calstock quay.

Immediately opposite Harewood House was the George & Charlotte mine, one of the oldest, and by the mid 1800's it took three large waterwheels and a steam engine to keep it drained and working. The fumes from all the steam engines along the banks were a cause of frequent river fogs, and the dust from the ore, and worst of all, the fine film from the arsenic refining process, spread all over the valley. What use those famed strawberry beds now?

It is hardly surprising that in 1867 Reginald Trelawny decided to sell.

Harewood as a school   (Calstock Parish Archive)

An approach was made to the Duchy, but this was unsuccessful and on 8th May, 1867 the property was put up for auction in ten lots – 300 acres and a 'Spacious Mansion House with Lawn' with orchards, gardens, wood, pastures, lime kilns and quays and cottages 'excepting all Royalties, liberties and privileges vested in HRH the Prince of Wales'.

The house was bought by the Revd. Thomas Jones, who moved 150 boys from their school at Saltash to found Harewood House Collegiate School. But after only three years this closed, possibly defeated by the arsenic fumes from Gawton.

For a time the house was occupied by Harry Sims, a mining agent, but by the

THE HAREWOOD ESTATE SALE.

Messrs. Ward and Chowen offered for sale, in the Ball Room of the Bedford Hotel, Tavistock, on Friday, the freehold estate known as Harewood, situate in the parish of Calstock. It comprises a magnificent site for a gentleman's residence (within one mile of the proposed new railway station at Calstock), farm, fruit, and accommodation lands, with cottage property, and valuable building sites, mostly with a southern aspect, sloping to the River Tamar, which surrounds the property. From this elevated position the lands command extensive views of the surrounding picturesque country. They include about thirteen acres of woodlands, a favourite resort for game. The whole estate contains nearly 200 acres. The auctioneer was Mr. Frank Ward, O.C., and there was a good attendance, but none of the property changed hands. The conditions of sale were taken as read. The Auctioneer said that the property was rather unique. It was close to the River Tamar, and would be near the Calstock Railway Station. It was formerly the seat of the Footes, then of the Trelawnys. It was a very fine site for a house, and within easy distance of Plymouth, from which yachts could come up. The climate was splendid. The property was first submitted in one lot, and the following biddings were elicited :—£3,000, Mr. Lawry ; £3,500, Mr. John Ward ; £3,750, Mr. Lawry ; £4,000, Mr. John Ward ; £4,100, Mr. Lawry ; £4,200, Mr. John Ward ; £4,300, Mr. Lawry ; £4,400, Mr. Orgel, of Plymouth ; £4,500, Mr. Lawry ; £4,600, Mr. John Ward ; £4,650, Mr. J. W. Spear, M.P. As there were no further offers for the time being, the Auctioneer proceeded to present the property in five lots. Lot 1 consisted of Harewood Manor House, commanding extensive and most picturesque scenery of the River Tamar and surrounding country, described as an ideal site for a mansion or residence ; together with Harewood Farm House and farm buildings, in the occupation of Mr. Frederick Knight. Cottage and outbuildings, and well-sheltered and very productive wall and other gardens, pasture lands and woods, in all about 74a. 0r. 3p. This lot was not sold, there being only one bid, that of Mr. Lawry of £1,200. Neither was Lot 2 sold, no offer being made. It comprised three fields and a marsh, measuring 46a. 3r. 20p. Lot 3, known as Harewood Cottage, in the occupation of Mr. William Sandercock, is a convenient nine-roomed farm house, pleasantly situated on the banks of the River Tamar, opposite Newquay, and, with the 74a. 2r. 5p. of land, forms a very nice little farm tenement. The bidding opened with £1,000, which Mr. A. Spear soon followed up with an offer of £1,100. The next figure named was £1,200, which Mr. A. Spear improved upon with £1,300. Mr. John Ward offered £1,350, and, after £1,400 had been bid, he further offered £1,450, but the lot was not sold. Lot 4 was described as a nice little tenement, late in the occupation of Mr. S. Spargo, comprising a four-roomed cottage, together with 1a. 1r. of land above the railway, adapted for fruit and market gardening ; also 1r. 11p. of land. Offers of £80, £85, and £90 were made, and then Mr. Ward passed on to Lot 5, consisting of five cottages and gardens, pleasantly situated at Okel Tor, in the occupation of Messrs. Geake, Wilton, Beale, Squire, and Gifford, together with three lime kilns, with garden in the occupation of Mr. W. H. Crocker, containing an area of 1a. 3r. 3p., the total rents being £24 18s. Mr. T. Bowhay bid £150, Mr. Paul £160, Mr. Bowhay £170. There was another bid of £180, and Mr. Bowhay offered £185. Then followed a bid of £190, and Mr. Bowhay offered £200, when the lot was withdrawn. Mr. Orgel bid £4,700 for the property as a whole, but it was withdrawn at £5,100, bid by Mr. W. Sanders Fiske, of London, solicitor to the mortgagee.

[handwritten notes]
August 1906
Harewood Estate sale
Bidding started at £3,900 & highest bid by Mr Orgel £4700 No sold
Then tried in lots
Lot one Mr Lawry only bid £200
do 2 No bid
3 started at £1000 highest bid £1450
4 £90
5 £200 nothing sold
Aug 1905 Mr Orgell £4700 not sold
offered 1911 Sir John Spear £650 do
.... 2550 8000, Paul

Press cutting of the sale – August 1906

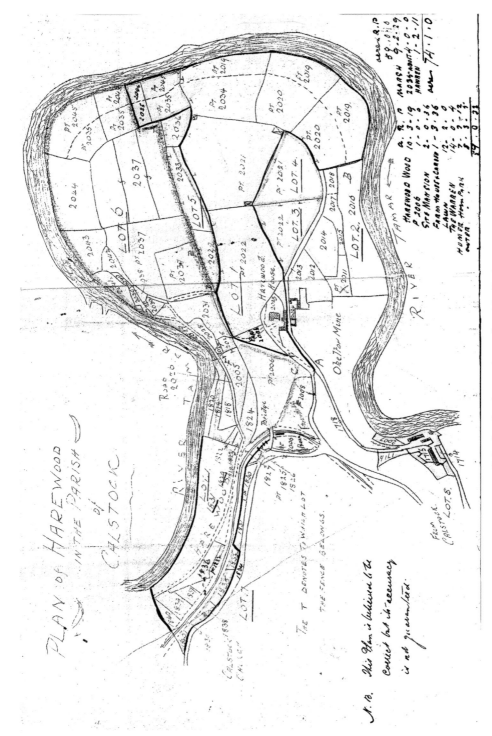

Sale plan showing purchasers from Mr. Paul
(Courtesy Brian Stanbury)

end of the century, Harewood was empty and becoming ruinous. When it was again offered for sale in 1906, the freehold estate was described as 'a magnificent site for a gentleman's residence – within one mile from the proposed new railway station.' The auction appears to have been a dismal affair. Bidding for the whole started at £3,000 and rose to £4,650 – and was then withdrawn, as were all subsequent lots. A further bid of £4,700 for the whole was put in by Mr. Ogel of Plymouth, capped by Mr. W. Sanders at £5,100 but it was withdrawn by Fiske of London, solicitor to the mortgagee.

A note at the foot of the press cutting records further offers in 1911, and 10th July, 1918 – £7,750, and then £8,000 by J. D. Paul. This is a reference to the second sale held on that day, when the estate was offered in eight lots. Lot 1 was the 'site of Harewood Manor House.' Mr. Paul was the tenant of The Warren, The Marsh and pasture land around the house and of Harewood Cottage Farm, a nine bedroomed farmhouse with 61 acres on the banks of the Tamar opposite Morwellham.

A subsequent estate plan indicates that J. D. Paul later sold on the farms and market garden.

Before the 1st World War a sale had been held at the house, which was stripped of its fittings – many of which ended up in properties in the area, including the granite quoins which were replaced with bricks. Harewood stood empty, a roofless shell in the middle of its once productive lands.

The porch survived! c1960
(Calstock Parish Archive)

Someone decided to demolish the upper storey and create an unimposing bungalow with one less window on either side, but the same front door and portico. Then it was reroofed and the upper storey rebuilt, and divided into two by demolishing the central portion, which is how it survives today an architectural oddity with a puzzling history.

The Trelawnys might have been at Harewood today if they had rented out the estate, for by 1900 it was all over. The coming of the railway, built between 1887 and 90, reduced the river traffic to a trickle. The Devon Great Consuls which, for a short period were producing more than half the world's supply of copper, peaked in 1862, and declined from then on, finally ceasing production in 1901. Peace returned to the Tamar Valley, but the Trelwanys had departed.

Mr Paul and his daughter in front of the ruined house.
(Courtesy Brian Stanbury)

Sources

Industrial Archaeology of the Tamar Valley, 1967; Frank Booker
'Tamar'. Journal of the Friends of Morwelham; The Trelawnys of Harewood, Jeanette Harris (No 27, 2005)
Harewood House, Canon G Running (No 11, 1989)
Notes on the Family of Carpenter, Alice Cann
Parliamentary Survey 1649

AD 305/1   AD 386/2
AD 1272/4 – 1998 sale catalogue   AP/F/842

Trebartha Hall   (courtesy Latham family)

Trebartha Hall, North Hill

As thou art, so was I,
And as I am, so shalt thou be

Henry Spoure, d 1603

Trebartha and its owners belong to that category of Cornish gentry who were content to live out their lives in relative obscurity, seeking neither wealth nor position but devoting their entire lives to their families and estates. The Rodds, the Spoures and the Trebarthas did just that – for around six hundred years. It is thought that the manor was granted to one Walter Reynell in the days of Richard I; a century later it became the property of a family who took the name of their new possession, and from then until 1940, Trebartha passed quietly down the generations. There were a few hiccups – twice the male line failed and the estates passed with the heiress to her husband, but few families can rival this record.

The earliest house was known to have been added to and 'rebuilt' at least twice in its history before reputedly being burnt down in the eighteenth century. A house of modern design was erected in 1720, of which only one drawing exists, dated 1750. This was later doubled in size and acquired various additions, including a new wing designed in 1812 by Jeffry Wyatt, later to acquire fame and title as the architect of Windsor Castle. And then came the second World War and for the first time in its history, Trebartha was put up for sale. The house was requisitioned, occupied by the Americans, and then a contingent of Italian prisoners – leaving behind a house that was fit only for demolition. And that might have been the end of the story of Trebartha had it not been for the Latham family who, looking only to buy the woodland, ended up with the whole estate just weeks after war broke out. They never moved in to Trebartha Hall, but they own the estate still – well on their way to clocking up their first hundred years.

Trebartha weaves a magic spell. It is easy to see why no-one has ever felt the urge to move away. Behind it are the barren, bleak uplands of Bodmin Moor, but Trebartha lies in the sheltered valley of the river Lynher. Beginning its long journey to St. German's and the Hamoaze, at Trebartha it is a young, joyful stream, fed by tumbling tributaries – a succession of pools and waterfalls, most notably the Cascade on the Withey Brook. Over the centuries its waters have been tamed to provide fishponds, then later confined to a straight channel running in front of the house, which feeds the atmospheric Swan Pool, before making its exit, now more of a river than a stream, to provide power for the water mill downstream. All these features have survived and have recently undergone careful restoration. Mature woodlands surround the water meadows where wildlife abounds, and narrow, winding lanes lead to hidden farms and cottages, and up on to the moor. Less than a mile away is the village of North Hill, a collection of cottages packed together around the parish church, where generations of the owners of Trebartha are buried. Pevsner, in his *Buildings of England*, states that the monuments are more, and more interesting, than in most Cornish village churches. That of Henry Spoure, dated 1603, aged 61, is very commanding with his coat of arms and the epitaph quoted at the start of the chapter, and mention of his five sons and six daughters. Richard Spoure, who died at the age of ten in 1653, has a remarkable monument, some 6ft long with the Spoure crest and a long inscription, still retaining the original colouring. His brother, Edmund, erected what has been described as 'one of the most endearing monuments in Cornwall', to commemorate his son, Henry Spoure, who died in 1687, also aged ten. Brightly coloured, it depicts the child and his sister, Mary, with their grieving parents kneeling in front, all dressed in Stuart-style clothing and brightly coloured.

It is not known when the peaceful site on the banks of the River Lynher was first chosen for a dwelling. The Trebartha knights continued in ownership until the end of fifteenth century, and it is reasonable to suppose that some kind of house existed. In 1498, the last of the Trebarthas, the heiress Anna, married Thomas Spoure, a captain in the army of Henry VII. Two centuries later the only known drawing of the house appeared in the *Book of the House of Spoure*. Dated 1694, it shows what was already an old house, with courtyards and gateways. There was a typical medieval garden, squares of grass or gravel with statuary in the centres and evergreen cones at the corners, with a pavilion on one wall, overlooking the valley. The house would have grown over the centuries, centred around the great hall, but the first real record we have from the *Book of the House of Spoure*, is of Henry Spoure (d. 1603) who 'built a great parlour and all the pile of building.' Henry struck lucky for he purchased the mines of Lemarne on the opposite bank of the Lynher. Tin mining had for centuries been active on and around Bodmin Moor; perhaps Henry went deeper for:

> *he got so much tin out of them as he gave a thousand pounds apiece to five daughters, and was the first thousand pound ever given to a daughter for a portion by any private gent of his quality in Cornwall, and erected a large pile of buildings.*

As well he might!

The Hearth Tax returns for 1660 record Trebartha as having ten hearths, which would have made it a sizeable house. It was to this house that Edmund Spoure (1654–96) brought his bride, Mary Rodd, daughter of James Rodd of Oakley near Exeter, and Mary Bampfylde. Almost immediately, Edmund set about renovating his home, adding

> *the stables, pound house, all the garden and Court Walls, besides wainscoting all the rooms and a great many other alterations and adornments, as paintings, landscapes and such like within the dwelling itself.* (Book of the House of Spoure)

Book of the House of Spoure
View from Hawks Tor
(courtesy Lady Rennell)

is the Landſhip and proſpect from the side of Hawkes Ter hill of Tre

the Villedge with the contrey round about

The chapel was repaired, and finally he placed a stone over the front door, dated 1677 with the initials E M S. It is this house that is pictured in the *Book of the House of Spoure*.

Edmund and Mary had two children. Their only son died in 1687, aged ten. There is a touching account of the boy's funeral in the *Book of the House of Spoure*:

> *His horse was covered with a rich velvet pall, with Scouchions on itt, he was born to his grave by five Esqrs. and three Gents ... which had all rings, Scarves, Hatbands and Gloves. His Funerall also was attended by a multitude of the Neighbour Hood round the Country; and there was a Handsome Treat of Cold Meats Propper for such an occasion provided for them and the meat in each dish adorned with streamers stuck in it with Escouchions on one side and deaths head on the other with this Motto: Memento Mori – and on some – prepare to follow H.S. besides Wine, some mull'd, some colde and such like, the great Parlor where the herse Lay was all hung with black with Scouchions all round the Roome, and eight silk Scouchions on the herse, the walls of the little Parlor and the Hall were also hung round with Scouchions with a large Hatchment att the higher end of the Hall. Likewise the Pulpit was hung with black with a Scouchion on itt, and the Spours Ile hung round with black with 12 Escouchions placed round about itt.*

It was to this child that the elaborate monument in North Hill church was erected by his father. This left their only other child, Mary, as sole heiress.

The Book of the House of Spoure is a beautiful thing. Knowing that he was the last of his line, Edmund Spoure set out to record the history of his family. It is richly illustrated, including the many coats of arms pertaining to the Spoures and their ancestors – the

Book of the House of Spoure
Mary Spoure
(Lady Rennell)

work of John Hellier whom Edmund employed as a ghost writer. The book is dedicated to Mary:

To my ever dear and Intirely belov'd
Peace, and Wealth in this World
And everlasting happiness and glory
In the World to come.

But Mary had a life full of tragedy. Her two husbands died untimely and both her sons died in infancy. Renatus Bellot died aged eight in 1712, shortly before his father, after whom he was named. Mary's second husband was Charles Grylls, who died in 1727, seven years after their son, George. Before she could marry her third husband, Captain Francis Rodd of Oakley, she succumbed to small pox and died in 1729. Mary's will had left her entire estate to her future husband:

provided he is not already married to, or shall not at any time take to wife, Jane Parker, living at Covent Garden.

Whoever Jane Parker was, the allure of Trebartha proved greater than her charms.

Francis Rodd and Mary were cousins; James Rodd (1611–1678) was grandfather to them both. By his second wife, Grace Bampfylde, he had a son, Bampfylde Rodd whose son was Francis, and by his third wife, also a Bampfylde, he had Mary, who married Edmund Spoure in 1675. The Rodds were to remain at Trebartha for six generations.

Francis was born in 1683, so he would have been 46 when Mary died. She was no longer young and children of the union would have been unlikely. It is interesting to contemplate who would have inherited Trebartha had she lived. Francis lost no time in finding a substitute for poor Mary, and his next choice was Alice Sandford of Exeter who provided her husband with a son and heir, born in 1732, and christened Francis, as were the next four generations.

The house Francis Rodd inherited was only a few years old, barely completed before Mary died. The old Trebartha is thought to have been destroyed by fire in 1720. The only drawing of the house built by Charles Grylls and Mary is tantalizing in its lack of

The 1720 house.
(courtesy Latham family)

16

Trebartha in 1850   (courtesy Latham family)

detail. It shows a plain house, not square, and was built to take advantage of the views down the valley and across to the moors. The original house had faced the other way, north, towards the then main drive from the road to Launceston. As was customary, the frontage was taken up with the medieval-style gardens with no access for carriages. The rear of the house was protected from the worst of the weather off the moors by the stables and outbuildings. By re-orientating the house, the main windows now faced south, with large windows.

> ***Trebartha Hall***, *the seat of Francis Hearle Rodd, esq. is situated at the foot of a mountain which faces the south, amidst a diversity of picturesque and interesting scenery. The venerable mansion of the Trebarthas and Spoures, together with a domestic chapel, were taken down by the order of the late Colonel Rodd, who erected on the site a large tasteless building, which appears to be deplorably destitute of architectural ornaments. The front opens into a large paddock, the soil of which is rather swampy, and a dampness prevails even in dry seasons. Near the house are good gardens and a shrubbery, with hot houses, and several neat gravel walks. The whole is surrounded by extensive plantations, the extremities of which are sheltered by an amphitheatre of bold hills, which bear on their bleak brows, tors of a most sublime and frowning appearance. From a stupendous elevation on the northern side, a considerable stream descends, and the roar of its waters in their falls over the different precipices, is heard at a great distance. The beautiful also, is here associated with the sublime; for the foliage of forest trees is seen delightfully clothing the sides of the heights, and forming pleasing contrast to the bare and bleak elevation by which they are protected.*

The above somewhat disparaging description comes from Gilbert's *Historical Survey of Cornwall, 1820*, and contradicts the view that the 'venerable mansion' referred to was destroyed by fire. Did Col. Rodd 'take down' the house built by Charles Grylls, and build a new house on a new site, or did he considerably enlarge it? Was this when the house was doubled in size, and an attic storey added? There is no record of any architect being employed, nor of the cost . Comparing the 1750 drawing with the view in 1850, the earlier house would appear to have been the right-hand half. The whole is indeed severe, and devoid of any architectural detail and appears to have been covered in some kind of rendering.

Francis (2) who was only four when he inherited in 1736, had a long and active life, dying in 1812. Not much is known of his childhood, but in common with many of his family, he left matrimony relatively late, marrying Jane Hearle in 1763. Their first son, Francis Hearle Rodd, was born in 1766, when his father was 34.

The diaries Col. Rodd and most of his family kept have survived – found by the Lathams in one of the outbuildings. These record an uneventful life, involved with the estate and farm visits. Social life consisted of trips to the theatre in Launceston, race meetings and local balls. He records that in April, 1765 they made various purchases at a house sale in South Hill, including china, a spy glass, an umbrella from India, cost one guinea, table cloths, and the complete furnishings for a bedroom for £27. The couple had another son, Edward, and two daughters, Jane and Harriet. It is probable that Trebartha was also home to his widowed mother, and his three sisters. These three girls seem to have been unfortunate; little is known of them except the memorial to their parents in North Hill church records that Bridget died 1765, aged 31, Elizabeth in 1803, aged 71, and Alicia 1816, aged 81. None of them married.

Col. Rodd was responsible for the construction of the pleasant drive along the river bank to Trebartha Mills. This necessitated removing part of the cliffs that formed the river bank and continued to Berriow Bridge. In 1785 he began work on the gateway and lodge at High Park and the new main drive, and in 1807 the family vault at North Hill church was constructed.

In 1780, his wife Jane died, aged 42. Four years later, Col. Rodd married Anne Sanford, who was 39 at the time. The diaries record the two families were friends, and also that a year later the two daughters were placed in a boarding school in Bristol.

The Colonel and his wife were regular visitors to Bath, where he attended the Pump Room in an attempt to alleviate his gout – a later entry refers to 'bottling off a pipe of port, which made 57 dozen bottles'. During the latter part of his life he was appointed a Colonel in the Royal Cornwall Militia, raised in response to the wars with France. He records that from 1781 to 89 he was much engaged with the militia and the diaries record his many activities.

Col. Rodd was 80 when he died in 1812; his father was born in 1683, so two generations spanned 129 years. Unlike his father, he lived long enough to see his first grandson born in 1806. This boy, Francis, was the son of Col. Rodd's second son, the Revd. Edward (1768–1842) and his wife, Harriet Rashleigh, whom he had married when he was 37. His elder brother, Francis Hearle Rodd (1766–1836) and his wife, Mary Coryton, had no children. This Francis, the third, appears to have lived a life

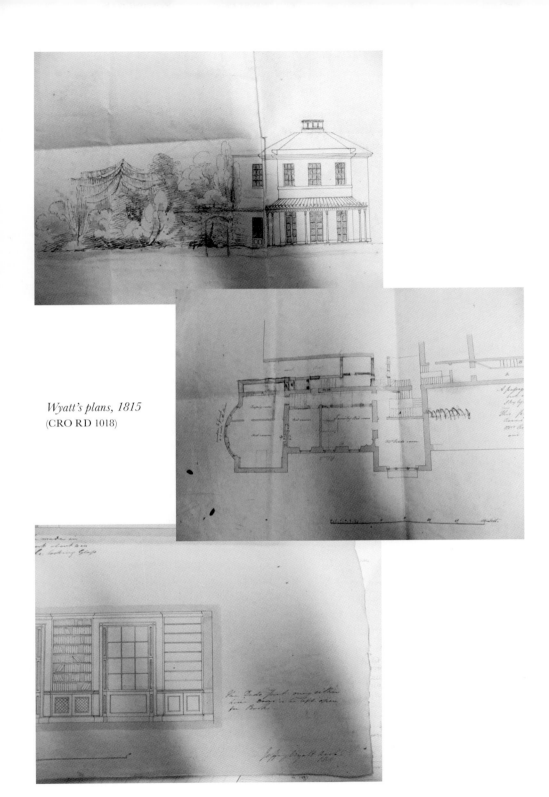

Wyatt's plans, 1815
(CRO RD 1018)

Kennedy's proposals for a gothic facade   (courtesy Latham family)

similar to that of his father. He was High Sherriff in 1818, a Deputy Lieutenant, and much involved in local affairs. It was this Francis who in 1815 employed Jeffry Wyatt to design a new front and extend the house. A new drawing room with a bow window overlooking the valley was added, with a library between this and the original hall. The library was book-lined with provision for large folios and tables between the windows. A note on the plan states that there was to be a passage on the chamber floor which would be convenient to lead to the rooms over the billiard room, and also to give Mrs. Rodd a direct way to the flower garden and green houses etc.

Proposals were also drawn up for alterations to the grounds. The landscape gardener, Lewis Kennedy (1789–1877), produced a lavish Repton-style book, written in flowery prose with several water colours illustrating his plans for 'this truly romantic and singular domain ... which would render Trebartha Hall to be rivalled by few in the county and in some picturesque effects, by none.' He notes that the present library is to be converted into a Hall and entrance and the present west wing be enlarged sufficiently to become a library with the best bedrooms, each with a dressing room, above. But, most interestingly, Kennedy inserted a scheme 'to show Trebartha in the Castle style at trifling more expense (than Wyatt's proposals) ... a design for the alterations of the building in the English style, commonly called Gothic which I have merely executed in a manner to show the effect such characterful buildings do produce when appropriately placed and of trivial expense to put an entire novel and as I presume finished, appropriate and elegant appearance upon the mansion which you will doubtless admit it at present wants from its marque and that local character which abounds so beautifully and abundantly in every part of this enviable estate.' It didn't work – Col. Rodd was not persuaded and Trebartha remained 'tasteless and devoid of ornament'.

Kennedy's proposals for the grounds included a new entrance drive from Five Lanes 'passing through a plantation to be made near the new Kitchen Garden keeping in a continued easy bend to arrive at the Lodge Gate and this would allow a large additional space to be thrown into the park and would do away with the back road close to the rear of the conservatory.' He also proposed 'that part of the grounds now occupied by various buildings next to the west end of the dwelling will form the flower gardens and be bounded by what is called an invisible iron fence and the private walk to the stables passing inside it.' The new drive was to terminate at the Hall, and return to the stables with a 'bridge of apparent ancient date and coeval with the alterations suggested for the house'. The path to the Cascade was to be adorned with a Sheep Shelter 'which looks very like a Swiss Cottage' to provide a resting place for visitors, and the rustic conservatory was to be surrounded by trees of various heights. An American garden and a Thornery were projected on the site up to the Cascade. The reference to the Conservatory implies it existed, at some distance from the Hall. Some of Kennedy's proposals were implemented – a new drive and bridge were built in 1819, and the American Garden was created in 1820. There are photographs of a 'Swiss Cottage' but not close to the Cascade and not on the scale of the proposed 'Sheep Shelter'.

Several diary entries record a close relationship between Francis (3) and his brother Edward, involving him, as his heir, in the running of the estate, which he inherited in 1836. Edward had taken Holy Orders and was rector of St. Just-in-Roseland. He

Rodd family by the Summer House

The new conservatory　(courtesy Latham family)

married Harriet Rashleigh when he was 37 – in keeping with family custom of leaving matrimony until middle-age! The couple had four sons, Francis (the fourth, 1806–1880) and Charles, Edward and John.

Francis was educated at Winchester and Trinity College, Cambridge where he gained a BA. He continued the family's keen interest in trees and gardening, planting large numbers of rhododendrons. He was probably responsible for the existing layout of the grounds, incorporating new walks and drives. Francis was fortunate – his diary records that in 1827 a rich new seam of copper had been found. Tin had long been mined in a small way, but the discovery of copper at a time when the world demand was rising, was good fortune indeed.

Francis was responsible for the addition of the grand new conservatory, supplied by Parham of Bath, which adjoined Wyatt's new front and overlooked the valley. The earlier detached conservatory seems to have disappeared.

Col. Francis, (4), married Mary Rashleigh, and their first son, Francis Rashleigh (5), was born in 1839, when his father was 33. She predeceased her husband, who died in 1880 after suffering ill health for some time so 'that his decease was not a matter of surprise'. His obituary describes him as 'Of commanding stature and dignified bearing, the beau ideal of a country gentleman.' He had served as a JP and DL, and High Sheriff 1845–6, and had been a promoter of the 'abortive Launceston, Bodmin and Wadebridge railway scheme.' He left £1000 each to his daughters Caroline and Harriet, and the sheet music and musical instruments at Trebartha – maybe some compensation for their single status.

Francis Rashleigh (5) appears to have lived a long contented life, dying in 1922, aged 83. He married, in 1882, (he was 43) Julia Graves Sawle, but there were no children. Various alterations were made to the grounds and surroundings – recorded in the diary for 1887:

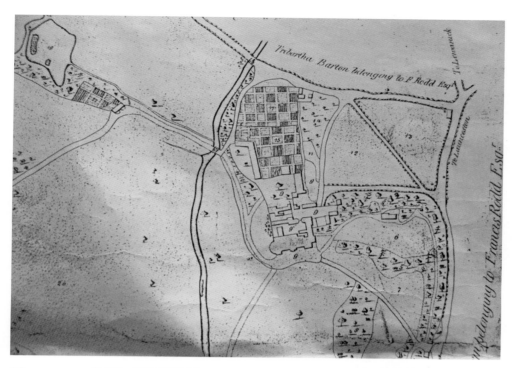

The estate map of 1856
(courtesy Latham family)

Raised terrace as to hide the old buildings in back yard. Built new paraffin house. Altered old house for lime and ashes, pulled down the old pigeon house by the stable yard preparatory to taking down old ash house, rabbit house, lime house and poultry court wall. Raised walk at back of old poultry court and enclosed hayrick etc with hedge (dry stone) and gates.

These would all have been part of the original medieval house. That was in September; in October Francis records that the lower pond burst – for the third time, and it took all hands a month to repair it.

By 1890, the dams commenced in the river were completed, and the banks raised on the Tinner's path side, so that the appearance of Trebartha today would appear to be largely this Francis' work.

He was a great tree planter; 200 larch were planted in the main plantation 'to fill vacancies'. He also records that the keeper caught a pole cat on 24 February (1890) – the first that had been seen for 25 years.

In November of that year 800 English oak were purchased, and 200 Balsam poplars for planting by the north drive, and 100 Auracarias (monkey puzzles) for the drives at the village, and two Luccombe and three Scarlet oaks. In December the planting of trees and shrubs in the village was completed – including Douglas, Noble fir, and larch. November of 1898 was a busy period; 1350 spruce, the same number of Scotch fir, 350 oak, 40 Douglas pine, 20 Weymouth pine and 6 Menziesii were planted. The Swan Pool was created at the turn of the century.

Francis' younger brother, Edward Stanhope Rodd, (1848–1928) inherited in 1922 – and continued the family tradition of not rushing into fatherhood; he was 38 when his son, Edward Francis Stanhope Rodd (1886–1947) was born. And here the male Rodd line finally dies out. Major Edward Stanhope and his wife, Florence Wynn, had four daughters. He lived at an unfortunate time. He served in the army in World War I, taking part in the disastrous Gallipoli campaign, accompanied by his groom. The horrors of that war remained with him, to such an extent that when the second War was declared, he ordered all his hunters to be shot. The suffering and slaughter of horses in the first War was horrific, when it is estimated that over one million horses went to the Front of which only a handful ever returned. The years between the wars were one of depression, and the rental income of the estate dropped to the levels of 1870. The running costs were increasing every year and continuing staff shortages with able-bodied men being called up all added to the problems, as did death duties. The house, by this time, was over two hundred years old and almost certainly suffering from neglect as the income from the estate dwindled.

Major Rodd would perhaps have envisaged desecration of the woodlands that were such a feature of Trebartha, and its possible requisitioning. He was 54. Perhaps it was a combination of all these reasons that caused Major Rodd to place the Trebartha estate on the market for auction on 25th July, 1940. The estate had never before been sold.

This brought Bryan Latham to view on behalf of the family timber firm, interested in the woodlands and plantations, some 500 acres. He asked if the whole estate was available – had he fallen under Trebartha's spell? This extended to nearly 4,000 acres along the north side of Bodmin Moor. A price was negotiated, but Major Rodd

Trebartha Hall

In the Parish of NORTH HILL and about 1 mile from the village,

TOGETHER WITH

The Gardens, Grounds, the Fish Ponds, Swan Pool, American Garden, the Park and Agricultural Land, and NINE COTTAGES, in all about

89a.   1r.   31p.

as described in the Schedule hereto.

Vacant Possession of the Residence and Lands in hand will be given on completion of the purchase,

---

The Residence

is approached by two principal drives which wind from the main road through beautifully timbered copses and open lawns planted with bulbs and flanked with ornamental shrubs.

The principal rooms on the Ground Floor are :

The Entrance Porch

approached by oak doors on the East and West sides, is 14 ft. x 10 ft. 9 in. Double glazed doors with leaded side panels lead to the Lounge Hall, 19 ft. 3 in. x 18 ft., with cut Cornish stone chimney piece and kerb, open hearth and iron fire dogs. The walls are panelled to height of five feet and the frieze and ceiling delicately moulded.

The Dining Room

35 ft. 6 in. x 19 ft. 6 in., with granite chimney piece and veined kerb, moulded cornice and massive 3-light candelabra from the centre of the ceiling.

The Library

A lofty well-proportioned room 34 ft. x 20 ft. 3 in. with marble chimney piece, kerb, and mirror over and with coloured marble window sills.

The Billiard Room

approached from the Library by double doors, is 36 ft. x 20 ft. exclusive of large bay window. It has an oak block floor surround, white marble hearth and fireplace and is fitted with three mahogany cupboards with glazed doors. On the North and East sides there is a balcony with hand-wrought iron work sides.

The Study

is about 20 ft. 9 in. x 12 ft. 9 in. exclusive of recesses and bay windows (glazed with concave glass. The walls are heavily panelled with teak. The fireplace is tiled and fitted with Cornish stone kerb.

Adjoining this room is a small Hall and lavatory with entrance from the Lawn.

The Morning Room

20 ft. 6 in. x 16 ft. 9 in., is fitted with cupboards and shelves in recess which is supported by fluted wooden pillars with carved capitals. Marble chimney piece and tiled hearth.

Fire-proof safe built into the wall.

There is also an Office and large Meeting Room.

The Domestic Offices

are well situated and spacious and comprise : Men's Room with door to exterior lavatory, staff-rooms, kitchen with two ranges, scullery, larder, and all the usual adjuncts to a house of this description.

Sale particulars   (courtesy Latham family)

The Bedrooms

are approached by two principal staircases and are eleven in number on the first floor.

The principal dimensions are :—

(1.) 19 ft. 3 in. x 18 ft. 3 in., with marble chimney piece and french windows leading to balcony over the front porch.

(2.) 21 ft. 6 in. x 16 ft. 9 in.   (3.) 17 ft. x 13 ft. 9 in.   (4.) 22 ft. x 19 ft. 6 in. exclusive of bay window.

(5.) 15 ft. x 13 ft. 6 in., with ante-room.

(6.) 20 ft. x 20 ft. with dressing room adjoining.

(7.) 18 ft. 6 in. x 17 ft. 9 in.   (8.) 17 ft. 3 in. x 10 ft., with ante-room adjoining.

(9.) 24 ft. 6 in. x 10 ft.   (10.) 19 ft. x 10 ft.   (11.) 14 ft. 6 in. x 13 ft.

Most of these rooms are fitted with fireplaces and some with cupboards. Also two bathrooms. lavatories, etc.

On the Second Floor.

A FURTHER 10 BEDROOMS AND BOX ROOMS.

There are commodious CELLARS under a portion of the House.

On the North side stands the Laundry built of cut stone with granite lintels, having a slated roof and clock tower. Coal house, wood sheds, tool house and out-of-door lavatory.

THE STABLING and buildings adjoining comprise : 5 loose boxes, 6 stalls, harness room and lofts. GARAGE, 34 ft. 6 in. x 38 ft. 9 in., with spacious yard and fore court.

The Walled Garden

approached by a wrought-iron ornamental gate is completely enclosed by walls to which fruit trees are trained.

The heated Glass Houses measure 24 ft. x 13 ft., 14 ft. x 15 ft. 9 in., 18 ft. 6 in. x 14 ft., 21 ft. 9 in. x 12 ft., 20 ft. 3 in. x 19 ft., and 32 ft. x 14 ft. 6 in. respectively, and include two peach houses and two vineries. Four large cold frames and soft-fruit cage.

A range of stone-built Potting houses and sheds, wagon house and workroom adjoining.

On the North-East side of the gardens is a well built Dwelling House, known as

Bridge House

Now in the occupation of MR. PERCY NORTHCOTT, which is suitable for Bailiff or Head Gardener on the property.

The Pleasure Grounds

comprise Shrubberies, Sylvan and Riverside Walks and Terraced Lawns.

Rhododendrons, azaleas, and a wealth of foliage plants enhance the natural beauty of the situation. St. Tawny's Well, noted for the exceptional purity of its water, is in the grounds.

THE AREA COMPRISED IN LOT 1 is about a. 89'446, and in addition to the Bridge House already referred to there are the following cottages :—

"HIGH PARK LODGE"

In the occupation of MR. CECIL BARTLETT.

No. 1, JUBILEE COTTAGES

(Part No. 1504). In the occupation of MR. H. LANDREY, JUNR.

No. 2, JUBILEE COTTAGES

In the occupation of MR. E. THOMPSON.

NORTH HILL LODGE

In the occupation of MR. WALTER BARTLETT.

In Part 1493 a.—

TWO COTTAGES

In the occupation of   (a.) MRS. W. BARTLETT.

(b.) MRS. RICE.

In Part 1493 a.—

TWO COTTAGES

In the occupation of   (a.) MISS SPOONER.

(b.) MRS. GOLDSWORTHY (now vacant.)

These Cottages are of superior character, well built and pleasantly situated.

never met the Lathams – and they never moved into Trebartha, which was indeed requisitioned. Initially it served as a hospital for evacuees from Dunkirk and was later home to American and Polish airmen. The last occupants were Italian and German prisoners. By then, Trebartha Hall was little better than a wreck.

Bryan Latham wrote an account of the estate and his family's involvement – *Trebartha – The House by the Stream* (1971). He gives a detailed account of the end of the house.

> *In the autumn of 1946 the Italian prisoners left for home, to the great regret of the local farmers who had found them willing and adaptable workers, so the manor house stood empty and derelict. The desolate wreck of a once proud manor house whose rooms had once echoed to the footsteps of the Spours, Tremaynes, Rashleigh and Rodds. Early in 1947 the War Office started a leisurely correspondence on derequisitioning the place. An inspector came and after seeing the damage, gave his opinion that the W.O. would take advantage of the clause in the Act and pay a total loss based on 1938 values. This was rejected by his superiors, although why in view of the ridiculously low offer they ultimately made, nobody can tell. So a surveyor came from Taunton and started valuing the dilapidations. After a few days he had had enough and reported back that the only possible base was a complete write-off. We asked for the sum we had insured the building at when we took possession in 1940 and I will not sully these pages by mentioning the sum the W.O. originally offered. I will merely say that after two years' negotiations we received the identical sum which I had written in my note book in July 1940 as being the value of the house and outbuildings. Clearly the place had to come down and the sooner the better, as it was being broken into and pillaged. We enquired amongst housebreakers and received two offers. The estate to pay £50 to have it demolished, and the other to receive £50. We quickly accepted the second offer and the contractors made a good job of the clearance. It was a time of shortages and they readily recouped their outlay by the sale of timber, lead and slate from the roofs and glass from the windows.*

The Western Morning News of 24th February, 1949, carried an account of the demolition:

> *The hall, which contained as many rooms as weeks in the year, is being dismantled until the substantial well-built walls have been reduced to a level of six feet. It will not be rebuilt.*
>
> *The greensward in front of what was a noble pile of building is cluttered with rows of slates stripped from the roofs. Stacks of timber grow steadily as the pulling down proceeds.*
>
> *Consignments of panelling, doors, windows, grates, timber, lead and other materials have already been carried away for building purposes locally and elsewhere.*
>
> *Every wrecked room is masonry and rafter-strewn, and the roofless interior resembles the aftermath of a bombing raid.*

The article cites the heavy expenditure necessary to restore the hall, and the impractability of converting it into flats as being among the economic reasons for its demolition. It then waxes lyrical about the setting of Trebartha and its reputation as a bird-lover's paradise. Noted visitors, it states, include a golden eagle, a bittern and a raven. Starlings first nested in Cornwall at Trebartha in 1854, followed by the greater spotted woodpecker, the stock-dove, rock-dove, the hobby and the redstart.

Edward Hearle Rodd had been a noted ornithologist, and author of *The Birds of Cornwall and the Scilly Isles*, and bequeathed his considerable collection of stuffed and mounted Cornish birds to Francis Rashleigh Rodd, and for some sixty years they were displayed in the Western or Museum room at Trebartha before being presented to the Royal Institution of Cornwall in 1940.

The last two paragraphs refer to the estate tenants;

> *for whom it was a sad day when the Rodds left. There was kindly consideration for them all. The veterans were allowed to remain in their homes rent-free for life and there was a similar rental concession over a stipulated term of years for the others.*

The memories of the 80 year old former gamekeeper, Harry Landrey, have a poignancy that sums it up. He had served under three generations of Rodds for 43 years, and his father for 21 before him. He recalled times when there were 30 or more indoor and outdoor staff, and the days of the shoots, and the house parties and Christmas celebrations. The loss of the house was something he never thought he should live to see.

Sources

Trebartha, House by the Stream Bryan Latham, 1971
Trebartha at the Turn of the Millenium Robert Latham. 2001
The Book of the House of Spoure, 1694, Lady Rennell of Rodd

CRO   RD 1018 – Wyatt plans
AD 40/1   RD 35
AD 648/20/21/22/23

Whiteford in 1824   (F W L Stockdale)

Whiteford House, Stoke Climsland

Anabob, according to the Oxford Dictionary, is 'a wealthy, luxurious gentleman, especially one returned from India'. The description fits John Call (1732–1801) perfectly and it was the fortune he brought home with him from India that enabled him to create the beautiful Whiteford estate. Gilbert gives it a good description;

> *By 1775 he had built one of the most elegant modern mansions of the neighbourhood, with shrubberies, lawns, Italian fountains, canal, bridge, cascade, hothouses.*

John Call, who became an MP, High Sheriff, JP and a baronet, came from undistinguished yeoman stock. His father, John Call (1704–66) came from Launcells in north Cornwall, but with connections to Tiverton where young John was christened and went to school. But instead of possibly progressing to university, he went, at the age of 17, to India, as so many sons of the lesser gentry did in the hope of making their fortune. Some did, many did not, killed by the climate and disease. John Call prospered. For 21 years he toiled in the service of the East India Company, during which time he rose to be chief engineer to Lord Clive, a colonel and member of the Governor's Council. He returned in 1770, following the death of his father a few years earlier. At 38 he was barely middle-aged and had behind him 21 most profitable years.

It would seem that whilst he was in India, John Call had an eye to his future back home and made plans to establish himself by purchasing a country estate. His father acted for him, and Whiteford was first considered in 1760, and was eventually purchased in 1763 for £7,101 1s 0d. The purchase included several of the surrounding farms.

The estate in the early seventeenth century was known as Whittavor and was owned by the Clarke family, one of whom has a memorial dated 1649 in Stoke Climsland church. It passed down to the Addis family who died out in the male line in 1741, and through the female line until it was sold in 1763, by which time it was let out. Only one illustration of the Elizabethan house survives in the Book of the House of Spoure, dated 1694. This shows a typical yeoman farmhouse, and the will of John Clarke, dated 1620, lists a hall, north, middle and south chambers, a malthouse, milk house and buttery with stables and a walled garden. Over the entrance gate were the Addis coat of arms. Only the walled garden survives of this earlier house, but it was thought to have been situated close to the present entrance to Whiteford; a map of 1784 shows three rectangular buildings and a courtyard close to the present entrance. It was here that John Call Senior lived until his death.

ns is the Draught of Whittavor in Stoahe Climsland the Ma..

..fe of Iohn Addis Gent: of Plymouth: which came to him by t..

..ghter and heir of Bond by the Daughter and heir of Iackm..

The exact size of John Call's fortune is not known. Certainly it was enough for the initial purchase of Whiteford and certainly he died a very wealthy man. Two years after returning home, John Call married Philadelphia Battie, one of three daughters of a wealthy doctor, Dr John Battie of Bloomsbury. Her sisters also married west countrymen – John Rashleigh and Sir George Young. By then Call had been appointed High Sheriff of Cornwall and he and his new wife must have decided they liked the Whiteford estate sufficiently to make it their home. Accordingly, the new house was planned, although there had been some doubt in Call's mind. The possibility that the nearby estate of

Whittavor from the Book of the House of Spoure, 1694 (courtesy Lady Rennell)

*Wm Gardner
1784 - detail*
(BL K Top
11.80.a.8)

*The sheltering
plantations are
shown with a
drive down to the
road, and another
to the viewing
platform, site of
the later temple*

Werrington might come on the market made him pause. In a letter to General Clive he writes 'I should be vexed if after I laid out £4,000 or £5,000 in adding to an old house, a better one and a good estate was to be sold in the neighbourhood.' So at that stage he was not contemplating a completely new house and was tempted by the parliamentary seat of Launceston. However, the proposed purchase fell through and by 1772 it had been decided to replace the old house and work had begun on a new site.

Somewhere along the line John Call had acquired remarkably good taste and an educated eye, not only for architecture but for all the internal embellishments that turned what might have been a typical plain Cornish Georgian house into something that was, by most accounts, outstanding. Did he make friends and visit other houses being built in the new taste? He didn't have any connections and it is interesting to speculate where he got his ideas from. No records survive of either the architect or the builder, but it was a well laid out house of only modest proportions. Unusually, it was T shaped with the main rooms forming the cross and the business and service areas in the long wing behind, rather than completing a quadrangle round a service yard. Considerable excavation was carried out so that the rear of the house was below ground level, but not built as a basement. A service road ran round between the kitchens and the retaining wall, and there may even have been a bridge at first floor level. The only surviving plan gives details of the ground floor only, but from prints of the house it would appear there were neither cellars nor attics to the main portion. The ground floor consisted of an entrance billiard hall, drawing and dining rooms and a library.

The house was built of granite from Kit Hill, probably surface stone as the quarry did not open until later. The sash windows were of mahogany as would have been the doors and the staircase, which was described as the finest in the county. One Walter

Wivel, presumably the joiner who constructed it, inscribed his name and date on it. Italian craftsmen came from London to model the plaster ceilings in the principal rooms, and the vaulted lobbies and corridors. On the first floor was an oval boudoir decorated with 'delicately painted shutters and ceilings, pretty guilt mouldings and decorated doors and looking glasses'.

The stables, built on the higher ground between the house and the walled garden, were of the same high quality. It is curious that John Call built his house at the lowest point rather than on the higher ground.

Temple before restoration

The grounds were laid out as befitted the surrounds of a gentleman's house, with several fine trees and plantations. The 1784 map shows many mature trees in the parkland which must have been planted by the Addis family, but Call added two major plantations. One swept round protecting the north side of the house and the walled garden rising to a viewing platform, and one on the southern side curving round the Lawn. He was known to be a keen tree planter, encouraging landowners in the drive to provide replacement timber for the huge quantities required by the navy. The stream was dammed so that the pond became a 'sinuous lake' with an island and a palladian bridge, and a sunken drive crossed the parkland, separated by a ha-ha, to the front of the house. Later, Sir John built the temple on the site of the viewing platform, around 1799. This became a much-used feature by later generations, and after years of dereliction has now been restored by the Landmark Trust – Sir John Call's only memorial on his estate.

John Call must have been a busy man. In 1782 he was appointed to the commission set up to enquire into the management of Crown lands. Two years later he became MP for Callington, and then his interests appear to move from Whiteford for he became

Palladian bridge

a partner in a London bank, Pybus, Call, Corant and Hale, and in 1785 purchased a house in Old Burlington Street. He is also recorded as having interests in plate glass manufacture, and copper smelting. John Call does not seem to have been content with just the life of a gentleman of leisure, spending his time on visits and country pursuits. A worker all his life, that was how he continued. In 1775 he was elected to the Royal Academy, and ten years later became a Fellow of the Society of Antiquaries. In 1791 he was created a baronet. For the last years of his life, Sir John suffered from cataracts which caused him to go blind, and he died in London in 1801.

His will, drawn up a year before his death, is very detailed. It begins with instructions for his tomb, to be erected on Kit Hill adjoining the castle he had built there, and not to exceed £500.

Portrait of Sir John Call, 1784 by Francis Alleyne
(Christies Images, Nov 1981

32

A marble slab was to be placed near his pew in Stoke Climsland church – or 'where his mansion house was when he died with arms cut thereon and inscription chosen by wife and executors'. Provision was made for his sister and her children, and his friends, John Coryton and John Rashleigh, were given powers over the estate acting as trustees – William Call being then a minor. Should the estate pass to the son of one of his daughters, then he was to assume the surname, crest and arms of Call by Royal Licence. To his wife an annuity of £200 per year together with coach horses, carriages with harness, and wines and liquors at Burlington Street. She was to have the use of the household furniture, linen and china. Then comes an interesting clause concerning his father-in-law's estate. 'Children surviving wife and two aunts would be entitled to equal division of late grandfather Dr John Batties' personal estate – probably £3000 each.' £40,000 was to be invested and the interest on £10,000 to be paid to each daughter until marriage, when it would be settled on her, with £300 for wedding clothes. His younger son, George Cotsford Call, was left John Call's share in the banking house, which was to be worth £6,000, and £4,000 share in the Stag Brewhouse in Pimlico. They were given powers to dispose of the £14,500 which formed his wife's marriage settlement amongst the children after her death – £1,000 each with the remainder going to William. He was indeed a man of substance.

A codicil was added later that year, leaving £2,000 for the use of his nephew, George Call, for his maintenance and education and promoting his appointment as Writer to the East India Company, his equipment and voyage.

Sir John Call
The good man's death is often a useful lesson to the living … whole life was dedicated to virtue … guileless to the end … act so conspicuous a part on the stage of life. Born of respectable but not affluent parents in 1732 at Fenny Park near Tiverton and destined for the church. At 17 appointed to writership for the Court of East India Directors and went out under Mr. Robins, celebrated for his mathematical and philosophical knowledge. Career in India well known for his probity and untainted honour. Engineer of the Fort of St. David at the age of 19 with charge of all the artillery carriages, buildings civil and military in the settlement and its dependencies. 1757 Chief Engineer on the coast of Corromandel. He was commended by the Board of Directors for his 'extraordinary services and useful talents in the raising of the siege of Madras after nine weeks in open trenches 1759. Lord Clive in 1765 commended him for his abilities in the public line and the esteem and warm friendship between them in private. After 21 years he returned leaving behind him an unblemished character and with an ample fortune which might have been much larger had he ever sacrificed one principle of probity … agricultural pursuits despite his blindness and Medal from the Board of Agriculture.
Obituary, *Gentlemen's Magazine 1802*

The tomb on Kit Hill was to be designed by Philip Stowey, but as he died in London, in accordance with his wishes he was buried in St. Margaret's Churchyard, Lee, Lewisham, where his son John had been buried in 1785, and where there is a fine monument to him. John Call must have died content in the belief that he had laid the foundations of a family estate and that the funds were sufficient to maintain it and his family, and that the future of the Call dynasty was assured.

But it was not to last. Only 70 years after the death of Sir John Call, the Whiteford estate was sold, the money all gone, and the last baronet, William Montagu Call, died in poverty without an heir.

John Call and Philadelphia had seven children, born between 1776 and 1785. The eldest son, John Battie Call, died at the age of 16 in 1785. That left four daughters and William Pratt Call (1781–1851) and George Cotford Call born 1783. William was 20 when he inherited. He continued in his father's footsteps, becoming sheriff in 1807, but seems not to have been interested in a parliamentary career.

William initially seemed content with the life of a country gentleman with visits to neighbouring gentry, and excursions to Bath and Truro. One of the few surviving documents, William's diary of 1809, gives a wonderful insight into their lives. He had inherited some eight years earlier and in 1806 had married Louisa Forbes, daughter of the Earl of Granard, (known as 'Snipe'). Three years later he embarked on a programme of refurbishment to Whiteford, of which he left notes.

New curtains were put up in the drawing room, and others were altered; there is a reference to grinding green paint, and furniture for the saloon. Later, he records he was 'watering flowers till dusk', whilst 'Lyle and three others were cleaning the walks, and 7 women cleaning the wood court.'

There were trips to Bath, London, Exeter and Cheltenham, where they took warm baths. Back home at Whiteford there were new draperies in Sir William's dressing room, the woodwork in the flower garden was painted, and he bought a blood mare at Tattersalls.

Hayman was washing down the nursery walls, and he gave Louisa '£15 as half years money for the children', and also £5 card money – which would seem quite generous by comparison.

Hayman – who seems to have been the general handyman – was kept busy putting up wires in the greenhouse, and stripping wallpaper in the yellow dressing room.

On the 26th June, he was 'up at 9.00, began mowing the lawn. Fished in the canal and caught some trout.'

July 4 – New Wine cellar – no further details. There is an intriguing reference to Hayman 'working about the bath' and later 'putting up curtains in the dressing room, and grinding white paint'. Then he was putting down the dining room carpet, and painting the traillage in the garden, which he had erected earlier.

On 17th he was 'up at 5.00 to see the colt gallop' before going off to Bude.

August saw him at Bodmin races all day, where his horse won.

In September, Hayman was putting down carpets, nailing down green baize and painting the iron railings. Sir William was enjoying himself putting wine into his new cellar.

Entries mention him fishing, shooting , playing whist, and hunting. Hayman was 'making frilly pieces for the blinds in the saloon' and flower stands – there seems to be nothing he could not do!

In October the reason for all this activity – and the new wine cellar –becomes clear – there was to be a ball.

Oct 27th 'At home all day taking out wine and looking over the rooms, checking the chalking of the ballroom.'

The day of The Ball arrived.

'30th Dined at 4.00 – 26 to the dinner, ball in the evening 44 to supper – a very pleasant evening.' The next day the guests went shooting and there were 16 to dinner; Lord Mt Edgecumbe sung and played.

Nov 1st Hayman putting things in order, while they went to Truro to a ball.

19th 'Went to Tehidy to dinner, very ill, stupid evening'

Shooting the next day.

23rd' At Carclew till 1.00, went to Heligan to dinner.' Later there were visits to Saltram, Pentillie, Mt. Edgecumbe, Tetcott and Sydenham.

'Hayman putting up shelves and making sofas.'

Followed by 'taking out window in Sir William's dressing room and putting up pieces to dam it up.'

1810

Feb – shooting in the deer park.

March – digging pits for apple trees. ' Spent all the morning planting by the Temple and pruning apple trees.'

23rd Measuring bookcases for the library.

Fishing at Bude

Trips to Bath, Salisbury and Weymouth are listed, and to Tavistock races in August.

Hayman took down the blinds in the drawing room and dining room, and repairing those in Lady Aylmer's bedroom. (She was Louisa, William's sister).

August 24 Hayman putting up curtains in the library, which was then fitted with bookcases and furniture – unspecified.

1811

Curtains in the white bedroom, books in the library

'April 3rd – sitting for my picture.'

Then comes the full itinerary for a visit to London, including waltzing at Lady Jersey's.

August – 'Hayman repairing the frontispiece of the house.' Annoyingly he gives no further details.

Sir William does not record how much he spent on the refurbishment, or the cost of the ball – nor does he reveal how much the inestimable Hayman was paid. But at the end of the diary he does record how much he paid the servants in 1809.

Hired Budge at 40 gns per annum

Hired a workman at 28 gns per annum

Godwin as cook and housekeeper at £35 per annum

Under gardener at 7shilling per week

Stablehand at 10s 6d per week
Stably boy at 14 gns, plus suit of clothes, stable dress, hat and boots
Footman 22 gns per annum 2 suits, hats, riding breeches.
Groom and postillions 24 gns, 2 suits, stable clothes, 2 hats.
A trip to Bath –horses, drivers, turnpikes and eating – £24 15s.
Bill for furniture and curtains £18 7s 0d.

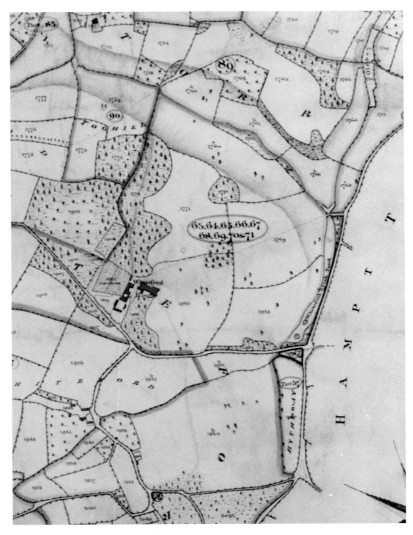

1815 map S Davis   (Cornwall County Council)

As well as improvements to the house, William Pratt Call further improved the grounds. He made a new entrance on the Stoke Climsland road, which crossed the parkland, giving visitors a good view of the house from the front – but Whiteford was never given an imposing entrance with stone pillars and gates, or even lodges. There was a circular carriage drive around the perimeter, lined with trees, and a bridge taking the new drive over the original sunken drive, to arrive in front of the house. The lake was enlarged and gained a couple more islands, and a cascade is mentioned. Kit Hill was, and is, the dominant feature with Sir John's castle forming a dramatic eye-catcher. It must have been a great favourite with the Call children and they must have had many picnics there amongst the 'ruins'.

In 1810 a tragedy struck the family. William's sister had married Benjamin Bathurst, who went missing whilst serving as envoy to Austria. George, a Lt. Col. in the army, resigned his partnership in the London bank to accompany his sister in her search for him. Sir William took over from his brother, and from then on the family divided its time between London and Whiteford.

Twycross describes Whiteford in 1846, the house and estate then in their prime:

> *A handsome building in the modern style with three regular fronts erected on a basement, and state floors with two upper stories. The internal decorations are gorgeous and elegant, the ceilings and door panels of the upper rooms being painted in a masterly style.*

> *Enclosed on the south side of a shrubbery in the centre of which is an Italian fountain of chaste and elegant design, and the other side is bounded by a lawn of considerable extent. To the north, the lawn is skirted by a thickly wooded plantation, and what adds much to the beauty of the scene is a large expanse of water in the midst of which are several small islands planted with fir trees. The gardens which are very extensive are particularly fine and contain several rare tropical plants.*

William Pratt Call died at Whiteford of dropsy in 1851 and was the only baronet to be buried at Stoke Climsland. His rule had lasted for fifty years and had seen the land holdings expand to some 2,500 acres. He was succeeded by his only son William Berkeley Call, then aged 36.

Whiteford still elegant

From then on it was downhill all the way. Something must have gone badly wrong for in 1853 an Abstract of Title to the Whiteford Estates was drawn up in favour of William Berkeley Call's godfather, Andrew Montague, of Yorkshire. Not much is known of the third baronet, other than that he served as High Sherriff. He was keenly interested in horseracing, a trait he sadly passed on to his only son, and this is believed to be the principal factor in the demise of the family fortunes. It was also a time of agricultural depression with falling rentals. By 1861, the census records only a housekeeper and two female servants at Whiteford, a sad contrast with earlier days. He was married to Laura Knight and they had one son. He must still have been involved in the family banking business in London, for it was there that he died in 1864, aged only 49.

There is always something sad about a family and estate in decline. William Berkeley Call was brought up in a house full of children and visiting aunts and uncle George. There would have been a cheerful bustle of servants, gardeners, stable lads and constant comings and goings amongst the neighbours. There were the frequent visits to the London house – and never any shortage of money. William Berkeley Call died only 13 years after his father, leaving the estate to his only child, William Montagu Call (1849–1903) then a boy of 15. Estate duty of £310 had to be paid on Whiteford, and £168.10s on lands at Stoke Climsland. The following year a sale of paintings was held at Christie's of London. In 1870, Sir William's wine was sold, and in 1876 further paintings followed. Would these sales have been on the instructions of Andrew Montague and the Trustees?

The decline was swift. The Calls left Whiteford, which was 'sold' to Andrew Montague in 1870, six years after the death of Sir William Berkeley. He tried to let what was by then a rundown house and estate, and finally sold the property to the Duchy of Cornwall in 1879. Prior to this, a sale of all the contents had been held. No catalogue has been traced, but there is a record of some fine Hepplewhite furniture

The fire damaged house

38

and the family portraits being bought by Admiral Sir William Wyndham Hornby, the husband of Augusta Call, one of the sisters of William Berkeley Call.

The Duchy, who had been primarily interested in the land and woodland, found themselves with a large decaying mansion, riddled with dry rot, for which they had no use. First to go was the rear kitchen block, demolished around 1900. Then a fire in the upper stories of the main portion settled the fate of the house which was knocked down in 1912. All that was left was the connecting wing, which became two cottages, and the stables.

The Stables

But parts of the house lived on, for in 1913 the Duchy was building a new Home Farm, on a site overlooking Whiteford. Much of the dressed stone, window surrounds, the porch, plinth and cornice were reused. Some of the mahogany doors, two Adam fireplaces and a fine staircase also found a new home.

Although the stables survived until the 1960s, the imposing arch and clock tower had already formed a central feature in the new stabling at the Home Farm. The final section of what remained of Whiteford was demolished in 1969, and the site sold to Mr & Mrs. Plant.

Today, the entrance drive leads down to the former stables, now converted into a pleasant house. There is some fine stone walling, and odd remnants of older buildings. Close by, still stands the walled garden, a survivor of the original Whittafor. New owners have replaced the Plants, the walled garden is beautifully cared for and the

All that remained of the house, post 1917

buildings in a good state of repair. The site of the Call's house was utilised to form an outdoor stage, for many years used for concerts – in a most lovely setting.

Postscript

The fate of the last baronet was sad, but not unusual. In 1880, Sir William Montagu Call, then living at an address in Pimlico, was declared bankrupt. But a few years later he must have got some money from somewhere for in 1886 he was charged under the contravention of the Foreign Enlistment Act in that he fitted out a vessel to form part of an expedition to sail against the administration of Venezuela. This proved a

Rear of the site showing steps to the stables

Site of the house when in use as a concert venue

complete fiasco, with the ship being handed over to a Venezuelan general who was then killed. Call blamed this as the cause for his second bankruptcy in 1888. He tried his hand at various enterprises, none of which prospered, and in 1897 he was declared bankrupt for the third time, involving the Trafalgar Cycling club and the Brighton Skating Rink, of which he was manager and had drawn an income of £1,200 a year. He had liabilities of £10,599. He died in 1903 without an heir. His wife, Marie de Mauleon, however, left her possessions to her only son, Albert Edward Call of Johannesburg, South Africa. All that can be traced is that in 1911 a man of this name was committed to a lunatic asylum in Praetoria following an incident at the Mali Dyke Mine where he had been working.

Sources

History Landscape Survey and Management Plan, 2004 Peter Dudley, MA, Dr. J. Mattingley (Cornwall County Council)
Diary of Sir William Pratt Call, 1809
Whiteford House, 1987 Alastair Forsyth

FS/3/1238 Diary of Sir Wm Pratt Call   CF 2225
AP/C/482   FS/3/1216 – Duchy Digest
CF 1283/1

Roscrow, Gluvias

According to poor Mary Granville, the only good thing about her new home was its position. A bride of seventeen, she had been married against her wishes to the elderly Alexander Pendarves, and her reaction on first seeing Roscrow was to burst into a violent storm of tears. A well-connected, well educated and very lovely girl, used to London society and being groomed as a possible lady-in-waiting to Queen Anne, she found herself a pawn in the age-old game of political marriage, banished from her family, friends and former life to a ruinous, remote Cornish manor with a morose and drunken husband, whom she referred to as Gromio.

Alexander Pendarves was born at Roscrow in 1662, the son of John Pendarves and Bridget Carew. He had two brothers, William, who died in 1693, and the Revd. John of Drewsteignton, who had an only child, Mary. The brothers lived through interesting times. Alexander Pendarves was born just after the Restoration of Charles II and by the time he died in 1726, the Hanoverian dynasty had been established for twelve years. Despite all the upheavals, Pendarves managed to serve as a Tory MP almost continuously from 1689 until his death. The Monmouth uprising, the Jacobite rebellion, the long years of war with France, and the ending of the Stuarts with the death of Queen Anne in 1714, all caused political minefields through which the leading figures had to tread warily.

Mary and her family were one casualty. Her father was the brother of Lord Lansdowne, the head of the once powerful Grenvilles (or Granvilles as they now spelt it) who had played such a major part in the Civil War as staunch supporters of the Royalist cause. The title of Lansdowne commemorated the battle in which his ancestor, Sir Bevil Grenville, fought so valiantly and won the battle but lost his life. The Grenvilles devotion to the Stuarts caused the new Hanoverian regime to view them with suspicion, and in 1714 Lord Lansdowne lost all his powerful offices of state on the accession of George I. Later that year he and his wife found themselves locked up in the Tower on a charge of high treason. He had married Mary Villiers, the widow of the Marquess of Bath, and on their release two years later without trial, thought it prudent to retreat to the Longleat estate. Alexander Pendarves by contrast, having served as a Stannator, was appointed Surveyor General of the Land Revenues of the Crown by the new monarch. He and Lord Lansdowne had long been friends, and Alexander Pendarves was a welcome guest at Longleat. Mary was already there, her wealthy relatives having taken pity on her now that her hopes of a position at court were gone. Her father was in dire financial straits, living on a very modest income, and gratefully accepted his wealthy brother's hospitality. Mary had spent a few weeks with her uncle, of whom she was very fond, and according to her diaries, she was enjoying herself greatly and making herself useful to her relatives.

That was until Alexander Pendarves arrived unexpectedly one evening whilst they were at dinner. This was her first impression;

> *He had travelled by horseback through the rain. I expected to have seen somebody with the appearance of a gentleman when the poor, old, dripping, almost drowned Gromio was brought into the room, like Hob out of his well, his wig, his coat, his dirty boots, his large unwieldy person and his crimson countenance were all a subject of great mirth and observation to me.*

Not for long – poor Mary spent the next two months trying to repulse him – under the 'dreadful apprehension, too well grounded' that she was the reason for his extended visit. The recollection of this period still caused her to tremble when she wrote of it years later. It was made very clear to her by her relatives that Pendarves' offer, when it came, was to be accepted. One view is that the Granvilles considered her position as future mistress of Roscrow was a good prospect, as it was assumed she would be left the estate on the death of Alexander Pendarves, then aged 56. A less charitable view is that Lord Lansdowne wanted the support of his influential friend at court; no more sojourns in the Tower. Either way, the seventeen year old Mary was, in her words

> *Sacrificed – I was married with great pomp – never was woe dressed in gayer colours.*

The estate of Roscrow had been in the Pendarves family at least since the days of Henry VI when Samuel Pendarves purchased it from the family of Roscrow. The antiquarian Norden, in his survey of 1507, lists Roscrow as belonging to John Roscrow. Back in the seventeenth century a younger branch had established themselves at Camborne at the property then known as Treslothan, but were considered the junior branch until the Roscrow Pendarves died out, and mining interests enriched the Camborne estate. Roscrow might have had a beautiful view – but there was a sad deficiency of copper and tin. The old Tudor house would appear to have been somewhat neglected, and according to Mary's account, had not been lived in for 30 years. Did Alexander and his first wife, Lady Dorothy Bourke, daughter of the Earl of Clanricarde, live in London? And if so, why didn't he take his young bride there? One account states that Pendarves, knowing he was the last of his line, planned to leave his estates to his niece Mary and her husband, Francis Basset of Tehidy – but he wanted Basset to change his name to Pendarves. Not surprisingly, Francis Basset was not agreeable, and some sources say that in a fit of pique Alexander decided to sell his property and live quietly in the country, and was on his way to carry out this threat when he stopped off at Longleat.

Judging by the description of Roscrow given by Mary in her autobiography, no wonder she had a violent fit of tears;

The castle was guarded with high walls that entirely hid it from view. When the gate of the court was opened and we walked in, the front of the castle terrified me. It is built of coarse stone, old and mossy and propt with great buttresses, and so had done for three score years. I was led into an old hall that had scarce any light.….on the left was a parlour, the floor of which was rotten in places and part of the ceiling had broken down and the windows were placed so high that my head didn't come near the bottom of them. My tears shocked Gromio … but I had not expected to see so ruinous a place. The rest of the house was answerable to what I have described.

Her shock must have caused a twinge of conscience for her husband gave her leave to fit up the house according to her fancy which, he thought, would help to amuse her.

The only known drawing of Roscrow (Courtney Library, RCM)

There is one sketch of the original Roscrow from the 1690s George Withiel map, depicting a typical medieval manorhouse. The Hearth Tax returns for 1660 list Wm. Pendarves, grandfather of Alexander, as having a property with twelve hearths – making it a sizeable house. The Poll Tax returns for the same year record 'The Worp. Wm Pendarves' as paying £10 in tax. His household consisted of his mother, Mrs Grace Pendarves, his two brothers, Francis and John, described as 'gent.' with incomes of £50 paying £1 poll tax; John Pendarves, gent., his son, and Bridget his wife paying £2, his children – it does not make clear whose – Nicholas, Meliox and Bridget, paying 1s, and Katherine Longford, niece, also 1s. The household was sizeable for the return lists the servants; three married couples, ten men servants and six female, all assessed at 1s each. Roscrow at this time was clearly a prosperous and bustling place.

44

William and Patience Salusbury Trelawny of HAREWOOD
(private collection)

TREBARTHA. Proposed Sheep Shelter, Lewis Kennedy, 1815

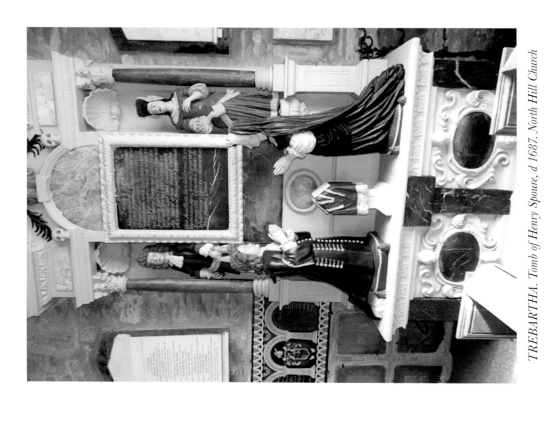

TREBARTHA. Tomb of Henry Spoure, d 1687. North Hill Church

This is the Draught of Trebartha Hall the Mansion House of the
Spoures: since they match with the Daughter and heir of Trebar[tha]
And is now Possest by Edmund Spoure Esq.

TREBARTHA from the Book of the House of Spoure, 1694

ROSCROW. Alexander Pendarves

ROSCROW. Mary Granville
(private collection)

PENDARVES. John and Susanna Stackhouse (private collection))

PENDARVES. Undated watercolour (Lucy Acton)

*TEHIDY. Francis Basset,
Lord de Dunstanville, d 1835*
(private collection)

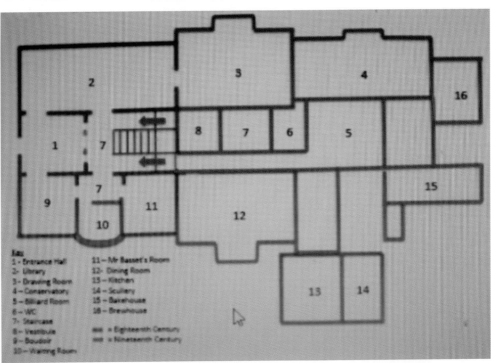

Key:
1 - Entrance Hall
2- Library
3 - Drawing Room
4 - Conservatory
5 - Billard Room
6 - WC
7 - Staircase
8 - Vestibule
9 - Boudoir
10 - Waiting Room
11 - Mr Basset's Room
12 - Dining Room
13 - Kitchen
14 - Scullery
15 - Bakehouse
16 - Brewhouse

▬▬ = Eighteenth Century
▬▬ = Nineteenth Century

*TEHIDY. Ground Floor plan of the 1863 extension interpreted by Patrick Newberry
(The Nineteenth Century House in Cornwall)*

CARCLEW. Sir Charles Lemon. Adam Buck
(private collection)

COLDRENICK. Charles Trelawny. (Robert Sneyd)

COLDRENICK.
Henry (Rooke) Trelawny,
Menheniot Church

THANKES. Admiral Lord Thomas Graves,
d 1802
(National Maritime Museum)

THANKES. Rear-Admiral Thomas Graves,
d1755   Thomas Gainsborough
(private collection)

STOWE. Prideaux Place — the room removed from Stowe (Peter Prideaux Brune)

Not long after they were married, in 1718, Alexander took his wife on a visit to Tehidy to stay with his niece Mary and her husband, whom Mary called 'Bassanio'. They were, she records, 'received coolly as they had hoped to inherit Roscrow and were both avaricious'. Francis Basset, who had been 'a man of gallantry in his youth', was impaired by ill health. The visit was marred by Alexander jealously regarding Basset's attentions to Mary and warning her that 'he had already been the ruin of one woman who was the wife of his bosom friend.'

Alexander managed to stay sober for the first two years of their marriage 'but then fell in with a set of old acquaintances, a society famed for excesses of wine and to his ruin and my misery was hardly ever sober.' When he wasn't drunk, he was sullen and sulked for days on end, according to Mary.

He was, however, content to leave Mary alone at Roscrow when he went to London on parliamentary business, and she happily entertained her own family, recording how she loved to ride on the beach as a form of escape. His business kept him away a full year, but he requested her presence when it seemed he would need to be in the capital longer. Reluctantly she went, and found the servants had been instructed to spy upon her. She described him as 'excessively fat, negligent in dress and took great quantities of snuff which gave him a dirty look' but that he was 'lively and sensible with an honest countenance, with a good nature and friendly'. Nevertheless she found his person 'disgusting rather than engaging'. Of his political activities she tells us that 'he was such a strong party man that he made enemies and was at one time involved in such difficulties it was with great good luck he escaped being discovered.' He was, she records, always out unless confined at home with the gout, sometimes for six weeks together. Then came the first hint of financial problems.

Hitherto I had lived in great affluence and I had never known want of money and was as prudent in the management of my domestic affairs as I thought our circumstances required … well furnished with clothes and pocket money by Lord Lansdowne and had no notion of ever wanting. Gromio complained of bad tenants and a cheating steward and some very near relations to maintain.

Mary does not specifically tell us the cause of this outburst but says 'it was the last misfortune I could have expected – I thought myself at least secure of an easy fortune.'

Then, in 1726, Alexander Pendarves died. According to Mary he had told her she was a good wife and he would like to reward her. Because of his ill health she persuaded him to defer to the morning 'signing his will' – by which time it was too late. Mary gives no account of his funeral, no account even of where he was buried. And there is no record that she ever went near Roscrow again.

(His obituary in the *Gentleman's Magazine* says he died at Beaufort Buildings, The Strand and was buried in the Savoy Church).

But then comes the twist in the tale. Alexander Pendarves knew there was nothing to leave his widow but a pile of debts. He had not even bothered to prove the will of his father, John, who died in 1682. It was left to Mary Basset, as next of kin and executor, to prove in 1727.

Francis Basset had died in 1721, leaving an heir, John Pendarves Basset, aged seven. An indenture dated 1734 quotes a memorandum of 1730; the Trustees of John Pendarves Basset and Mary Basset would ...

> *pay all debts of John Pendarves late of Roscrow and of Alexander Pendarves, son of John Pendarves and should pay an annuity of £370 to Mary Pendarves, widow of Alexander Pendarves in lieu of her jointure and that Mary Basset should convey all the estate and estates of the late Alexander Pendarves to John Pendarves Basset and his heirs forever.*

Then followed a list of bonds raised by Alexander Pendarves that had been paid off by the Trustees and that 'he had paid out several large sums of money ranging between £960 and £40.'

An old legal document exists listing creditors of John and Alexander, brought by Mary Pendarves and others against the beneficiaries and executors of the late Alexander Pendarves. These debts were in the nature of loans from their contemporaries and the names include Enys, Hawkins, Dennis, Trefusis and Kempe. The amounts range from a modest £12 to £1,560 – loaned in 1687 by Honor Gregor of St. Just. The first loan was in 1684 – £400 from Dorothea Trefusis, and the last in 1706, £1,400 from Margery Smith. Several women were persuaded to lend substantial sums to Alexander – was he an early example of a con man? Certainly he knew when he married Mary that he was heavily in debt, for the amounts totalled almost £6,000.

Perhaps it was as well Alexander Pendarves never altered his will for at least Mary had an income for life. She later married Dr. Patrick Delaney and became a celebrated writer and artist, dying in 1806.

To the Bassets, Roscrow was just another house. The new owner, Mary Basset, lost no time in finding a tenant and in June, 1730 a 99 year lease was drawn up between herself and William Plummer who for £62 leased;

> *All that Barton, Mansion House and land previously held by Thos. Pellowe, except the coach house and stable and part of the mansion called the little parlour and wing adjoining together with the Green Court, Bowling Green and Mount Garden with liberty for her to take them into her possession and use them at any time, paying 40 shillings yearly.*

This would imply that Plummer was the second tenant, and that Mary Basset wanted to be able to make use of Roscrow. He was still there in 1752 when he paid 4s 6d as half year's window tax. The Basset accounts show items for surveying Roscrow and the 'sale of goods there' in 1740, and for maintenance and repairs at Roscrow, using bricks from Tehidy. Interestingly, Mary's annuity did not stop on her remarriage in 1743, for in 1752, 53 and 54 Mrs Delaney was paid £370. And in 1753 an entry reads '1 yrs ground rent for Roscrow new house, pd Plomer £2 0s. This is the only intimation of the rebuilding that must have taken place, to alter the 'ruinous place' that Mary described into the neat house, described as a 'modern square shooting box' in a later account.

The *Book of Properties of Sir Francis Bassett* drawn up in 1793/4 records the Roscrow Estate: 'The Mansion House, Courtledge, Bleeching Yard, Pleasure Grounds, Kitchen Garden, Fore Meadow' and other acreages, totalled 38 acres. Roscrow Barton, the

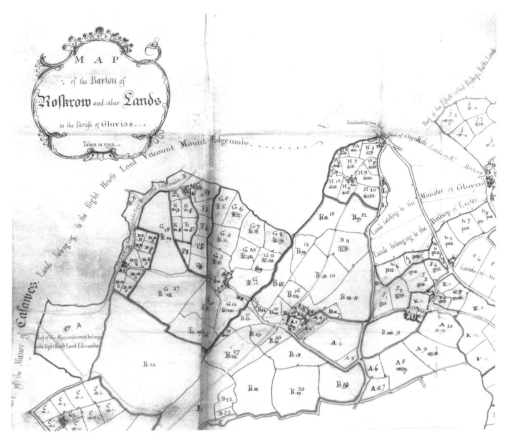

Estate plan of the Roscrow Estate, 1793. (CRO AD/894/7/52)

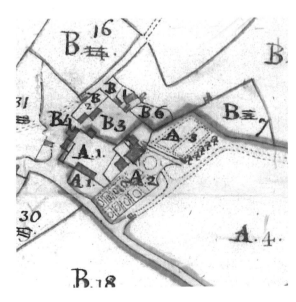

Detail showing house and grounds

home farm that backed on to Roscrow itself, with a dwelling house and small grounds, totalled 191 acres, so it was never a very large estate. The plan shows a compact block fronted by a carriage circle with two drives. The Pleasure Grounds are divided into several compartments each with a central oval – a style which was by then out of date.

Towards the end of the century the Plomers were still there for Samuel sublet part of Roscrow – to an interesting tenant. A document, was drawn up in March, 1795 between Samuel Plomer, tenant of Roscrow, and the Commissioner for Sick and Wounded Seamen and for exchanging prisoners of war, 'for taking the premises for the purpose of converting into a prison for one year certain and for longer … All the new stable barn and coach house and courtyard and also the wing of the dwelling house formerly known as a brewhouse and the room over 'for the annual rent of £100.' How long the Commissioner made use of Roscrow is not known, but in 1814 the tenant was Mr. R. Fox.

The property did, however, feature in the Marriage Settlement drawn up between Francis, Lord de Dunstanville and his young bride, Harriet Lemon in 1824. The estate was to be hers for her lifetime, along with the not inconsiderable sum of £2,000 per annum, increasing to £2,200 after her husband's death. During her long widowhood, it is not known whether Harriet ever lived at Roscrow, but it must have been in a habitable condition and of reasonable standard to feature as a dower house.

In 1856 a visitor – the editor of Mary's autobiography – described the modernised Roscrow. She was convinced that at the heart of the modern looking building was the kernel of the old mansion -

> modernised after being deprived of its quadrangle, gateway and courtyard, for the walls, the chimneys and even two or three of the rooms are the same, as also a small staircase which leads to the bedrooms and which formerly must have been one of many; one or two mantelpieces and ceilings remain unchanged in the lower rooms. There was a closet which matched Mary's description. There are still evidences in the foundations of Roscrow having been a very considerable pile of building though a passing traveller might at a distance take it for a square modern shooting box.

There is one picture of the 'modern shooting box' in decay, but it was quietly allowed to deteriorate until in 1890 it was demolished. A new house now occupies the site.

A rare photo of Roscrow in its shooting box style

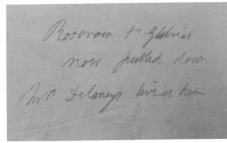

Sources

Autobiography and Correspondence of Mary
    Granville, Mrs Delaney. 1861
Cornwall Record Office
B/1/14/8
B/1/114/41
J/1/1746/1742
J/1/1746

J/1/1796
AD 1147/2
AD 894/7/52 – Estate map 1793

Royal Institute of Cornwall (Courtney Library)
HB/16/74

Pendarves in the 19th century   (courtesy Acton Family)

Pendarves, Camborne

Pendarves is a very private place. The estate is surrounded by protective belts of woodland and there are few signs that here was once a great house, home to one of Cornwall's historic families. One is the long winding stone wall enclosing the parkland, around which the parish road must travel, and the entrance gates and lodges, which no longer give access to the world within. It is still a private world, but a modern house occupies the terrace where once the family strolled, and where once they would have looked out over the parkland with its ancient trees, fields of daffodils now flourish.

The final end of Pendarves was unusual. According to a newspaper cutting of the time, it was 'the first major West Cornwall mansion to be razed to the ground by picks and shovels of a breaker's gang'. The year was 1955, a bleak time for country houses whose owners found them unsustainable.

Pendarves had not been lived in by the family since 1930. It had been used firstly as a school, and latterly by the military, including Patton's Armoured Division, prior to D Day. With their departure, the house was boarded up, awaiting its fate. The farms and 1,630 acres had been sold off in 818 lots in a four day sale in June, 1930, when the estate was advertised as having a rental value of £3,422 19s 7d per annum. But no attempt was made to sell the house and parkland either then, or after the War. There was no well-advertised demolition sale to mark its end, just a gang of breakers, with various materials going to whoever made an offer. A sad ending for long centuries of history.

The Pendarves family could trace their descent back to 1134 and were thought to have come to the Camborne area in the days of Elizabeth I, and their original home to have been at Treslothan. One account states that the family resided in the manor house of Treslothan, a short distance to the east of the present mansion, and that 'amongst other ruins there remained the walls of a chapel'.

Alexander Pendarves is the earliest recorded as 'of Pendarves'. He died in 1624, the estate passing to his son and then to his grandson, William, who died without issue in 1682. Camborne church contains a memorial to him, but little is known of him except that he was a Sheriff of Cornwall. Not for the first, or last, time the estate went sideways to his nephew, Richard, but he died unmarried at the age of 21 in 1706, so it is unlikely that he had any impact on the house. The next to inherit was nephew William, son of Thomas Pendarves, the rector of St. Columb Major, and his wife, Grace Hoblyn. This William, (1689–1726), concerned himself in local affairs, and represented St. Ives in Parliament. He was knighted by Queen Anne when he was just 23 but his career was cut short, for he died in 1726, aged 37 and he, too, was buried in Camborne.

Sir William would appear to have been quite a character – 'an offensive, hard-drinking man'. In her autobiography, Mary Pendarves, widow of Alexander Pendarves of Roscrow, gives an insight following a visit in 1718;

> … a very handsome man with a moderate understanding who has been 10 years at court. He was younger than his lady who was neither young nor handsome. It was therefore presumed that he married her for her fortune and connections … after her death Sir William's house was made the rendezvous of a very immoral set of men. A copper coffin was placed in the midst of the great hall and filled with punch …

Unfortunately, she did not describe the house.

Sir William had married Penelope Godolphin, widow of Robert Hoblyn of Nanswhydden, who had died after just two years of marriage leaving a son, Robert, who presumably was brought up by his mother and Sir William, so it is likely their time would have been divided between Nanswhydden and Pendarves. There were no children of this marriage, so on Sir William's death the estate went to his sister, Grace. She had married firstly Robert Coster, and secondly Samuel Percival, a Bristol merchant.

The earliest picture of Pendarves House is a drawing by Dr. Borlase dated 1758. It shows a plain Georgian house on a rusticated semi-basement, with a few simple steps to a modest front door. Concealed in the engraving behind groups of trees are two structures on either side of the house; one appears to be attached, with a tall chimney, and that to the left could be a walled garden. To the front is a plain lawn, with an exedra with six classical statues, separated from the parkland by a ha-ha – an early

51

Pendarves Wm Borlase, *Natural History of Cornwall*, 1758 (courtesy Acton family)

example in the county. However, there is some doubt as to whether this view existed, or if Borlase was depicting a possible future scheme, as there is no mention elsewhere of the statuary or the ha-ha, nor does it feature on any map.

A delightful painting, still in family ownership, dating from the end of the 18th century shows the south west elevation; four bays with a central canted bay, set on a hillside overlooking the lake. In the foreground is a palladian bridge and a small classical temple. (See colour section).

What is uncertain is who was the builder of this house? Did Grace, sole heiress of her brother, decide to move from the Tudor house at Treslothan and erect a modern building on a new site? Sir William Wynne, writing in 1755, described Pendarves as 'a fine seat of Mr. Percival, new fronted and good gardens.' This would imply that the house had been there for some time and that the Percivals had made alterations. Grace was certainly responsible for the grotto, which Dr. Borlase described;

> *Mrs. Grace Percival has offered us a fair pattern by fixing side by side in her Fossilary an infinite number of crystals of various and the clearest waters, in all shapes, single and in clusters, mostly out of mines in her own lands, all out of her neighbourhood. So many rich subjects will well remunerate the attentive inspection of every inquisitive Fossilist.*

But the 'mines on her own lands' might give a clue. Although mining returns had not yet reached anything like the peaks of the mid nineteenth century, they were certainly repaying any investment, and Sir William was described as a renowned copper smelter – one of the first in the county, with the copper coffin no doubt coming from his own mines. But with no children of his own, and interests mainly in London, it seems likely he died before embarking on building projects, and no reference has been found linking him to it. Perhaps the two of them, knowing Grace would inherit, planned the house together.

A Deed of Revocation between Pendarves-Coster-Percivall, dated August 1757, makes interesting reading. Based on the 1736 marriage settlement of Grace Coster, widow of Robert Coster and sister and heir of Sir William Pendarves, there being only one surviving trustee, the Deed appoints Grace and Joseph Percivall as trustees and cites property in Treslothan, Helleggan, Illogan, Redruth, Gwennap, St. Agnes, Crowan, Gwinear, Camborne and Gwithian inherited from Sir William, to receive revenues and profits for lives, then to use of John, second son of Revd. William Stackhouse, then to his sons, etc. And ends with Grace's tin bounds in Illogan, Camborne, Crowan, Wendron and Kenwyn (except Pendarves lands in North Downs) to uses as above.

A letter from Grace Vyvyan of Trelowarren, a Hoblyn relation, written to Jane Quicke of Nanswhydden in 1760 refers to Pendarves. She writes to thank the Quickes for their hospitality and recounts ;

> *Mrs. Percivall appears greatly elated upon being returned to Pendarves and at present finds, after so long an absence, many material repairs, absolutely necessary to be done to her house, and particularly, the essential one of new roofing it, as the rooms in some parts of the house receives the water in; this job she chooseth to inspect the doing of, and which she says will detain her home.*

She goes on to mention a visit to Tehidy with 'Mr Basset behaved with the utmost complaisance, Mrs. Basset and her sister all elegant and easy, and after dinner the child appeared, a sweet little thing, the express image of her mother tho' only two years old.' The letter finishes by saying how much they missed Mr. Percival's company – it would have been his illness and death that had kept Grace Percival away from Pendarves. If the house was in need of re-roofing, it would imply that it was already of some age – the builder remains a mystery.

Although Grace was the mistress of Pendarves for nearly 40 years, her husband's business interests were in Bristol, and he was described as 'of Clifton', where presumably they had a house. Pendarves was, perhaps, only occasionally occupied. Grace died in 1763.

Her will, dated 1761, states she is to be buried at Camborne;

> *… in linen not dressed for grave but to be wrapped in a clean sheet and to be seen by very few persons and to be buried in Camborne parish church as near my late husband and Honoured Mother.*

She states that the heir to the Pendarves estate is to

keep in repair and beautify the monuments and tombs of uncles Alexander and William Pendarves, and of her dearly beloved brother, Sir William Pendarves, in Camborne church, and also to beautify, repair and keep clean her father's honoured monument in the church of Higher St. Columb, and also the altar piece in Camborne church. The pictures in Pendarves House to remain as heirlooms and Pendarves House to be kept in good repair. Twelve poor women of Camborne to carry her to her grave and receive three guineas of gold and a pair of gloves.

She left the residue of her personal estate to John Stackhouse, Fellow of Exeter College, Oxford, her great nephew. John Stackhouse of Trehane, (b.1741), was a descendant of Dorcas Pendarves, sister of the first William. Her daughter had married John Williams of Trehane, which estate passed to their daughter, wife of Revd. William Stackhouse of St. Erme. Their son, William of Trehane, married Mary Rashleigh of Menabilly and it was their second son, John, then aged 22, who inherited Pendarves. He would appear to have been something of a prodigy, matriculating from Exeter College at the age of 16, and becoming a Fellow until 1764, upon his inheritance of Pendarves. John then spent the next three years travelling around the Mediterranean, pursuing his study of marine biology, on which subject he was to become an acknowledged expert. But he lost no time in setting in hand improvements and alterations on a large scale. Perhaps Pendarves had been neglected in the latter years of Grace's life, much of which had been spent in Bristol.

The steward's accounts for this period have survived, and as early as 1764 references are made to digging clay for making bricks and to the 'Brick Moor'. The total paid in July the following year for making 40,000 bricks was £6 13s 4d. In December another entry reads 'Paid Thomas Rickard in all £16 5s 5d in full for making 47,675 bricks', the burning of which required 3,000 wood faggots (£2 9s 6d) and 2,500 furze faggots (£8 2s 6d). This would all indicate a major building project was in progress. Other entries refer to glass works at Pendarves, masons and carpenters work, and right up until November they were still making bricks. John Stackhouse must have had great confidence in whoever was in charge of the building operations in his absence, and it may be the house was rendered uninhabitable.

Work was also being carried out around the grounds. Several entries refer to hedges being planted, and to six stones being cut for landmarks between Sir John St. Aubyn's land. In July two guineas was paid for making the new road and again, in August, a further three guineas for the new road and the new pond. In March, 1768, eight days were spent clearing out the foundations for the brick wall to 19 inches and later that year the garden wall was built.

During his tenure, John Stackhouse considerably enlarged Pendarves, more than doubling it in size – but photographs show a house faced with stone, to which there is no reference in the 1765 accounts, although when the house was demolished, a quantity of granite was noted. Perhaps this was the new front mentioned in 1755. Twycross in 1846, (quoting from Hitchins' 1824 account) describes the house:

present mansion is extensive and elegant with two handsome fronts of granite, the view across the western part of the county is of considerable extent and the southern front overlooks a large sheet of artificial water. The house contains some very splendid apartments in which there are several good pictures and a valuable mineral cabinet.

But he states that Pendarves was enlarged by John Stackhouse in 1790, so were there two building projects?

Map showing 'Property of John Stackhouse' 1778   CRO PD 90

Two estate plans give some help. That of 1778 shows an outline with two plain sides, and a series of additions to the other two. By 1842, the outline has simplified, with a new addition on the west front – the large *porte corchere* shown in the photograph. The 1778 map lists a poultry court, the deer park and a mowhay. In all, eleven ponds or canals are named.

On the later map the old village of Treslothan is still shown, with the Chapel of Ease. A new entrance drive is shown in dotted lines, leading in from the north west, curving in front of the house. A new stable block is shown with considerably more outbuildings, and part of the rear of the house has gone.

In 1773, John Stackhouse had married Susanna Acton of Acton Scott in Shropshire,

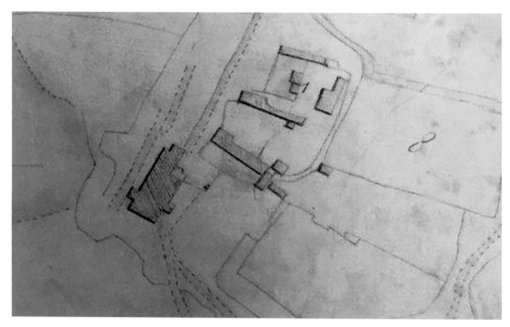

Estate plan dated 1842   CRO

heiress to a considerable estate. Two years later, their son John was born, the first direct male heir for almost two hundred years, and a year later, Edward followed. John did not survive boyhood (d. 1782). However, it would seem that Pendarves did not entirely suit the couple for in 1775, the year Susanna inherited the Acton Scott estate, they built themselves another large house on the cliffs above Prussia Cove, called Acton Castle, specifically so that John Stackhouse could study marine biology and seaweed at first hand. The bay beneath is named after him, and it is said that there was a tunnel to the beach. Built in the cellars were two lead tanks in which to keep his specimens. He was increasingly prone to rheumatism and spent time in Bath taking the waters, which led to him employing John Wood to design this new house, which was sold in 1802, and is now an hotel.

A few details of the estate were recorded in a surviving account book for 1785–88. £144 19s was spent on the purchase of a ticket in the English lottery – and the coal merchant was paid £15 10s. The gardeners' wages came to £18, and three guineas were given to 'the poor'. In 1786, £13 4s was spent on book binding and six guineas on a set of library steps. Then in April, John Stackhouse, on account with Messrs. Leigh and Sotherby, sold off a large portion of his library – including books from the important collection acquired from Narcissus Luttrell – a forebear. This realised just under £1,000 which was spent on the purchase of stocks and consols. Later that year another lottery ticket was purchased, and the year's window tax came to £17 6s 5d. The account book ends with the totals for 1788 – income £1537 11s 6d, expenditure £1500 4s 9d.

Narcissus Luttrell (1657–1732) – of Holborn and Kentisbury (Devon) deserves a

56

mention. His mother was Catherine, daughter of Narcissus Mapowder of Holsworthy. He was briefly MP for Cornish constituencies but it was for his chronicles of parliamentary proceedings – the only record of this period, 1678-1714, that he was well known. He had a legal background and was a historian who spent largely on his collection of books – by 1706 it was estimated he had spent £1,500.

As well as inheriting the Acton Scott estate, in 1789 Susanna also inherited estates in Hereford from her uncle. Much of their time must have been spent travelling between their many properties, as well as trips to London and increasingly to Bath where John Stackhouse sought relief for his rheumatism. But his study of marine biology continued and in 1795, the year he was elected a fellow of the Linnaen Society, he published *Nereis Britannica, or a Botanical Description of Marine Plants*. It was a masterly work, superbly illustrated by Stackhouse. In the early years of the nineteenth century, John and Susanna decided to simplify their lives; 1802 saw the sale of Acton Castle, and following the marriage of their eldest surviving son Edward in 1804, they passed Pendarves over to him and moved to a new house in Bath.

Edward would appear to have been of a scholarly disposition; Harrow was followed by Oxford, where he gained an MA and became a Fellow and sub-warden of All Souls until his marriage. In 1804 he married Tryphena Trist from Bowden in Devon, of which she was the heiress. Although he appears not to have actually become an MP until 1826, he actively supported the Reform Act, working for it from 1811 with the Friends of Parliamentary Reform. He was also active in the founding of London University. As well as representing the county in Parliament until his death – he was re-elected unopposed at every election – he was on the South West railways committee,

Edward William Wynne Pendarves
(courtesy Acton family)

and served for many years as a magistrate. Edward supported the Repeal of the Corn Laws in 1846, and in 1852 was made a Special Deputy Warden of the Stannaries. He refused elevation to the upper house with the title of Lord Camborne

This diligent and public-spirited man was twice to inherit sizeable estates. In 1814, a relative, the Revd. Luttrell Wynne died, leaving all his estates in Cornwall and Hereford to Edward, who added the name of Wynne to his own. Then in 1819, his father died and Edward inherited the Pendarves estate. Unlike his father, he decided to change his name and assumed the arms and titles of Pendarves, perhaps because he was born there and felt keenly associated with the estate. His younger brother, Thomas, also changed his name on inheriting his mother's estates at Acton Scott and How Caple in Hereford.

In 1821 a London house, 36 Eaton Place, was purchased – close to his mother's house in Cadogan Place. There is reference to plate from 36 Cadogan Place in an 1809 record, so the family may have had a London home for some time. Property in Whitechapel and Aldgate is also mentioned. This was a period of great prosperity with Cornish mines producing much of the worlds' copper supply, and the Pendarves income would have reflected this.

Edward Pendarves embarked on some ambitious plans for the estate. In 1840 Treslothan was chosen as the site for a new church and a model village. A chapel of St. James existed in 1427, when it was granted a licence, but it had fallen into disuse and become ruinous. The architect George Wightwick drew up the plans. A new vicarage and a schoolmaster's house were built, and a pair of cottages were added in 1845, and also a farm a short distance away. At least one of the lodges dates from this period – the original house had none.

Any former cottages were swept away, the road widened with a broad sweep in front of the church, which was connected to Pendarves House by a private drive. This, and the endowed school that had been built close by, funded by Grace Percival, has disappeared.

The only plan of Pendarves House known to exist is dated around 1850 when the same architect, George Wightwick, was called in to draw up alterations to the house. This shows the principal floor, with the Justice Room still marked. The domestic area takes up the whole of the rear portion, so it would seem that the semi-basement contained only cellars. Pendarves House appears to have been simple, and quite plain. Nowhere is there any reference to plasterwork, panelling or quality doors or woodwork. Nobody commented on the interiors, and prior to its demolition, no-one thought of taking photographs to record it.

Edward had a long tenure at Pendarves until his death in 1853 – the only owner to be born and die there. As well as building the chapel and altering the house, he took a keen interest in the gardens which became famous, and were included in Loudon's top ten Cornish gardens listed in the *Gardeners Magazine* of 1837.

Edward Pendarves has greatly improved this place by extending the grounds and giving them a park-like appearance, altering the approach on the south west and adding another on the north east.

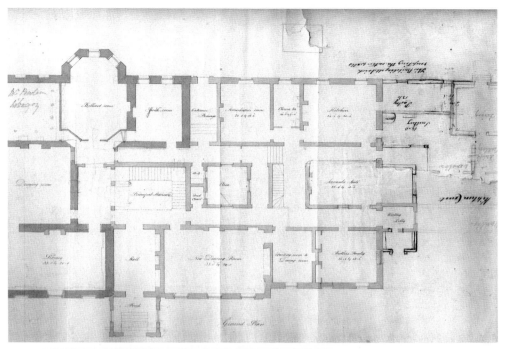

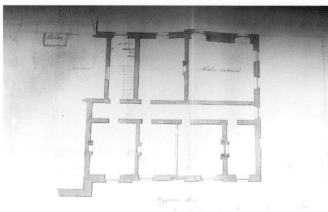

Plans of the proposed extension, 1850 'This building all brick except the outer walls.'

Kelly's directory for 1919 refers to the gardens, 'which were formerly mere barren wastes strewed with granite' as laid out by the late Edward W.W. Pendarves and near which 'is a curious grotto built entirely of Cornish minerals.' So Grace's grotto was still in existence one hundred and fifty years after her death, and amazingly, a small fragment still survives – or did in the 1990s.

The sale plan of 1930 shows the estate as Edward Pendarves left it. Shelter belts of trees are marked around the perimeter, the house is surrounded by trees and the grounds laid out with drives and walks. It was probably he who altered the ponds, and the whole park was, and still is, enclosed by a stone wall.

The two censuses of 1841 and 1891, chart the changes taking place. In the first, Treslothan is listed with seven families named. Of the men, 13 were listed as working in the copper mines and several of the women dressed the copper ore. Pendarves itself had a game keeper, gardener, housekeeper, bailiff and an agricultural labourer. Fifty years later Treslothan had shrunk to just two families. At Pendarves Lodge lived Francis Davies, the butler, and his family. Also living in lodges were the gamekeeper and the gardener. William Cole Pendarves, of Chelsea, was living at Pendarves House 'on his own means' and a housemaid and laundress were named, and three female servants. At the farm was the bailiff, Thomas Tripp, and a gardener, and the stables housed the coachman and carpenter. John Rodda, the land steward was in the office and James Reed, with a large family, was at Pendarves Mill. Although there is an absence of indoor servants such as cook and housekeeper, maids etc. who were possibly away at Chelsea, the size of the estate had grown.

In 1853, Edward Pendarves died – 'full of years and full of honour', but childless. 'Another of the old and staunch reformers of this county has been taken from us' his obituary went on, referring to his strongly held liberal principles before such views were valued. In the long history of Pendarves, Edward stands out as the only owner who considered the estate his home and where he spent much of his life, during which he greatly enhanced it.

The estate passed to William Cole Wood (1841–1929), the grandson of his eldest sister, Mrs Barnard Coleman, and he also assumed the name of Pendarves. Edward's widow, Tryphena, lived on for another 20 years, dividing her time between Pendarves and Tristford, where she died in 1873, aged 95. She had erected a mausoleum at Treslothan in memory of her husband, where she was also buried. She seems to have been a woman of great influence whose presence was felt in the area, a benefactress of the school and the tenants, who held her in high esteem. Her will of 1860 states that her heir to the Tristford estates shall change his name to Trist and bear the arms of that family – failure to do so would mean the estate passing to the next in line. Tryphena then goes on to list items at Pendarves Mansion House – plate, linen, china, books, pictures, minerals, statues, marbles, bronzes, two portraits of her late husband and a picture of

Our Saviour by Raphael, three family rings – all to be held as family heirlooms upon trust and within three years of her death an inventory of such heirlooms was to be made and a copy placed with the trustees and with the muniments of title to the estate. She wished to be buried in the same vault as her late husband at St. John's and to be carried there by estate servants without ostentation as with her late husband.

Following her death, an inventory of the contents of the house was made. In the absence of any plans or sale catalogues, this gives the only description of the interior. Outside was a stable, smiths' shop and yard, dogs' house, wood house and greenhouse with 100 plants. Inside the inventory starts with the 'downstairs' rooms – servants' hall, butler's pantry and a run of pantry, scullery, dairy, wash house with lead trough and copper boilers. The kitchen had a roasting range, and a small oven – 6 ' 6" long. The china cupboard had only 'old and odd items' and the pantry an 'old dinner service' of 150 pieces. The glass cupboard housed 'old decanters and coolers' and there were 100 old plates. Only a small number of silver knives and forks are listed. The cellar, however, still seemed well stocked with claret, sherry, Madeira etc., listed in 100s of bottles.

The inventory then moved 'upstairs' to the dining room, and drawing room with 164 yards of carpet. More details are given of the library, which contained 2,498 books, catalogued. These were housed in oak bookcases, 6' long by 12' high with four doors with brass wire panels, 18'6" with 16 doors, 13' 8" with 10 doors, 12' 9", and 12'. The curtains were of silk damask and there was 18 yards of carpet. The table in the billiard room was 12'x 6', and the curtains were 'motheaten'. The entrance hall contained a Specimen case with glass doors, 5'6" x 7' x 21" deep, full of specimens – presumably minerals, although this is not specified – and with coconut matting. Then came the hall and staircase, with 12 yards of carpet. The house still had a Justice Room, and gallery

The house surrounded by trees

61

containing a mahogany case of 5 maps with spring rollers, 700 ft of shelves and 1800 books. In the Terrace Entrance were yet more book shelves with 370 large books, and beyond were the housekeeper's room, a store room and linen cupboard. Above were 19 bedrooms and 6 servants' bedrooms.

The itemised furniture was the usual mahogany tables, chairs and chests with little detail given, and the number of paintings in each room is given, but no clue as to whether they were portraits or landscapes, or of the artists. The only two described were the 'large painting of Napoleon, 9' x 10' in a gold frame' above the Best staircase, and, right at the end, 'Portrait of Mr. Pendarves in gold frame' – but not which Mr. Pendarves. (The Pendarves had spent some time in France and met Napoleon during his Consulate).

A picture emerges of a house not much used, of a house that was perhaps of secondary importance to an ageing, childless woman – for the second time in its history.

'Uncle Pen'   (courtesy Acton family)

William Cole Pendarves and his wife, Alice Farrar, had a son, John Stackhouse Pendarves, within a year of their marriage in 1893. He would appear to have carried on the family tradition of public service – chairman of the county council, High Sheriff, Deputy Lieutenant and Chairman of the Magistrates – but not Parliament. He provided scholarships for the sons of working miners and was Governor of the School of Mines in Camborne. Pendarves seems to have jogged along, surviving the First World War unscathed. He is remembered as a caring, kindly man – Uncle Pen to his young relatives, one of whom remembers visiting Pendarves and feeding the swans on the lake and dining in the servants' hall. He died in 1929 and, unlike his recent forebears, was buried with some ceremony – his coffin draped in white borne on a purple-covered wagon.

William Cole Pendarves with his wife Alice and son John in front of the temple; this survives as the front porch to the former stable block (courtesy Acton family)

John, who had followed his father to Harrow, and later to Oxford, served in the Life Guards during the War and was severely wounded. He seems not to have been interested in Pendarves, and following a secret marriage in 1919 to Elfreda Stephens, he set up as a racehorse trainer with stables at Epsom.

In 1930, one year after the death of his father, the entire estate, with the exception of the house and park, were sold off. Then in May, 1936, Sotheby's were instructed to sell 'Valuable Books the property of John Stackhouse Pendarves including the second portion of the library of Narcissus Luttrell'.

Perhaps the estate was struggling. The steward's accounts for 1918 give an insight into the costs of running such an estate. The weekly wage bill was just over £20, of which the gardeners were paid £5 5s, the farm workers £4 17s 4d, estate workers £4 18s 6d, game keepers £1 15s 4d, masons £1 12s 6d and the laundry £1 12s 6d. Other outgoings included £41 16s for stable oats, £38 14s 7d for house coal for September, £2 10s for Spratts game dog biscuits, and rates payable to Camborne, £89 11s 4d.

A summary for 1918 records that the estate received payments for the sale of potatoes (£376 1s), cattle and pigs (£1006 19s 8d), dairy (£123 19s 11d), stables (£93 10s), poultry (£56 10s), gardeners dung (£4 10s) and other items, in all totalling £1,610 10s 3d. The rents and dues totalled £6,897 4s 1d. Major expenditure for the year, which totalled £4, 323 10s 6d, included £130 5s 1d in rates, £878 11s 5d in income tax and £423 16s 3d in tithes, National Insurance £9 17s 5d and a bill for wages and repairs of £1,912 16d 9d. Interesting items were £16 15s 2d for car hampers – the maids board and wages were £18 9s 4d – and £5 1s 4d for papers. During the year, William Pendarves had paid money in to keep things running, but between July and December, £5,900 5s 2d was paid into his account. This shows an estate just ticking over with little money for repairs and no profit for the owner. At a time of national crisis and depression, to a young man with seemingly no attachment to the place, it would be more of a millstone than a welcome inheritance. So the last of the Pendarves sold what he could and shut up the house. The War Department requisitioned it – but the writing was on the wall.

John died in Switzerland of tuberculosis in 1938, leaving his elder daughter Winifred to inherit. She married Captain Warwick, who added Pendarves to his name, and they had a son, Philip Warwick Pendarves.

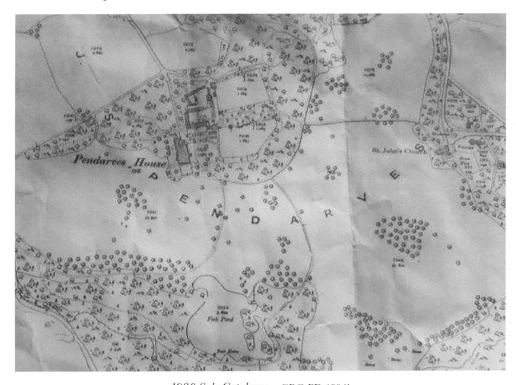

1930 Sale Catalogue   CRO PD 489/1

The temple relocated

The bridge shown in the 18th century painting.

With no estate left, and having no feeling for Pendarves, Winifred had the house demolished in 1955 – and it ended its days as hardcore for a road improvement scheme.

There is some public access to the estate for the Duchy of Cornwall now own some of the woodland and the lake, which are managed as conservation areas, and from which visitors can look across the lost parkland and try to imagine Pendarves House as it once stood.

In a sad corollary, the Pendarves archive has now been dispersed. Originally it was deposited at the Cornwall Record Office where it was available to interested parties, including myself. Then in June 2013, it was put up for auction in its entirety. Among the lots were the remnants of Narcissus Lutrell's books, mining documents, estate records – and the portrait of Alexander Pendarves of Roscrow, which now hangs above the backstairs of a former Cornish rectory.

Sources

John Stackhouse and a Tale of Five Houses
   Lucy Acton. Unpublished Ms 2007
Acton Family Archive

Cornwall Record Office
GHW/13/2/5/6/1

GGHW/13/2/3/14
PD 90 – 1778 estate map
PD 345
RP/4/30/6
X 84/24
AD 2258/1/43/44/45 estate maps

Nanswhydden Wm Borlase, *Natural History of Cornwall*, 1758

Thomas Edwards

Tehidy was one of a trio of houses built in the first half of the eighteenth century with two things in common – all suffered disastrous fires, and all were the work, partly or in whole, of a little known architect, Thomas Edwards. These were Tehidy for the Bassets (1735), Nanswhydden for the Hoblyns (1740), and Carclew for the Lemons (1749), featured in Borlase's *Natural History of Cornwall (1758)*. Two handsome town houses in Truro, and two churches are surviving works of Edwards. He was also involved at Trewithen, built for the Hawkins' family in the 1730s, which had two large flanking pavilions connected by colonnades and with basement corridors, a feature repeated by Edwards in his designs.

Thomas Edwards was not a prominent architect, and seems to have dabbled, rather than making it a serious career. His home was in Greenwich and he had interests in shipping and mining, which could have brought him into contact with the Cornish gentry. He died in 1773, and his will makes reference to his mines, which were to be sold, and various properties he owned. It is not known when he was born, but his children were born between 1746 and 59, so the youngest would have been 14 at the time of his death. This would mean that either he married late in life, or he was a young man at the time he was designing his Cornish houses. Edwards is known to have been an admirer of the work of Palladio, subscribing to his book of designs published in 1738, and of the English architect James Gibbs, whose designs harked back to Wren and the Baroque.

The three houses have similarities. The regular fronts were broken by a central section with a pediment on a rusticated basement, with the entrance on a *piano nobile* reached by a flight of steps. Typical Georgian sash windows had keystones, and the angles were of dressed quoins. The designs were simple and plain, with no embellishments, except for the portico at Carclew. As if to break the severity, Edwards added flanking pavilions. Those at Carclew were connected with colonnades; Tehidy was given four much larger structures of two storeys, obviously intended to serve some function, and each with a highly decorative cupola, in the earliest drawing shown concealing the chimney stacks. Nanswhydden made do with two very small structures, completely out of scale, connected to the house by blank walling and, oddly, with crenellation round the roof, one of which is almost all that survives. Tehidy was by far the grandest of the trio, but as no original drawings or plans have come to light for any of the houses, one can only speculate as to whether they were by the same hand, and whose that was.

Edwards was involved in building work at Trewithen certainly between 1738 and 1740 according to account books kept, and possibly earlier for the house dates from the 1720s. Tehidy was begun about 1735 and John Pendarves Basset may have been influenced in his choice of Edwards by his Hawkins relatives. Architecturally, Tehidy is extraordinary, and something of a one-off in the county. Only the very grandest of houses were built with substantial flanking pavilions – but they were always linked to the main house in some way. It would seem Edwards and John Basset were prepared to build in a new and innovative style, and on a grand scale.

Carclew Wm Borlase, *Natural History of Cornwall*, 1758

Tehidy   Wm Borlase, *Natural History of Cornwall*, 1758

Tehidy, Illogan

Tehidy is the story of one extraordinary family that for at least six hundred years lived out their lives on their estate within a few miles of the windswept north Cornish coast. The estate passed down the generations in unbroken male line, and never once came on the market until 1916. The Bassets were ordinary squires for the most part, serving king and county, their history following a similar pattern to that of many of their fellow Cornishmen of the landowning class. Their unbroken tenure marks them out, although the thread was perilously thin on more than one occasion. Wives came from the neighbouring gentry families, who in turn married Basset daughters. Four times the estate was managed by trustees when a minor inherited – several of the Bassets died untimely – and more than once a cousin inherited. Fortunes began to rise with increasing agricultural values, but what really brought about the major change was the discovery that below the thin, stony soil lay major deposits of first, tin, and then copper. Unimaginable wealth began to pour into the Basset coffers. The boom years lasted for almost a hundred years, with copper producing the greatest rewards.

It was this money that enabled the Bassets to build their mansion, and lay out the grounds, although the source of this wealth resulted in anything but an attractive landscape, as this description from around 1824 highlights:

> *When viewed from the summit of Carn Brea it appears like a well-cultivated garden in the midst of a barren desert, the whole extent of the park and grounds was about 700 acres, of which 150 are lawn and sheep walk; 130 of woodland, 90 of which have been planted by the present nobleman, by whom the estate has been greatly improved.*

The nobleman was Francis Basset, Lord de Dunstanville, who had inherited the estate when he was twelve, some fifty years previously.

It is generally thought that the Basset's long tenure began around the middle of the twelfth century with the marriage of William Basset to Cecilia, heiress of de Dunstanville of Tehidy. Certainly it was in Basset hands when Sir William Basset was given licence to crenellate his house in 1330, so it would have been of some size. From medieval times a castle or hunting lodge existed on the height of Carn Brea, a site also favoured by Neolithic Iron Age and Roman occupants, with a deer park on the lower slopes, which were thickly wooded. But the site of the first Basset house is not known.

The estate passed down through the generations, with Bassets acquiring land and manors, the squires taking part in county affairs and making judicious marriages, John Basset (d 1485) especially so. His bride was Joan, daughter of Sir Thomas Beaumont who brought with her the estates of Umberleigh and Heanton in North Devon. For the next three generations, the Basset squires would have had the choice of Cornwall or their Devon lands. Tehidy must have seemed the least attractive, remote, exposed with only poor agricultural land to support it, and an ancient house dating from at least the days of Edward III. Umberleigh was styled their principal seat, beside the river Taw surrounded by lush farmland. All that remains on the site is a pleasant farmhouse, but in its heyday it was a large mansion with its own chapel. Heanton, on the Taw estuary, was within easy reach of the market town and port of Barnstaple and close to many of their numerous relations. This branch of the Bassets died out in 1802 and Heanton has been a hotel for many years. Sir Arthur (d 1586), grandson of John and Joan, inherited all three estates and in 1558 he passed Tehidy over to his uncle, George, with no idea of the wealth that would soon transform those barren acres. George was perhaps living at Tehidy and would appear to have been based in North Cornwall as he represented Launceston in Parliament; perhaps some kind of deal took place. From this time the two branches of the family went their separate ways.

George Basset (d 1589), was succeeded by his son, James, (d 1604). His bride was Jane, daughter of Sir Francis Godolphin, who brought several valuable manors to further increase the Basset lands. Their son, Francis, like most of his fellow Cornishmen, was fiercely loyal to the King and their peaceful existence was rudely shattered by the Civil War. He and his brothers took part in several of the local battles, two of them commanding divisions, and one, James, was killed at Braddon Down in 1643.

At considerable expense Francis defended St. Michael's Mount, then a Basset possession, for the king, spending some £1,620 on the garrison and guns alone. He died in 1645, ignorant of Cornwall's eventual defeat and his monarch's fate. His second son, John, succeeded, and it was he who paid the price for his father's loyalty, despite never having borne arms himself. He was briefly imprisoned and to pay the fine imposed by the Commonwealth, he sold St. Michael's Mount for £2,100 to the St. Aubyn family. Other properties also had to be sold and 'his descendants were distressed for many years.'

It is intriguing that there appear to be no records of the Tehidy of this period. Until their fortunes took a blow from supporting the Royalist cause, the Bassets were a wealthy family, well connected by marriage. There is reference to early mining activities in the vicinity of Carn Brea, which led to its deforestation, particularly during the Civil War, and the moving of the deer to a new park by the house — but no description, or painting, of what must have been a substantial dwelling, although there would have

The completed Tehidy   Engraving by Watts, 1781

been no money available to spend on new schemes. The Basset possessions have been so dispersed over the generations that it is possible a sketch or small oil painting may be hanging somewhere, unidentified.

Then followed a period of stagnation; the estate had been impoverished by the Civil War, and wisdom would have decreed they kept a low profile, having been such strong Royalist supporters. The death of John's son, also Francis, in 1675, leaving a year old son as his heir, meant that the estates would have been in the hands of trustees for the next twenty years. Another Francis, he married twice, and it was the son of his second wife, John Pendarves Basset, who was to transform Tehidy.

In his will, written in 1718, Francis left £7,000 to be divided equally between his younger children when they reached 21, hoping they will be 'brought up in a Godly and religious life and I beg they will live with their mother so long as it is consistent with their education if she continues a widow. Wife to have mansion house of Tehidy with furniture, gardens and orchard during her widowhood also coaches and horses. I would advise her never to drive with more than a pair, which will not be very expensive.' He specified small amounts for mourning and £5 to each parish for charity schools. This would indicate that the house that existed at that time was substantial; and it was the clause concerning his daughters that was the cause of later acrimony, resulting in law suits in 1722 and 1723 brought by the legatees of Francis Basset against John Pendarves Basset (infant) and the trustees.

John Pendarves Basset was only seven when his father died in 1721, aged 47. His mother, Mary, was a Pendarves, heiress to her uncle Alexander of Roscrow. The family

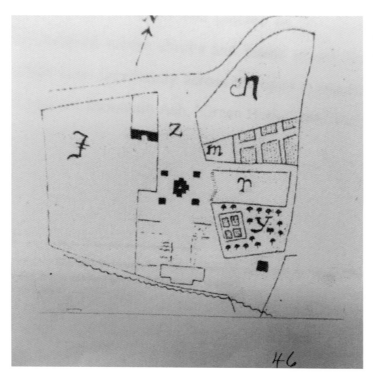

fortunes were already beginning to be influenced by the growing mining activities, although the returns were negligible compared with what was to come. However, during his minority, it was estimated that around £45,000 accrued, and it was this that enabled him to build on such a lavish scale. The family were frequent visitors to Bath so that the new styles of architecture would have been familiar to them. George I had accepted the throne in 1714, and the country was enjoying a spell of peace and prosperity. All over the country landowners were rebuilding or restyling their houses, and most chose the new classical style. There was also a sense that the country was entering a new phase – a new monarchy and a new Whig government – and a break with the past was needed.

Work must have progressed very quickly at Tehidy, from 1734 when the search for a source of clay for the bricks began, to early 1739 when much of it was habitable. The local clay proved insufficient, and 12,000 bricks were imported from London, shipped to Hayle and dragged to Tehidy by cart. Portland stone, 74 tons of it, and 30 tons of Bath stone, arrived by the same route, and much use was made of the local granite from Carn Brea. The Day Books for the period give some details. Between March 1736 and 1740 'by agreement with John King' £1,332 15s was spent. Entries include a reference to 'an addition to the Bowling Green by 100 odd feet in length', and work to the slope and ha-ha! at the end of the green – totalling over £100. Then 'to the contracts for the fruit garden £50.0s 0d'. In August 1736 is an entry 'To the Court before the house and the circular parts between the courts and the Bowling Green, also that space of ground where the coach office now stands and 59 feet beyond' but does not specify what work is being undertaken. In December there is reference to the 'terrace and mounds above the Green'. In 1737 'To the space of ground where the kitchen office now stands and the north courts and the whole hill'. In June, 1738 'Wilderness, flower garden and water £338 1s 8d and enlargement of the plan £204 10d.' The river was enlarged for 15 feet 'from the nursery to the wood.' Hedges were removed from 'the old coach house' and 'three further hedges around the farm office, smiths shop and pigsty'. The old mowshed was 'carried away' and the dry house, stables, coach house and pigs house and the old pound hedge were all pulled down. Although there is no reference to the old house these entries would seem to indicate that it, and its ancillary buildings, were on the same site. Then comes:

Digging and carrying away the grounds for the subterranean passages 187½ feet
   £318 1d
digging for the cyder vaults containers   256½ yards   £5 6s 10½d
Grand total £1486 12 6

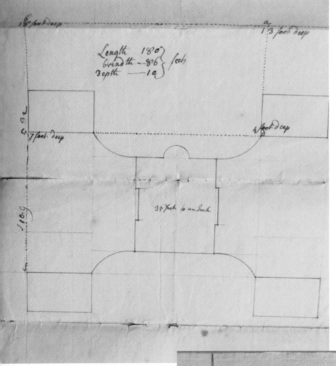

Outline plan of the house and pavilions 18th century   CRO

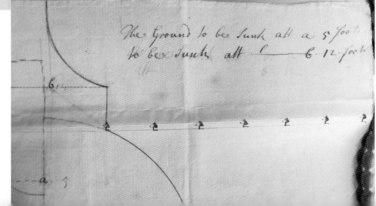

The foundations were dug for the poultry courts, and on the north side of the house '12 trenches and filling with good earth for the trees, 1372 yards. Dig and take away the ground at the west end of the terrace to the bowling green, 666½ yards. Laying drains, moving earth, levelling, watering trees – Grand total £1,616 4s 6½d.' But John Pendarves Basset did not live to see his ambitious new house completed, for he died on 19th September, 1739 at the age of 25, of small pox.

From the inventory taken at the time of his death, it would seem that John Basset was temporarily occupying an attic room, furnished with walnut and mahogany chests and tables, with a large feather bed with bolster and ten pillows, a settee bed, easy chair and six walnut and rush chairs – and an iron stove and grate. Small pox was a terrible disease and highly contagious. Poor John would have been kept completely isolated, banished to this attic, and denied the comfort of his wife and family as he lay dying. The account book records a payment of seven shillings paid to Pattience Mager for the eleven days and three nights she cared for him.

Even in death the risk was still considerable, for two masons were paid to wrap the dead man in waxed cloth. The entry continues with a payment of ten guineas to Dr. Colwill for 'attending the deceased' and recorded that the sum of £401 3s was found in the desk, and £10 14s in gold coins was found on the deceased and a further balance of cash at time of death was £318 15s 9d.

John was given an appropriate send off. The account book gives a long list of payment for mourning clothes, presumably for the servants, and then records 'paid John Taylder, the Haine at Tehiddy, for the use of the Barton £72, and silver £11 14s', and a further sum of £17 16s for his Bill for Carriage and use of the building. 'Haine' at one time was taken to refer to the Master of the Feast, or Ceremonies, and as it would seem that the main house of Tehidy was incomplete, it seems feasible that the nearby Barton was made use of to entertain the funeral guests. Other entries refer to eight days work at the church and 'about the grave', and then in September 1740, a year after John Basset's death, the sexton was paid for taking down the mourning about the church.

> *Who amidst ye temptations of youth, affluence of Fortune, and the examples of a dissolute age, was blessed with that purity of mind, and integrity of manners, as to practice the duties of modesty, temperance, justice, and piety, with great affability, and sweetness of temper.*
>
> *Reader go and do likewise.*

So read the inscription on his 'sumptuous monument' in Illogan church.

Only seven days prior to his death, John Basset drew up his will. He left annuities to three aunts and then states:

> *my will is that in case my dear wife shall be … the time of my death whether of one or more child or children be borne alive then the residue of my personal estate shall not be distributed as aforementioned but put in trust; otherwise half to my brother Francis and half to my dear wife and four sisters.*

The inventory of 1739 gives an insight into the furnishings and contents of a gentleman's house at that time – but with a twist as the main house was not finished, and it is possible that the family were occupying one of the four pavilions. Thus we find that the 'circular attic room' was being used as a picture store with 30 or more family portraits and several 'landskips'. Another contained bolts of bedding, quantities of chintz, damask, Indian dimity, calico, tape and 'about 500 curtain rings.' Was this new material waiting to be made up – or curtains from the previous house? The housemaids' cleaning equipment was in the cupboard in the gallery – 'brass payle, dust shovels, two large scrubbing brushes with lead, and seven white chamber pots with wash basons.'

The south west parlour would appear to have been the dining room, containing twelve walnut and leather chairs, a dining table and side table, and the 'Lady's Tea Room' was the living room with a harpsichord, card table, tea table, backgammon box and dice, and portraits of Sir Francis (full length) and Lady Basset (half length). Both the North East chamber and the South East chamber were listed as bedrooms.

The servants' quarters seem to have been much nearer completion as full lists of the contents are given of the Housekeeper's and Steward's parlours, the Butler's room and cellar, and the Servants' Hall. The coach house and office had a 4-wheel chaise and harness for a pair of horses, and the beds and bedding in the gardeners' chamber were 'all old'. There was a long list of the linen in the laundry, some of it 'much worn.' And the equipment needed for its care included a long deal table, a horse for drying cloths, four box irons with eight heaters, six smoothing irons and iron horse for heating them – and three old Turkey work chairs for the exhausted laundry maids. There was a brewhouse, a washhouse and a dairy. The kitchen office contained 'an iron jack with weights, pulleys and chains, 4 spits, trivets, copper ladell, plate warmer, hand toaster and large quantities of china 'some with arms, some without.' There was also a clock with a large dial plate – to ensure meals were on time – and a coffee mill. Mrs. Hughes – presumably the housekeeper – had her own room with storeroom containing a spice box and set of scales and weights. Most of the cooking equipment in the scullery was of copper or brass, and then followed the interminable warren of rooms – a bread room, still house, slopp house, maids room, etc. – considered essential for the running of a mansion the size of the new Tehidy.

Outside were a kennel, and a gardeners' room with the equipment for making cider. Then comes a long and detailed list of all the plate in the butler's pantry, giving weight and size, and the china ware in the housekeeper's parlour – but without details, so whether there was a special dinner service, or any fine china, is not listed. There is also a long list of books and of sheet music, and a few personal items of Mr. Basset's – a gold watch and chain, a shoe buckle, silver buttons, and a silver vice-admiral's seal and silver-hilted sword.

An additional inventory refers to a 'Great Staircase sent from London' and lists double deal shutters, mouldings, soffits, mahogany and wainscot doors, with precise measurements; all at Tehidy but not fixed, nor were the marble fireplaces for the library, common and best parlours, best chamber, two bedchambers and the hall. There was a run of carved architrave, carved ovals over the mahogany doors, ogee friezes, ogee carved mahogany rail, fluted pilasters for the best bedchamber and a run

Undated drawing by Wm. Borlase showing rectangular pavilions
DRO Z/19/16/1 (Devon Archives & Local Studies Service)

of Ionic capitals, 9 inches in diameter, for the hall and staircase, all awaiting their final positioning in the house. Outside was a 'Bridge of Moorstone' and a 20ft length of elm pipe.

The completed building was some 70ft by 60ft with five bays on each front and a colonnaded pediment on the entrance front, raised on a half basement. The pavilions were 32 ft by 50ft and housed the kitchens, the steward's office, the washhouse, and one was intended for a chapel.

Tehidy must have been nearing completion, but it would have been with great sadness that the young widow moved into the house that had been her husband's great project and pride. The posthumous birth of a son nine months later would have been a cause for rejoicing, though possibly not to brother-in-law Francis who had expected to step into his brother's shoes. This he did in 1756 when young John Prideaux Basset was taken ill whilst at Eton, and died aged just 16. His mother, Anne, presumably had to move out, but it is said she 'acquired £100,000 in mineral profits and rents'.

Until the death of John Prideaux, the Hawkins family and the Bassets had been closely intertwined. The Trewithen estate, acquired by Philip Hawkins in 1715, who 'much improved' the house, passed in 1738 to the son of his sister Mary who had married a kinsman, Christopher Hawkins, and it was he who managed the estate until 1744 when Mary's son, Thomas, came of age. Christopher Hawkins is important, because he also oversaw the completion of the building work, and managed the estate of Tehidy for almost twenty years after John Pendarves Basset died in 1739. When uncle Francis finally inherited almost the first thing he did was to accuse Christopher Hawkins of mismanaging affairs so that they favoured his late nephew's widowed mother. She was Anne Prideaux, and her mother was sister to Philip and Mary Hawkins, and a trustee of the estate until her death.

A document drawn up a year after young Basset's death as part of Francis Basset's action against the Trustees, sets out the State of Personal Estate of John Pendarves Basset. It gives the value of Tin and Copper Ore on the grass at the Testator's death as £6,063 16s 2d. £600 was advanced for 'arrears of Lady (Anne Basset) Prideaux' annuity'; £699 had been raised by the sale of plate and household goods from Roscrow to which Mary (Pendarves) Basset, widow, was entitled for life. Household goods, linen and books were listed and 'goods brought from Lady Prideaux of Tehidy since Testator's death all of which remain there; books in testator's study consisting of old books and pamphlets, watches, buckles, buttons and other toys in the bureau; plate and goods from Roscrow after Mr. Basset's death', were all valued at £1,308 4s.' Materials provided by the Testator at Tehidy, London and elsewhere for furnishing his mansion house at Tehidy and not set up at his death, value £973 9s 2d.' Then came a long list of bonds and loans, some over £1,000, with interest at 5%.

Then comes an item referring to John Pendarves three sisters, Luce, Eliza and Anne, who, under the terms of their father's will were owed £1,881 6s 1d each, and Francis himself, John Pendarves brother, was owed £450. Mary Pendarves, widow of Alexander of Roscrow, was due £92.10 (she had an annuity of £370). A list of small bequests and money owing to tradesmen followed, and the funeral expenses of providing mourning rings, gloves, milliners bill and 20 servants at £5 each for the day, and the monument (£119) totalled £556.6s 3d. Mr. Hawkins, executor in Trust, received a legacy of £1,000. The total due (from the estate) was £44,408 18s 2d, and the balance after payments of outstanding rents etc was £18,432 3s 9d. One tenth share of the balance of the personal estate, £2,029 4s, was due to Anne Prideaux in her own right.

It was during this period that mining began to play a spectacular part. Mining activity had been carried out for centuries in a small way, but it was new technology and increased demand for copper ore that caused the surge. Dolcoath, on Basset land, has been named the 'Queen of Cornish Mines'. It was a very early mine, a Basset possession from 1588, and the Adventurers, who worked it, were granted a new lease for 21 years in 1748, for one sixth of the dues. Francis Bassett took a keen interest in the development of new machinery, including the Newcomen engine which revolutionized the mining industry, and he also encouraged and supported Richard Trevithick, the mining pioneer. He built the harbour at Portreath in the 1760s to facilitate the export of ore – road transport at that time being virtually impossible. But the boom years were yet to come, and a slump in prices in the latter half of the eighteenth century made mining uneconomic until the last year of the century when the price of copper rose steeply, and Dolcoath was reopened. For the next century, mining was to shape the fortunes not only of the Bassets, but for much of Cornwall.

Francis Basset was yet another to die young, in 1769, leaving his son, also Francis, to inherit at the age of 12. He had married Margaret St. Aubyn, who had died a year earlier, and some have suggested that with her an unfortunate strain of mental instability came into the family. Their second son, the Revd. John Basset died in an asylum, and his son, also the Revd. John, committed suicide in 1843, but not before fathering four sons, of whom two died insane, and four daughters.

But there was nothing wrong with young Francis. When he died in 1835, aged 77, he had held sway at Tehidy for over fifty years. King George II died three years after his birth, and he died two years before Victoria became Queen. He had seen the loss of the American colonies, and the beginnings of Empire, and the huge expansion of overseas trade that brought much prosperity. He had seen the increase in his own fortunes and the expansion of the population and of the towns. But he had no son.

His parliamentary career began when, aged 21, he was returned for Penryn in 1778 and became part of Lord North's coalition government, active on the French Revolution, and against the peace with America. In 1779 when the combined fleets of France and Spain threatened Plymouth, he marched his miners to the city where they quickly threw up defences, and at the same time made defences for the small harbour of Portreath. For this he was created a baronet. He was just 22. His political career was rewarded by Pitt, who created him Lord de Dunstanville in 1796, but apparently he took his seat in the House of Lords prematurely for 'in 1807 a private act was passed to relieve him of the disabilities he had incurred by taking his seat before taking the oaths'. His 'princely income', derived mainly from the mines which lay within site of his mansion of Tehidy, enabled him to devote considerable sums towards developing the mining interests of Cornwall and the moral and social welfare of the miners. He also improved the means of transport, and in 1809 laid the first rail of the tramway designed to connect the mines to Portreath. Carew's *Survey of Cornwall* was published at his expense in 1811.

A handsome silver candelabra was presented to Lord de Dunstanville on 19th June, 1828 by the miners of Dolcoath, made from silver from the mine, acknowledging 'the zealous advocate of the mining interests by the Adventurers as an acknowledgement of the protection they have invariably received and of their admiration of his lordship's many public and private virtues.' A man highly regarded among those who depended on him for their livelihoods, it would seem.

An insight into life at Tehidy at that time comes from the *Diaries of Joseph Farington*, a landscape painter of London who visited Cornwall in 1810.

> *Being without company today the family lived thus; After a few glasses of wine, coffee was brought to the dinner table, & in a little time the Ladies walked out, before tea which we had at 8 oclock, Lord de Dunstanville also walked out saying he had a weak stomach & the open air was necessary for him. We retired to bed at 11 o'clock.*

He recounts rides on the cliffs and along the beach with Lord de Dunstanville and a visit to Carn Brea where he describes the 'Druidical ruins.' His host at dinner told him of his experiences, when a young man, fighting in Germany with the Prussian army they were challenged by a far superior force of Cossacks. Prince Henry of Prussia told him to flee, but instead he joined in the fighting until they were rescued by two cavalry regiments. During the course of a conversation the next day following the death of

Lord Camelford in a duel, Lord de Dunstanville condemned the practice saying if it was left to him, he would hang anyone prepared to shoot another. Intriguingly he adds, 'Lord de Dunstanville never alluded to the duel he had lately had with Sir Christopher Hawkins.'

After church at Illogan – where the two Misses Basset had established a Sunday school – he was taken to Portreath where they had a cottage 'delightfully situated under rocks near the sea side. Here they have everything for a breakfast or a repast with books to amuse … near this place in Baths formed in the rocks Miss Basset frequently comes to bathe.'

Another entry refers to the prizes Lord de Dunstanville awarded to the tenants for the best husbandry and management of their smallholdings which was encouraging to their efforts. A Chapel of Ease had been built about a mile from Tehidy to which his lordship liked to walk 'as an example'. And reference is made to the chapel in one of the wings in which 'there is a neat altar and altar picture painted by the Honble. Miss Basset. At prayers the whole family of servants attended.'

Farington also notes that once a week there was a 'public day' at Tehidy when anyone who chose could be entertained. In consequence they dined at half past three.

A little light is shed on the duel in an account by Mary Dunstan in her notes for an unpublished biography of Lord de Dunstanville, 'Francis Basset; Patron of the Cornish Renaissance'. The dislike of the Hawkins family, stemming from their time as agents during the minority of John Prideaux Basset resulting in lawsuits, was increased by the 1806 Election when Christopher Hawkins was accused of bribery. She tells us that Hawkins sent a note to Lord de Dunstanville, and that his reply amounted to a challenge. Basset settled his affairs, added a codicil to his will, and arose at six o'clock – and did not tell his wife. With his second, Admiral Sir Edward Buller, he proceeded to Westbourne Green, Paddington. Hawkins' first ball touched the hair of his opponent and after two shots, the seconds halted the duel. 'The two men parted unsatisfied and never again had any friendly dealings.'

A pocket description of Francis Basset is given in the *Dictionary of National Biography (1885 edition)*. He was educated at Harrow, Eton, and King's College, Cambridge, and in 1877 made a Grand Tour of Europe. He was described as a patriot, political writer and patron of science, literature and art. In 1783, aged 26, he wrote *Thoughts on Equal Representation* – something which wasn't achieved for another century – followed by *Observations on a Treaty between England and France*, and *Crimes of Democracy (1798)*. He was interested in agriculture on which he also wrote – *Experiments in Agriculture (1794), A Fat Ox, Crops and Prices (1800)*, which appeared in *Young's Annals of Agriculture*.

From this brief paragraph, a picture of a well educated, intelligent and thoughtful man emerges, with a wide range of interests. He married Frances Coxe of Ston Easton in Somerset, and in 1781 their only child, a daughter, Frances Susan, was born. By now, the family had not only a town house in Portland Square, London, but also a property at Twickenham, Radnor House, next door to Horace Walpole at Strawberry Hill. This was sold in 1795 and a property bought in Upper Grosvenor Street, London and it was there that Lady Basset died in June, 1823. She had suffered increasingly from rheumatism and was painfully crippled. It had been the custom to spend part of the winter in London, but despite a specially constructed coach that allowed her to travel lying down, she could not make the return journey to Cornwall that spring. Her body was brought back to Tehidy for burial, followed closely by that of her great friend, Lady Lemon of Carclew, who had also died in London. It was one of her daughters, Harriet, who Lord de Dunstanville almost immediately courted. They were married in July the following year and Frances Basset was said to be 'as Cross as the Devil'. To be supplanted as mistress of Tehidy, and see her mother's jewellery etc. in the possession of a girl her own age must have been galling, not to mention the £2,000 per annum jointure settled on Harriet. A sort of truce was apparently reached whereby Harriet 'reigned supreme' in the Knightsbridge house, while Frances reigned at Tehidy. If Lord de Dunstanville had hoped for a son and heir by his young wife, he was disappointed, for there were no children, and he died at his London home on 14th February, 1835, aged 77. He had become increasingly frail in the preceding months and had to spend several weeks at his nephew's in Exeter before he was strong enough to continue his journey to London.

The passing of such a prominent man was marked by a funeral procession of great magnificence, on a scale accorded only to royalty and national figures today. His coffin was brought back to Cornwall by carriage, with plumed horses travelling at walking pace. It took twelve days to reach Launceston, where it lay in state over night, and the same was repeated at Bodmin and Truro. In each town the mayor and corporation accompanied the procession, the bells tolled and the shops shut. Reports of the time state that not less than 20,000 people filled the park at Tehidy for Lord de Dunstanville's final journey to Illogan church and the family vault.

A lasting memorial was erected – a large granite cross high on Carn Brea overlooking the vast estates of the Bassets – and was paid for by public subscription. Carn Brea dominates the landscape in this part of north Cornwall. Naturally defensive, there were remains of a castle, mentioned in the *Itinerary of Wm Worcester*, in the days of Edward IV, as being the property of Sir John Basset. In 1820 it, or part of it, was still standing, considered as an ornament to the deer park and an object of interest when viewed from Tehidy.

A wonderful description of the landscape in 1865 comes from Elihu Burritt, an American philanthropist who travelled from London to Land's End. He mentions that miners were paid 16s a week, and women 8d a day, and the St. Just mine employed around 500 men, women and children – some of them far under the sea, digging by candlelight day and night, summer and winter.

Carn Brea, a capital observatory with a vast concentration of views. The whole region is disembowelled and the surface is piled thick and high with mounds of the earth's vitals still red and reeking. The entire district is studded with shafts, like grain elevators around Chicago. The clatter and chatter and banging of machinery pumping water, drawing up ore, pounding it to dust and the squashy, splashy sound of the washing all unite to make it an area of the roughest and noisiest industry. Within a dozen miles there are 20 men 100 fathoms below the surface facing downwards towards the central flues, where there is one on the surface looking up to heaven. Beyond this rough noisy place, you have a beautiful vista of well cultivated land showing all the picturesque patchwork of English crops, beyond again is the still blue sea with fishermen plying their nets.

The increase in mining produced a dramatic increase in the local population, which had to be housed. Three acres of land were offered by the Bassets to anyone who would cultivate it and erect their own cottage on it, with an additional three acres when the first was under cultivation. After a term of three lives, the land and cottage reverted to the Bassets – a not uncommon practice -and it was estimated that between 1798 and 1842, 400 acres were farmed providing homes for some 2,000 people.

Drawing by Thomas Allom from Cornwall Illustrated 1831

During his long tenure, Lord de Dunstanville made some alterations to the house, principally the addition of a new dining or banquetting room with a prominent bow, which destroyed the symmetry of the original house. Reference is made to this in Mary Dunstan's notes for an unpublished biography *Francis Basset: Patron of the Cornish Renaissance*, when she refers to the purchase of new furniture. Such an extension is shown in Thomas Allom's etching, published in 1831, filling the space between the main house and the south west pavilion. Allom's etching also shows only one pavilion – five bays wide – as having a cupola, whereas Borlase gives all four of them a clock turret. The pediment and coat of arms above the main entrance with a raised attic storey are shown in the drawing published in C. S. Gilbert's *Historical Survey of Cornwall*, 1817. The pavilions are something of an enigma; the earliest drawing – Borlase – shows them five bays by three; then in his later drawing, 1758, three by three; Gilbert shows them three by five, and Allom five bays wide.

A fine collection of paintings was built up, which included family portraits by such fashionable artists as Van Dyke, Lely, Kneller, Reynolds and Gainsborough.

Drawing showing the altered entrance front   (C.S. Gilbert, Survey of Cornwall, 1820)

There were a large number of Italian works, perhaps acquired on the Grand Tour. The collection would have been even more extensive had not the greater part of his hoard ended up in Spanish hands when the *Westmorland* was captured, sailing from Italy to

Britain laden with the collections of several noble Englishmen returning from the Continent. One item that never made it back to England was a striking full length portrait of Francis in a scarlet coat painted by Pompeo Batoni, now hanging in the Prada, Madrid.

Another loss was the set of drawings for a new chapel in one of the pavilions at Tehidy. These had been attributed to Christopher Ebdon, an architect who was based in Florence at the same time that Basset would have been there.

Portrait by Batoni of Francis Basset in Italy on the Grand Tour in 1778
(Museum National del Prado, Madrid)

Elevation showing the altar attributed to Christopher Ebdon 1777
(Real Acadamia de Bellas Artes de San Fernando)

Floor plan of proposed chapel attributed to Christopher Ebdon 1777
(Real Acadamia de Bellas Artes de San Fernando)

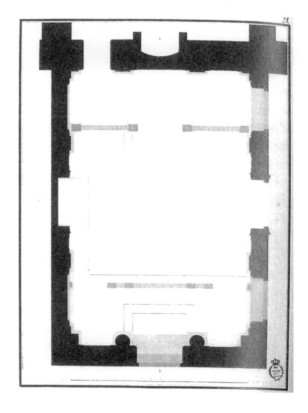

Ebdon is also quoted as being the architect of two of the gate lodges at Tehidy which he visited in 1783 – but did not recreate his chapel designs.

The drawings show a simple, classical interior with Ionic pillars and pilasters, and brass railings. No definite location is given – not even that it was for Tehidy – but the chapel measured 30ft by 20ft and was 20ft high so it would have fitted neatly into one of the pavilions. The catalogue from the 2015 exhibition *The English Prize* states that the painting above the altar comes as a surprise; it was of the Holy Spirit in the form of a

83

dove amid a starburst surrounded by clouds and was thought to be an extraordinarily Catholic image to be found in many Italian churches including St. Peter's in Rome. Did Basset own such a painting? Was it also on the *Westmorland*? When a chapel was created it had to make do with an altar painting by Frances Basset, and it would seem that this was the pavilion that was lost when Tehidy was extended in 1863 as it does not feature in the sale particulars.

Lord de Dunstanville, as was likely from someone interested in tree planting and agriculture, did turn his attention to the grounds. The medieval gardens and barns that had surrounded the earlier house had long been banished, replaced by smooth expanses of grass. A windbreak had been planted on the high ground to the north, and over a thousand trees, including horse chestnut, rowan, holly and firs, were planted. He continued extensive planting, using firs as nurser trees, explaining his methods in one of his articles in the *Annals of Agriculture;*

> *I find the pinaster tree answers best, because it stands our north-west winds and penetrates the bed of spar stone more easily than any other tree. Under its shelter I plant silver spruce, Weymouth firs, larches, Spanish chestnut, oaks, planes, beech, lime, birch, sycamore etc.*

He gave the pinasters a two year start, and advised preserving the furze etc, as added protection, and 'never destroy the weeds as they-keep the roots of the trees moist'. Clumps of trees adorned the park, and avenues were planted along the new drives he built. In the kitchen garden were ranges of glass houses, with hot houses, and frames. There was also an ice house – everything, in fact, that a well-equipped country estate of that period was expected to have. Lord de Dunstanville was also responsible for a new road connecting Tehidy with the main road to Redruth, and one to Illogan Downs, complete with new lodges at the entrances. One delightful circular carriage drive followed the river down to the coast at Godrevy, back over the downs and across North Cliff, where there was also a private drive. This was the unlikely site of the new deer park.

The original deer park at Carn Brea had been moved closer to Tehidy in the previous century. In 1779 a ditch was constructed to keep the deer away from the old bowling green in front of the house, but deer were not compatible with the extensive tree planting, so Lord de Dunstanville enclosed the moorland on the cliffs. Hedges were planted, old quarries reopened to provide 900 loads of stone for walling, and new stock brought in. Because of the poor nature of the soil, the deer had to be fed – oats, hay and corn – and then they had to be caught with nets. So the deer were neither ornamental, nor for sport – just a very expensive source of meat, which lasted around twenty years.

Similarly short-lived was the temple erected 1778-81, on the slope behind the house. At a time when landowners were adorning their estates with quantities of 'eye-catchers' in the form of obelisks, temples, mausoleums and classical bridges, Lord de Dunstanville was surprisingly restrained at Tehidy. The temple was described by Gilbert as 'a Grecian temple, dedicated to Bacchus and social mirth. Over the pediment stood a jolly god, and at the entrance were the figures of two lions, carved in stone'. It was reached by an avenue cut through the plantations to the 'Temple Field' and was provided with a fireplace, plumbing and glazed windows.

In 1808, for some reason, it was pulled down at a cost of £25. One suggestion was that the building was used for less than decorous pursuits and that Lady Basset objected.

Frances Basset could not inherit her father's title, but in 1797 he had been created Baron Stratton with a remainder for his daughter, and for the rest of her life she was known as Lady Basset of Stratton. Even though one source describes her as 'ugly as sin', it is surprising that she never married. A vast fortune was usually enough to overcome such a slight disadvantage. But she did not, living on at Tehidy until her death in 1855, when her cousin, John Francis, could inherit. For those twenty years, the house must have been in something of a time warp – for Harriet seems to have spent most of her time in London, where she died in December, 1864 and was buried at Kensal Green.

The glory days of Frances' father, when the house was filled with guests, and the servants were kept busy with constant entertaining, with sporting activities and expeditions, were a distant memory. One dwindling old maid rattling around in all those rooms. Very little is known of her, except that by the end of her life she was nearly blind. Did she keep her cousins at bay – or were they welcome guests in the property that would one day be theirs?

With the succession of John Francis, Tehidy entered upon its final era that was to last for just over fifty years. Little, if anything, would have been spent on the house since the death of Lord de Dunstanville, and with an income of some £20,000 per annum from his mining interests alone, John Francis decided to spend on his new home. Tehidy was by now over 100 years old, and his marriage to the Hon. Emily Vereker in 1858 could have been an added incentive. In 1863 he chose a London architect, William Burns, to draw up plans, and although they were largely sympathetic to the original house, its symmetry was destroyed, not least because the new extension was only three storeys whereas the original was four. A complete set of plans exist in the Cornwall Record Office, including floor plans, sections, details of the necessary reinforced joists and girders, roofing details, and elevations, beautifully presented. They also show the extent of the original house, which was not excessively large. On the ground floor this had a library on one side of the entrance hall and staircase, Mr. Basset's room, a waiting room and back stairs, and a boudoir on the other. Below at basement level were two wine cellars, still room, shoe room, large brushing room, steward's room and a men's bedroom. The original kitchens had been in one of the pavilions. The plans clearly show the sunken corridors linking two of the pavilions to the basement mentioned in the accounts of 1737.

The house was extended westwards, almost doubling it in size, and demolishing de Dunstanville's dining room. There was a grand new staircase, a new drawing room, dining room and billiard room – all of large dimensions – and necessitating the demolition of one of the pavilions. A new library was formed by knocking two of the rooms in the original house into one. The principal rooms all had ornate ceilings, crafted by Italian workmen, and marble fireplaces. A billiard room with smoking room adjoining, top lit and also with decorative ceilings were added and a conservatory completed the ground floor extensions; with modern heating methods and plate glass,

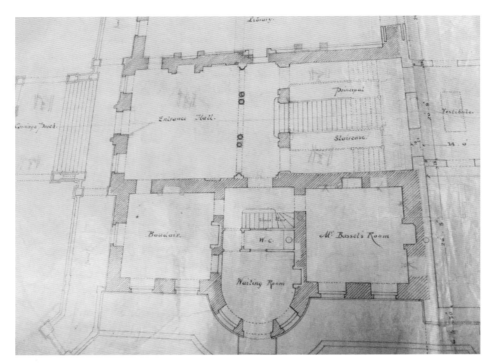

The original house – William Burns proposals 1863   CRO

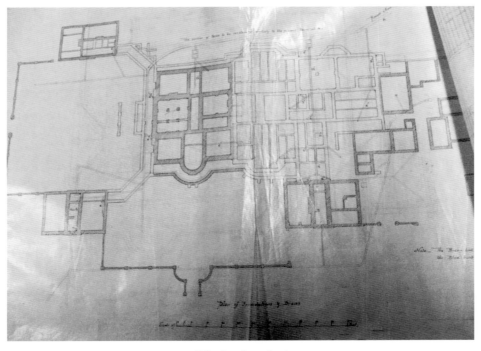

The foundaton level

The lake elevation – Wm Burns 1863   CRO

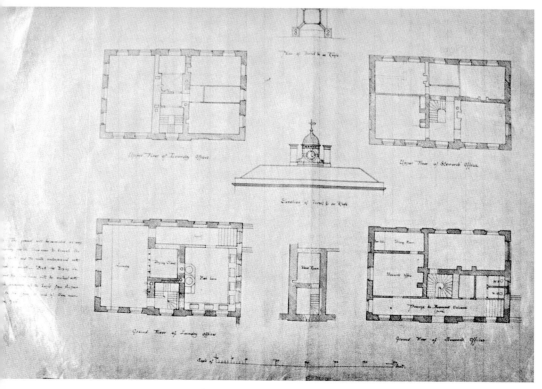

Plan of Pavilions – Wm Burns   CRO

this was the very latest status symbol. Beneath were modern kitchens and servants' quarters. The entrance front was remodelled with a *Porte cochere* of Portland stone, with the Basset coat of arms set into the pediment. The whole was reroofed, and gas lighting installed. The cost was at least £150,000, though it is not clear whether this included the work of the Italian artists creating those lavish ceilings.

Like his predecessor John Pendarves Basset, the first builder, John Francis did not live long to enjoy his grand new mansion, dying in 1869. He had no children, so the estate passed briefly to his brother Arthur, who committed suicide in a mental asylum just over a year later. Gustavus, the third brother (b 1834), became the next lord of the manor.

This was a relatively peaceful era for the estate. Gustavus took a keen interest in his mining interests, and contributed towards experiments with rock drilling and improving facilities at Portreath harbour. He appears to have taken his duties seriously, being instrumental in the setting up of miners' hospitals which he visited regularly, and taking an interest in the affairs of the miners generally.

By 1883 it was estimated that Gustavus was receiving £20,000 in dues from his many mining interests, of which £8-£9,000 came from Dolcoath. That year the Adventurers negotiated for a new lease, and the first hint of a different relationship between landowner and miners crept in. Gustavus demanded a 'fine' of £40,000 and that a new shaft be sunk. Acrimonious negotiations led to the temporary closure of Dolcoath with the real possibility that it might not reopen. Six hundred miners marched through Camborne in protest and, in the end, the Adventurers gave in; the economy of the area was grinding to a halt and the miners needed paying. The lease was renewed for £25,000 but only for 4½ years. (Falling copper prices caused the mine to close in 1921 – long after most other Cornish mines had ceased, overwhelmed by foreign competition and exhausted lodes). Gustavus' health had been impaired during service in the Crimea and, as a result of frostbite, he was confined to a wheelchair in the latter years of his life. His obituary commented that 'Owing to ill health, Mr Basset did not fill his place in public life of the county as it was hoped he would.' He died of throat cancer in 1888, leaving an only son, Arthur, aged 15.

An Inventory of the furniture had been made in 1882 – possibly for insurance purposes. The total for the house came to £12, 684 4s, and for the kitchen quarters, laundry, and stables, £2,617. 9s 6d. The plate and linen totaled £2,128 – and the turret clock was valued at £200. Hall – £1773.2s, Drawing room – £2573.6s, library – £2150, dining room – £925.

With the death of Gustavus, Tehidy entered into its final, sad, phase. Although there is no proof in the public domain, there was a widely held belief at the time that Arthur, who was an only child, was not a Basset at all, but an adopted son who came to Tehidy when his mother returned from a holiday abroad. Much of his later behaviour was attributed to him 'not being a proper Basset'. This seems unlikely – if it were true surely some evidence would have come to light? He did, however, have a marked dislike to being photographed.

The old house was still the centre of the neighbourhood and was to have a few more glory years. Arthur's coming of age party in 1894 must have been one of the most

Mrs. Basset.   A. F. Basset, Esq.

Arthur Basset and his wife, Rachel Buller, around 1900   (Royal Cornwall Museum)

lavish celebrations ever staged in the county. Arthur was 15 when his father died, so he was also celebrating taking over his vast inheritance, which included most of Perranaworthal, large chunks of Falmouth, St. Gulval, Meneage, Tywardreath and an ancestral mansion at Whitsone. He was also the first direct heir to inherit for three generations. All the county gentry would have been invited and would have marvelled at the 100 ft pavilion with sprung floor and electric lighting specially erected for the festivities. Temporary dormitories housed the extra fifty or so people specially engaged in all the preparations and on the night itself. It must have been the social occasion to trump all others and would have been the talk of the county for years after.

On 5th January, 1898, Tehidy Park was again *en fete* for the homecoming of Arthur Basset and his bride, Rebecca Trelawny, after their honeymoon. Over two thousand fairy lights decorated the house, and welcoming garlands and more fairy lights were strung out along the drive. The platform at Camborne station had been carpeted and the couple were greeted by a brass band. They were then escorted by a mounted troop of yeomanry as their carriage passed between cheering crowds, and at South Lodge, as was customary, the tenants took over from the horses and pulled the carriage the rest of the way to the house, accompanied by flaming torches. No doubt the celebrations went on late into the night.

Life continued much as before, but there was an underlying current of thoughtless extravagance that had not been present before. Arthur's overriding passion was for all things horsey – hunting, racing, betting – and one account states he returned from his

The library in the original house showing the plasterwork to the ceiling   CRO

honeymoon with five thousand guineas-worth of race horse. The Bassets had always been keen horsemen. Lord de Dunstanville kept a string of race horses, exercised regularly on the North Downs where race meetings were also held, but Arthur took it to new heights, with horses kept in several stables around the country. He would be away from Tehidy for long periods, either hunting or racing. When he was at home, the lavish entertaining of the period continued. As well as the beautiful grounds, guests could now enjoy tennis on asphalt courts, squash on courts built in 1911, riding over the cliffs and

Carriage and Pair outside the front entrance   CRO

90

Grand Hall CRO

*Detail of the Dining
Room Ceiling* CRO

Drawing room CRO

along the carriage drives, and even a game of cricket. As ever, shooting parties were the mainstay of the country house circuit; at Tehidy it was taken very seriously, with a large number of keepers. It was recorded that during one three-day shoot in 1899, a total of 2,597 pheasants were despatched. The cost of rearing each bird was estimated at 4s 6d (1914), which made it a very expensive hobby. Keeping race horses was even more costly – without taking into account any betting losses.

Arthur built garages and workshops for his fleet of impressive motor cars, and also installed the electric plant that replaced the gas lighting in the house.

And yet the days of Tehidy were numbered. Arthur was the last Basset to live there, and it was he who brought to an end nine hundred years of continuous ownership when, in 1916 he put the house and estate on the market. He could hardly have chosen a worst time.

For some years the income from the Basset's mining interests had been declining sharply. And yet Arthur, brought up to expect everlasting wealth from mining, seemed unaware of the impending change in the family fortunes – perhaps like all gamblers, hoping something 'would turn up'. In 1899 he had sold his mother's jewellery, raising £2,000, but the writing was on the wall, and even without the cataclysmic effects of the First World War, the Bassets and Tehidy would have had to part company. Arthur spent the early war years in London as a recruiting officer and at some stage the decision was made to abandon Tehidy. He bought Henley Manor near Crewkerne, and began a series of land sales which raised around £250,000. In 1915, the house was vacated, and the tenants pensioned off. Sold a little later were the mining interests, and in 1920 a sale of the family paintings at Christies raised £4,382.

The house was first offered for sale by private treaty, and one clause shows that Arthur was oblivious to the conditions of the time and that the Basset's extravagant lifestyle was unsustainable;

> the purchaser of the mansion will have the option until May 11, 1916 of taking the furniture therein, subject to certain reservations, by valuation.

No-one bought either the house or the furniture, and in an auction that lasted six days, one of the largest estates Cornwall had ever seen was broken up into 396 lots and sold off. It was somewhat ironic that the auction was held in Camborne, in the very Town Hall that the Bassets had built in 1866. Lot 1 was the mansion house, woods and home farm, around 875 acres with an estimated rental value of £1,422 per annum, and Lot 396 included Godrevy Island, leased to Trinity House. In between were numerous small parcels of land, cottages and properties in Camborne and Redruth, and oddities such as the urinal at the Market House, the Mission room at Nancekuke, a roadside waste depot and a stone depot. The catalogue, beautifully printed and bound, gives a wonderful insight into such an estate, and the many pages devoted to the house itself give a picture of a life long gone.

The size of the rooms was on the large side, with high ceilings. The entrance hall (26'6 x 24') had a marble floor and pillars with a magnificent oak staircase, seven feet wide with a heavy oak balustrade and galleried landing, lit by a circular lantern at a height of some 40 ft. The dining room (40'6 x 26') was nearly 19ft high and had a ceiling described as 'sumptuous with foliage design filling geometric panels with the Basset arms all in gilt and white on sky blue'.

The drawing room was even larger with an inlaid patterned oak floor and an astonishing ceiling created by Italian craftsmen with a large central painting, gilt coving and small circular painted panels. The library was huge (53' x 18') and was connected to the drawing room and conservatory so that a ballroom some 100 feet long could be created. All the principal rooms had Adam-style marble fireplaces, and heavy six-panel mahogany doors and 'the whole scheme of decoration is in excellent taste and displayed to perfection in the method adopted for electrical lighting'. The conservatory must have been quite something; heated by hot water with a mosaic floor and fish pool in the centre, with doors leading to the terrace, and an aviary. It was a massive 52' x 25' with a domed roof. As was customary, the billiard room (30' x 20') was set apart, reached down a short corridor and included a 'gentleman's lavatory with 2 Shanks pedestal W.C's and lavatory basins each having h&c water', and a smoking room (18'9 x 18'6) with panelled coving ornately decorated, and top lit. The Boudoir (18' x 13'9) was decorated in gold and white with recesses for displaying china, and painted panels to the walls and ceiling with festoons of fruit and flowers. The study had a bow window with steps leading down to the north west front of the mansion, and close by was a lobby with the telephone, and fire alarm connecting to the stables.

Upstairs were numerous bedrooms, described as 'Chintz', 'Red', 'Crimson' – all around 20' x 18', and most with their own dressing room, and two with their own bathrooms – an unusual feature at that time. One bedroom, the South East, had a mauve marble fireplace, statuary marble frieze, hand-painted panelled doors and an 'ornate dentilled cornice to the ceiling with delicate hand-painted decoration.' There were two guest bathrooms, a heated towel rail and three W.C.s. The housemaid's room had a sink and drying coil, and there was a service lift. Tehidy, it would seem, had become a well appointed house with every modern convenience to ensure the comfort of the inhabitants and their guests.

Five bachelors' bedrooms were on the top floor, as was the nursery suite with school room, pantry, bathroom, lumber room, luggage and coal lift.

> *An efficient system of Fire Hydrants is provided on each of the upper floors and communication is by means of speaking tubes between school room and boudoir, principal bedroom and maid's room etc.*

The wings, or pavilions, housed the servants' bedrooms, the estate office which included a terrace room and gymnasium, and a kitchen wing, and there were five bedrooms for men servants in the half-basement, with a bathroom. The Basset servants, and visiting staff, would seem to have been well provided for – most of the rooms were of a good size with a fireplace and a plentiful supply of bathrooms and W.Cs.

The rest of the catalogue details the below-stairs world inhabited by the servants, so essential to the well-running of a house the size of Tehidy, where guests would have been numerous and frequent. The 'Domestic Offices' were situated in the well-lit half basement and included a huge kitchen (25'9 x16'6) which was described as lofty with two gas stoves and a smoke jack, with two copper petrol gas stoves in the scullery. Equally large were the rooms of the housekeeper, the steward, and the servants' hall. The kitchen maids had their own sitting room, as did the housemaids. The linen room was heated by electricity and there was a separate drying room with heating coils. The still room had a petrol gas range and an oven. There was a strong room, boot and knife holes, a brushing room with portable safe and fitted with an electric iron, a lamp room with a sink, and a huge Butler's Pantry (32' x 15'6) with four sinks (h&c), a plate cleaning room with adjoining strong room, and two W.Cs. The butler would also have been in charge of the two brick-binned wine cellars and two stone ditto. Wood and coal were also kept in cellars and two stoke-holes were used in connection with the hot water apparatus.

Outside, described as 'Out Offices', were the larders for game and meat, the gun room, carpenter's store, a coal house with 45 tons capacity, a mess room, lumber shed, fire engine house, two W.Cs, a large galvanised iron wood shed, and five dog kennels.

The 'Well Equipped Laundry' was kept well out of sight in one of the pavilions, connected to the main building by 'a sunk passage'. It had five tubs, with water laid on, two coppers, a large ironing room with hot air drying cupboard fitted with slide racks, a stokehole with boiler and four laundry maids' bedrooms. The amount of laundry must have been prodigious – sheets and pillow cases for all those bedrooms, including the servants' own; linen table cloths and napkins washed daily, towels, and starched aprons, collars and cuffs. The heat and steam must have been appalling. The wing was surmounted by a turret clock.

The Basset servants, according to the catalogue, were well housed and cared for. The butler had his own double-fronted house of 'fairly modern construction' with two sitting rooms and three bedrooms. The head chauffeur and head gardener were similarly housed and there were eight cottages for under gardeners and estate workmen, and for the forester and the head and under keepers.

A magnificent stable block was situated at a short distance from the house and 'quite out of view', with provision for 21 horses, complete with saddle room, washbox, lamp and harness room, blacksmith shop, and a mess room with seven men's bedrooms and a bathroom. Reflecting Arthur Basset's passion for racing was a new stable block for 16 horses with a groom's room – and there were cottages for the stud groom and head stableman. The motor car was catered for with a garage for 'six or more large cars' with a large pit and engineer's workshop. The traditional existed alongside the modern – a petrol house and pit with cart sheds, a weighbridge house and an iron trap house.

The house must have been one of the earliest to have installed an electric light works with two 20 brake horse power engines, two dynamos, switch board, magnetic clock and 54 batteries – and suction gas generators. Water was supplied from two wells, pumped by an automatic water wheel to a large covered reservoir in the woodlands to the north of the mansion. The drainage and fire appliances were described as 'modern and efficient.'

Tehidy was surrounded by 300 acres of parkland, with a wealth of trees and shrubs. The pleasure grounds included a squash racquet court and asphalt tennis court and

Garage and Stable Yard CRO

Glass houses in the walled garden CRO

a 'capital cricket ground and pavilion'. The kitchen garden covered three acres and had the usual extensive range of glass houses – peach, melon, vinery, camellia – with propagating, forcing and stove houses. Four ranges of pits 'were heated by 'nearly new boilers in good condition.' There was a Fancier's Fowls house, a mushroom house, a packing shed, fruit room and store rooms. The woodlands were described as 'well managed with a capable staff of woodmen' with their own glass house and mess room.

And there were unlimited pheasants in the coverts with hare, woodcock, wild fowl and rabbits.

Remember, this was Tehidy in 1916. It was self-contained, a community capable of supplying its own needs. The number of people who relied entirely upon it was huge. Had the Bassets remained, most of that army of male servants would have disappeared to fight in the trenches, and by the end of World War I, such an establishment was no longer possible, except for the very wealthiest of families. The detail given in the catalogue brings vividly back to life the last gasp of the Edwardian era – the

Plan of the estate from the sale catalogue, 1916   CRO

organization, the huge statistics, the strict hierarchy, and vast amount of work involved just in the day to day running of such an estate. And no-one seemed to envisage that it was ending, and no-one would ever again want to live on such a scale. The sale catalogue in itself is an important link to that era; ten years later such a sale would simply list the number of rooms and suggest an institutional or educational use might by appropriate. Failing which demolition was the usual option.

The Bassets had held sway over this corner of Cornwall in a tenure that stretched back to Norman times. The manors of Redruth, Camborne and Illogan were Basset country, run along ancient feudal lines with a continuity of ownership rare, even by Cornish standards. What must it have felt like, waking up to a world without the rule of the Bassets, a rule that had dominated the area for so many centuries and had entered every phase of their lives? Was there rejoicing at a yoke shaken off, a feeling of liberation – or a sense of sorrow and loss, and fear for the future? One moment you were fed, housed, clothed and employed; the next it was all over and you were on your own. It is hard to imagine what it must have meant to have been so dependant on one family for so long.

Arthur Basset died in May, 1950. His obituary recorded that he lived at Norcott Hill, Northchurch, Hants, and was formerly of Heath House, Stockbridge, and Tehidy, and that he owned Dr. Dolittle, worth £10,000 in stake money and had been associated with horse racing for 50 years. He left £204,852 gross, £189,795 net. He left £24,500,

96

After the fire

his car and certain effects to his wife. All his bloodstock, mares, foals, yearlings and horses went to his son Ronald, whose address was given as Craigallachie, Banffshire, Scotland. There were various bequests to his butler, grooms and other staff, retired or otherwise, and £5,000 to his daughter, Patience Agar-Robartes.

Tehidy Park and its grounds were bought in 1917 by a London syndicate (Messrs A. H. Bond and R. Hamilton Edwards). As was so often the case, it was the valuable timber that was the reason, not the ancestral home of the Bassets. Felling began almost immediately, and the once beautiful grounds were reduced to the appearance of a logging camp. The syndicate offered the house and 250 acres to the County Council for £10,000, for possible use as a hospital. A deal was struck, whereby the County Council agreed to take over the maintenance of the building which would be run as a sanatorium for TB sufferers. Public subscription was to be the method of raising the funds, and considering the country had just come through four years of war, it is amazing that the considerable sum of £18,000 was raised in a few months – the hospital was to be a War Memorial. By January, 1919 the work of conversion was almost complete, with the main rooms becoming wards. The conservatory was used as a lounge, and the billiard room as a games room. Additional huts were erected in the grounds. On 23rd February, just before the first patients moved in, the Basset coat of arms was removed from the entrance front. By some, this was considered prophetic, for within two days, on the night of 25th February, the mighty mansion of the Bassets was reduced to a gutted, smouldering shell. A sleepless patient fortunately noticed smoke and raised the alarm, so that there was no loss of life. Despite the efforts of every available fire engine in the neighbourhood, by morning it was obvious that Tehidy was no more. What had not

97

been destroyed by the fire and heat was damaged by water. The entrance porch and, amazingly, the statue of Flora survived. The billiard room, a single storey addition, was largely untouched, as was the smoking room with its ornate ceiling.

A moving description of the ruined house is given in a novel written by Mary Dunstan – the pen name of Patience Mary Basset, Arthur's daughter. Called *She Was Always There* it recalls Pengarrow House – Tehidy – seen through the eyes of the retired Nurse.

> *They had come out of the wood now, and were walking down a wide gravelled path between huge rhododendron bushes spaced out evenly. The house lay in the hollow below. It was lit by the sun on its downward course, which threw patches of deep blue shadow across rough grass beyond, where there had once been lawn. A jagged outline of great walls, where, through blank windows, the sky showed through. Blackened timbers tilted into space, forming bizarre patterns. High up against the inner wall, seen through a gap like a chasm, a fireplace of marble, remote in isolation. And a stone staircase with wide treads, leading nowhere. At the foot of the walls, piled high in confusion, rubble, plaster, girders and panels scrolled in dull gold, charred and warped, cast down in groups so that they looked like giant playing-cards, dealt unevenly. A smell in the air of stale smoke, of ashes and decay. And silence, broken only by the distant cry of rooks on homeward flight. A scene of utter desolation.*

It must have been an interesting time for the patients housed in huts in the grounds, who had expected rest and recuperation; one month after the first big fire, a second

Tehidy as a hospital after the fire   CRO

broke out in one of the pavilions where many of them had been moved. But the hospital board persevered, and a new building was constructed on part of the old. The front range of drawing room, library and billiard room became a sunken garden. The new Tehidy utilised much of the stone, and the entrance pillars of the old, so that something still survives, and no doubt it was much more convenient than the miles of corridors and basements that had been converted. The new building had cost £35,000, over £12,000 more than the insurance, and running costs were rising, and the Health Authority started to grumble.

The locals, many of whom were former tenants, viewed the rebuilding with suspicion and the superstition that no-one but a Basset could live at Tehidy was popularly held. According to Mary Dunstan, none of them would work there and the labour force had to be imported. From the start there was opposition – an article in *The Cornubian* of 11th March, 1922 asked 'Will Tehidy shut down?' and called it 'A Great Cornish White Elephant, completely unsuitable so close to the damp sea air.'

> *The expenditure of £66,000 chiefly connected with rebuilding and refurbishing this 'gift' is a disgrace to Cornwall County Council ... a sanitorium could have been built for far less than this sum.*

The article stated that the number of patients was limited to 64 who appeared to be male only, as provision had to be made for 16 women to be cared for elsewhere and 'it would probably be much cheaper to treat the men and women elsewhere and shut Tehidy.'

In 1988, despite protests, the hospital did close, and the buildings lay empty for five years. By 1991, the health authority had sanctioned redevelopment and in 1995 the site was acquired by a property development company for £275,000. In an ironic twist, the County Council raised some £80,000 to buy back 257 acres of woodland surrounding the hospital – land which had come with the original purchase. This is now run as a Countryside Park, with much new planting of trees, and dredging of the lake.

There is nothing romantic about Tehidy Park today with its manicured lawns and street lights and abundance of 'Residents Only' and 'Private' signs. The hospital building has been divided into houses, and all the outbuildings – stables, workshops, electric plant, etc. converted, and there are a number of neat new homes. The old walled garden remains, but between the development and the country park and lake, a thick belt of trees and shrubs ensures the privacy of the residents. Almost all trace of the once mighty Bassets has gone.

Sources

The Landed Gentry

Tehidy and the Bassets Michael Tangye

Farington Diaries; J Farington 1810

The English Prize; The Capture of the Westmorland, an Episode of the Grand Tour Catalogue of the Exhibition at the Ashmolean Museum, Oxford 2012

Francis Basset; Patron of the Cornish Renaissance Mary Dunstan

She Was Always There; Mary Dunstan 1951

Cornwall Record Office

TEM/1/304/305/306/307
   309/310/311

X62/17/2

X 229

J/1/1724/1725/1729/1730/1742

J/1/1755/1796/1781/1789/1791/1794/1816/ 2263

C 211/37

CN/3526/2

T/1371a

H(2)/46 – early plan of foundations

B55 – photographs of interior

AD 894/7/13 – inventory & accounts 1780

AD 894/11/20/28/29

LIB/2247

AD 55/9/10/11 – 1736 sketch plans

AD 19 – plans etc 1861

AD894/7/7/50

AD 894/11/39/58

BY 382/383/391

CC/8/3/5/16

H/127

RS/107

TEM/17

TEM/11/17/18

X 1254/22/2

T 833

CC/8/3/5/16

RP/4/30/6

RS/107 – photo of house, 1860

X 84/24

AD 2258/1/43/44/45 estate maps

Nanswhydden (Wm. Borlase *Natural History of Cornwall* 1758)

Nanswhydden, St. Columb Major

The third Cornish house Thomas Edwards was called upon to build was Nanswhydden, begun about 1740. A plain rectangular block of classical design, the only embellishment was a pediment over the central three-bay portion. As if to break the severity, Edwards added flanking pavilions as he had at Carclew and Tehidy. But Nanswhydden was given two very small structures, completely out of scale, connected to the house by blank walling.

The only published view is an engraving included in Dr. Borlase's *Antiquities* of 1754, which shows the house as newly built, looking somewhat austere. Today, the semi-circular sweep in front of the house and its ha-ha are evident, one of the earliest in Cornwall, and the ruins of the circular pigeon or dove house on the hill are just discernible. Little more than the bare outline of the right-hand pavilion remains, stranded in a paddock together with the grand arch to the stables, but the left hand one is now a dwelling, attached to the farmhouse that was so carefully concealed by the trees in the engraving. Remnants of the stables, including the entrance arch, lie behind the farmhouse, and past an extensive range of farm buildings is the walled garden, beautifully constructed of brick.

The history of Nanswhydden is a long one, first mentioned in 1323, and does not end with the loss of the house. The later chapters include an entail, an elopement, the dramatic decline of the family fortunes, a law suit between father and son, and an heir

101

apparent in America who declined to take up his inheritance, so that what was left of the estate was administered by the Official Solicitor in Chancery Lane – it could have come straight from a novel by Charles Dickens.

The exact date of the original manor is not known, but it was bought in about 1581 from the Nanswhydden family by Richard Hoblyn. According to C. S. Gilbert (*History of Cornwall*), the family of Hoblyn were originally from Brodbane in St. Pinnock where they 'had flourished for several generations'. John Hoblyn, who is thought to be the first to settle at Nanswhydden, was the son of Thomas Hoblyn, (d 1635, buried at St. Columb Major.)

Known as the Barton, a schedule of the lands and their value survives in an ancient Rent Book from the time of James I.

Item I was the Dwelling, Garden, Pear Orchard and one Little Orchard, value per annum £5; Item 2 was the Nursery, Pidgeon House, Orchard with Pidgeon House, ¾ acre, value £5; item 3 was the Lower Orchard, Hopyard, 1½ acres, value £10, item 4 was the House park (¾ acre) now an orchard, also the grove adjoining, 4 acres, value £2. There follow various Meadows, Parks, Orchards, totalling 149½ acres with an annual value of £98 3s 4d. Also mentioned was 'The Quarry close beside the Way.'

This describes a property clearly superior to a farm and omits any reference to farm buildings. Judging by the number of orchards listed, it would seem that the situation was favourable for fruit growing, and the mention of not one, but two 'pidgeon houses' underlines the status of Nanswhydden. At that period such structures were usually the perquisite of monastic establishments and the manorial or squire's properties.

Little is known of the family in the intervening century and a half, living contentedly at Nanswhydden for long generations, leading the lives of country gentlemen. They seem to have avoided involvement in anything contentious, steering clear of the religious conflicts and letting others fight for King or Commonwealth – the Hoblyns stayed at home whilst the Stuarts came and went, and the Hanoverian age began.

Then followed several generations of Robert Hoblyns; the third of this name (1658– 1706), appears to have been a gentleman of some standing who left his mark upon the county. He was educated at Oxford, gaining a BA in 1678, and MA in 1681, and spending in all six years there in scholarly study. As the younger son, he was destined for the church, and became rector of Ludgvan. His elder brother, Richard, died childless in 1689, and from then on Robert seems to have become heavily involved in county affairs as a magistrate and commissioner of taxes. He kept diaries which record his involvement with the mining industry; he was a major shareholder in two mines and concerned in the running of them and would appear to be the first Hoblyn to acquire significant wealth from this source. He died in London in January 1706, aged 47, his body being brought back to St. Columb Major for burial. He left an only son, Francis, aged 19. He, too, studied at Oxford returning to Nanswhydden on the death of his father. By the time he died in 1711, Francis had been appointed both a JP and a Stannator and had married Lady Penelope, daughter of Sydney Godolphin, a most prestigious match. The birth of his son, Robert, in 1710 was followed by his death at the tragically young age of 24.

This Robert, the builder of the mansion, would have had a childhood quite different from his forebears. Left a fatherless baby, his upbringing would have been solely in the hands of his well connected mother. Three years later, in 1714, she married Sir William Pendarves, himself the owner of a large estate near Camborne, and so Robert would have been familiar with the houses of the Cornish gentry, and may have spent more time at his step-father's house than he did at Nanswhydden, which must have begun to look very old-fashioned and outdated.

Robert was given a scholarly education – Eton followed by Christ Church, Oxford, where he gained a degree in law. As a young man he travelled abroad and it is in Italy that he is thought to have begun his remarkable collection of rare books, which by the time he died amounted to some 2,500 volumes. In 1745 he was elected a member of the Royal Society, a distinction which must have delighted him. His wife was Jane Coster, only child of Thomas, a wealthy Bristol merchant who had left her £40,000 in 1739. The Hoblyns had business connections with the Costers, selling much of their tin to their foundry, and from then on the couple divided their time between Bristol and Nanswhydden. It is interesting that Grace Pendarves, sister of Sir William, was married to Robert Coster of Bristol, possibly Jane's brother, and that the mother of the two Pendarves was Grace Hoblyn of Nanswhydden. Robert Hoblyn was to represent Bristol in three parliaments, and acted for many years on the Commission of the Peace.

Robert's contemporaries, many of whom would also have made a 'Grand Tour' of the Continent, were indulging in a rebuilding pandemic throughout the country. The Hanoverian accession meant peace and a respite from the unsettled times of the Jacobite rebellions. The countryside was prosperous, and the new Palladian architecture sweeping Italy would have had a strong influence on the many English visitors. They returned home to quaint medieval or Tudor manor houses, with small windows and small rooms, and a clutter of additions and outbuildings surrounded by walled gardens. Some decided on a new house on a new site, allowing the original home to decline to farmhouse status, but many rebuilt on or around their original home. And that is what Robert Hoblyn decided upon.

A good description of Nanswhydden is given in Davies Gilbert's *Parochial History of Cornwall* (1838):

> The basement story was built of granite, the upper part of a light coloured slate or killas, and the whole lined with brick: the door cases, windows and pediment, and balustrades were of the Ionic order. The shell of this structure, was erected by that able architect Potter, and was allowed to have cost about £15,000, and the finishing and compleating as much more. The chimney pieces, which were finished in Italy, were remarkably elegant, in respect of the richness of marble, the delicacy of design, and the excellence of the sculpture. The library occupied two rooms, the largest of which was 36 feet long, 24 broad and 16 high, and all the other apartments were equal in design and furnished throughout in a style in which elegance and comfort were alike combined.

The library is again described, with an additional note in Polwhele's *History of Cornwall* (1810), detailing some of the books and stating that 'Mr. Hoblyn was a sedentary man who amused himself with books and buildings, but destroyed all documents relating to the price of either'. It was the account books kept by Thomas Edwards that gave details of the cost – and evidence of Edwards' involvement . Until these came to light, Potter, the builder, was thought to be also the architect.

Mr. Hoblyn's books were intended to be 'as general and useful a collection as possible' and included a number of rare Italian works collected on his travels. 'The books were collected on a very liberal plan and were designed as a standing library for the county, to which every clergyman and author, who had the design of publishing, were to have the readiest access' – and apparently local clergy and antiquaries, including Dr. Borlase, 'availed themselves much.'

Polwhele also makes reference to Mr. Hoblyn pulling down the old house 'to add a regular body of another wing corresponding to the first building, which made one regular whole.' This seems unlikely, as the classical façade was Edwards' work and surely there would have been no need to pull down an older wing if it had already been encased? And was the original house on the same site, or was it part of the adjoining farmhouse, which is more substantial than the usual Cornish farmhouse?

Dr. Borlase' engraving shows a somewhat severe house with little decorative detailing except for dressed quoin stones, and a rusticated basement. The ha-ha – which survives – is clearly shown, as is the columbarium, and the plantations behind the house. He describes it:

> *A large house well completed, rooms and handsome apartments, some very good portraits, no landscapes, good plantations rather pretty than grand, great variety of hilly slopes in the grounds, in the valley little falls of water into basins edged with turf. The house sits on the edge of a hilly lawn and this narrows to a plain before the front. The hill behind the house is thrown into slopes planted with evergreens to prevent its approaching too near and sudden to the house which it does in some measure.*

Robert Hoblyn was evidently not entirely happy with the engraving and had some observations to make to Dr. Borlase, to whom he wrote in October, 1756;

> *I should have been glad to have shown you a point of view from whence I think the best prospect might have been taken and to have shown you some plantations already made and others to be made this year which perhaps may have escaped your notice now, though they would not have done so two years hence. Likewise fix on a place for making a piece of water in the bottom which though not yet executed should not be omitted if it comes in view as I imagine it must. The length of the principal front is 110ft, the height to the top of the cornice I take to be 40-41 ft, and the depth of the building is 80ft. The height of the rustic basement is 10 ft and the height of the main body from the rustic basement to the cornice is 26ft. The eastern front has seven windows and is 80 ft in length. Your drawing seems to have allowed for only five windows. The house being seen so near and the exact proportions preserved in the drawing makes me mention that the steps going up to the house, though of moorstone, are not rustic and therefore with the balustrade upon them*

they together hide what little rustic would appear in the compartment under the pediment. The steps project 10 ft from the house and the balustrade on top hides the bottom of the doorway which is of the Ionic order.

But Robert did not live to see those plantations mature, for he died that same year, aged 46. He had no children, and the estate was cursed with an entail. Nanswhydden went to the descendant of Thomas Hoblyn of Tresarren, the Revd. Robert Hoblyn, Curate of Gwennap. But he did not get the famous library – that Robert left to his wife Jane, probably with much else from the inside of the house. She remarried, John Quicke of Exeter, who, in 1768 produced a complete catalogue of the books, entitled *Bibliotheca Hobliniana sive Catalogus Librorum.* It would seem that Jane and her new husband remained in occupation of Nanswhydden for in 1769 the King's Librarian travelled to Nanswhydden to view it. He commented most favourably, as was recorded in a letter from the agent to John Quicke:

> *I desired him to examine Danu: Mys: Panneo: which he found greatly exceeded that in the Kings library, and thinks that £200 is about the mark by what I can at present judge. The collection is far more valuable than I apprehended. He repeatedly asked me what I might think the value of the whole, or whether I have ever heard. I told him I could not possibly say as I was no judge of the one, nor ever heard the other. If you should approve of selling the whole and the King should accept them, he says he should come down again and stay for four or five days.*

But the library was not sold to the King, nor to the Bodleian Library, who also expressed interest. It remained at Nanswhydden until 1778 when the decision was made to sell the library and the plate, and they were carted off to London. In a sale lasting 25 days, the collection raised £2,500. And at some stage that glorious library which would have occupied most of the east wing, was divided up.

Memorial bust of Robert Hoblyn d.1756
(Royal Institution of Cornwall – Courtney Library – Henderson Antiquities – Vol III)

Nanswhydden in 1800   (Courtney Library HOB/52)

Robert was buried in St. Columb Major, his life commemorated in a wall plaque with a very lengthy eulogy –

> *His learning was extensive and solid, and in divinity, history, philosophy and languages, both ancient and modern, his critical skill, sound judgement, comprehensive memory, and elegant taste, were the admiration of scholars in every profession …*

and surmounted with a bust and the arms of the Hoblyns – azure, a fesse or between two flinches ermine. However, this and many other memorials were thrown out by the incumbent in 1845, so there is no record of the once prominent local family. A bust of Robert was at one time housed in the Royal Cornwall Museum, possibly that from the church, but is no longer there.

There is one other known drawing of Nanswhydden, dated c 1800 inscribed *from Anne's Water Coloured Drawing with her love – The Seat of the Rev. Robert Hoblyn.* The windows are shown with glazing bars, which gives the house a much softer look, and surrounded by mature trees. Three floor plans of the house, amateurish in execution, but giving a good insight into a house of this period are possibly by the same hand. Each floor is accompanied by a legend of the rooms – and it is noted that windows are represented by circles, and fireplaces by ovals. The ground floor, which was semi-basement at the front, was entirely given over to servants' quarters, and the enormous number of cellars etc. necessary for the running of a large establishment. The cellars directly under the centre of the house were all vaulted, as was the beer cellar under the library. There is reference to the 'old servants hall' but the plan gives no indication of any older building. The kitchen was built across the back, enclosing the 'larder court 'which appears to

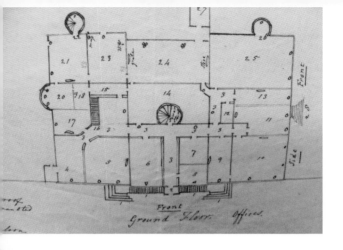

Front
Ground Floor.   Office.

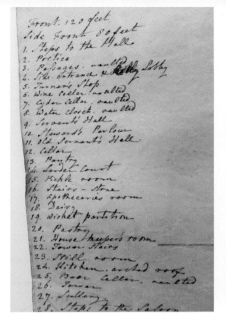

Front. 120 feet
Side Front 80 feet
1. Steps to the Hall
2. Portico
3. Passages. vaulted
4. The entrance & Lobby
5. Turner's Shop
6. Wine Cellar vaulted
7. Cyder Cellar vaulted
8. Water closet. vaulted
9. Servant's Hall
10. Steward's Parlour
11. Old Servant's Hall
12. Cellar
13. Pantry
14. Larder court
15. Pickle room
16. Stairs - Stone
17. Apothecaries room
18. Dairy
19. Wicket partition
20. Pastry
21. House keeper's room
22. Tower Stairs
23. Still room
24. Kitchen. arched roof
25. Beer Cellar. vaulted
26. Tower
27. Scullery
28. Steps to the Saloon

Floor plans c.1800
(Courtney Library HOB/53

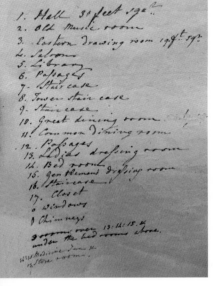

1. Hall 30 feet sq.
2. Old Music room
3. Eastern drawing room 19ft 5ft.
4. Saloon
5. Library
6. Passages
7. Stair case
8. Tower Stair case
9. Stair case
10. Great dining room
11. Common dining room
12. Passages
13. Lady's dressing room
14. Bed room
15. Gentlemens dressing room
16. Staircase
17. Closet
0 Windows
9 Chimneys
9 rooms over 13.14.15.16
under the bed rooms above.

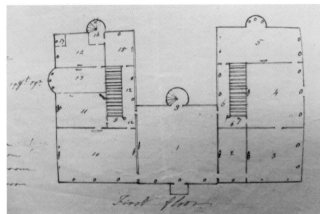

First Floor

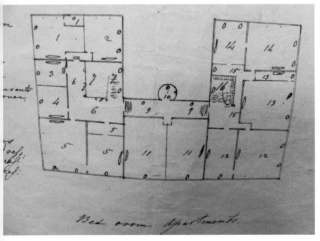

Bed room Apartments.

1. Crimson & dress. room
2. Bed room
3. Bed room
4. Yellow Bed room
5. Green & dress. room
6. Passage
7. Staircase rooms over
8. Rails & Pillers
9. Gallery
10. Tower Stairs
11. Servants Rooms
12. Poppy room & dress.
13. Tapestry room & dress.
14. White room & dress.
15. Passages
16. Staircase

107

have been under the courtyard, and opening onto a rear yard. It was arched, with a stove at one end and a grate at the other, and was single storey and appears not to have any windows. An unusual feature was the three circular towers at the rear, two containing spiral stairs – that in the inner court giving direct access to the hall, and rising to the first floor. The only other service staircase was of stone rising from the lobby in the west wing to the dining room passage above. On the principal floor, the drawing room, saloon and library all interconnected. The hall was a vast 30 foot square and would appear to have been double height with a gallery. It did not, however, contain a grand staircase, the two wings each having a simple flight to the floor above. On the upper floor were five main bedrooms each with its own dressing room, with servants' rooms in the attics. Pamela Dodds in her study of the work of Thomas Edwards, refers to an older house being incorporated in the new, and the turret stairs could be an indicator. Were there plans for a grand staircase in the large hall, which otherwise seems somewhat pointless?

And then came the tragedy:

My dearest Love,

We have met with a very severe accident at Nanswhydden which you must summon up all your fortitude to hear, but I must not mince the matter lest it should be represented to you worse than it really is.

The fact is that I was called up at 1 o'clock this morning by Francis with a cry of fire, and on going downstairs I was encountered by a volume of smoke and fire in the passage near the men's room, which seemed to proceed from the pantry. Finding no hopes of extinguishing the fire, which had perhaps been burning for some hours, I endeavoured to save what furniture and movables I could; and I succeeded in saving all the books and papers, all your drawers and the furniture of our bedroom and dressing room, the piano forte and harpsichord, the contents of the cellars, but all the furniture of the eastern part of the house is destroyed.

We have no clue to find out how the fire began, Francis went round the house in the evening after the men were in bed and the pantry locked, and did not perceive anything amiss. I have moved all the goods saved into Mr John Jewell's house in St. Columb and am now at Mr Warnes, and Francis at Mr. Hawkeys.

The goods were a little wetted by the morning rain and we were afraid to place them in any house till the fury of the flames was abated, but they did not reach to the offices or stables.

I sent off some provision article this morning and received your letter announcing the receipt of the former parcel. I hope this will have no great affect on your spirits. I am perfectly well, and resigned to my misfortune and bear it with the spirit of a philosopher. Best love to yourselves and to my dear daughters.

Yours,
My Dearest both in prosperity and affliction,
Robert Hoblyn

Thus did Robert Hoblyn break the news of the disastrous fire to his wife in a letter dated 1st December, 1802.

It is hard to imagine the feelings of himself and the servants as they stood by helplessly, watching whilst the great house – their home – and all their possessions were destroyed. It was just as well that Robert Hoblyn's famed library had been removed. However, three large lockers containing his records of the Stannary convocations over which he had presided, and other records of public interest, were lost together with a fine collection of minerals.

The Hoblyn who suffered this grievous loss was yet another Robert, the Revd. Robert of Gwennap, who had inherited in 1756. His wife was Mary Mallet of Millbrook, and they had nine children, though fortunately it would seem only Robert was at Nanswhydden that fateful night. Had it not been for the man servant rousing the occupants, the event could have been even more tragic with loss of life, for in houses such as Nanswhydden once a fire got hold it would have spread rapidly, the staircases acting as chimney flues, and the heavy curtains and large quantities of panelling and wooden shutters feeding the flames. A contemporary newspaper account put the blame on a boy servant who was in the pantry as late as 11 o'clock, but this was not corroborated by Robert Hoblyn.

The family abandoned Nanswhydden and made their home in Bath, where Robert died in 1839. And here the succession takes a knock. The couple had three sons. Robert, the eldest, predeceased his father, leaving Edward and William. Edward began a liaison with a young lady in Bath, to whom his parents took exception. It was not because she was of low birth, although her family were not wealthy, but because she was ill mannered and forward, according to his mother's somewhat hysterical account of the affair. Edward was threatened he would be disinherited if he married her. In the summer of 1808, news of an intended elopement reached his father early in the morning and servants were despatched to the neighbouring churches, but they were too late. Edward and his Mary were married – and he was indeed disinherited. A long and bitter correspondence ensued between Edward and his parents, but to no avail. It was brother William who inherited on the death of his father in 1839, aged 87.

What effect would his father's decision have had on William? Edward became rector of Mylor, and he and his wife had a large family of four sons and seven daughters. Was there any contact between the brothers? It cannot have been a happy situation and it is easy to imagine the resentment Edward and his family must have felt towards the brother in possession of his inheritance. However, Edward does not seem to have been too impoverished. The living at Mylor was in the gift of Sir Charles Lemon of Carclew. He was a contemporary of Edward and had considerable mining interests; the two men would seem to have been friends, and Sir Charles came to his rescue. Edward Hoblyn was rector of Mylor from 1823 until his death in 1868 and lies in the churchyard in a substantial tomb. The vicarage behind the church was rebuilt – replacing a smaller, decayed building. It is a large handsome Georgian-style building with lovely views, so Edward does not seem to have come off so badly after all.

The Nanswhydden estate at this time was said to be around 3000 acres with an annual income of £1,450. The first Revd. Robert had added the Barton of Colan in the adjoining parish to the Hoblyn lands, which, prior to that, had ended at the river Porth in the valley. This meant they owned the whole valley – an extra 1000 acres and nine farms. The second Revd. Robert married Frances Paget and their only son was neither a Revd. nor Robert. He was William Paget Hoblyn who inherited in 1846. His father had left the estates in such a way that he was 'tenant for life' and any son would become 'tenant in tail', possibly to make sure Edward's children could not make a claim.

And here the story of Nanswhydden might have ended. In 1820 it was recorded that 'the walls of the mansion are yet standing entire, and at a distance appear in a perfect state; but on a nearer approach, the gaping windows and tottering mouldering point out the ravages of the destructive element …'

1888 map of Nanswhydden

The family, when they visited, would have stayed in the farmhouse 'next door'. This, so carefully hidden in Borlase's drawing of Nanswhydden, is a sizeable house, very plain. It is possible that this was the site of the original manor house, but if it does date in part from the 17th century, or earlier, then substantial alterations have been carried out, whether at this time or later, is not known. At some stage the ruins, which must have been a constant reminder and an unwelcome neighbour, were demolished and some of the stone was taken to Trelowarren, home of the Vyvians, on the Lizard, where it was used to create a long ha-ha and garden walling. Suspiciously good quality stonework is to be seen in several local buildings. And, again with no certain date, the Nanswhydden estates were sold to Miss Brune – but not the lands at Colan.

What survives today? The farmhouse is reached down a long drive; there was no lodge, or imposing gates, and the original drive wound through the belt of trees to pass the entrance to the stable block before arriving at the house. This entrance is listed – double gateway with tall square brick pillars – and leads to a former courtyard with some interesting remains built into the rockface. The coach house of slate stone with granite dressings, has three carriage entrances and is now used as a farm building,

*Surviving side wall of
the left hand pavilion*

*Remains of the
right hand pavilon*

restored after a recent fire, and the kitchen garden walls, of red brick, over 13 ft high are also listed.

The surviving pavilion is not listed, neither are the remains of the columbarian on the edge of the trees. If this is one of the 'pidgeon houses' mentioned in the Hoblyn rent book of the 1600s, then it is very old indeed. Several sources mention that it contained a fireplace, an unusual feature, but as the undergrowth is encroaching rapidly it is difficult to see if this survives.

The view out across the valley, where the terraces and herb garden once fell away, is lovely, although the Hoblyns would have been surprised at the expanse of water created when the river Porth was dammed to form a reservoir. Did Robert ever create his own 'piece of water' mentioned in his letter to Dr. Borlase? If so, it could be submerged beneath the waters of the reservoir. The remnants of the drive down to the river can be traced and in the rising woodland beyond are intriguing remains. The broad ditch

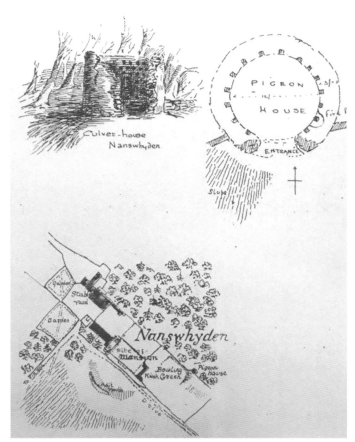

Plan of Nanswhydden and the culver house
(Courtney Library – Henderson Antiquities Vol III)

running towards the reservoir is all that remains of the Edyvean canal. Begun in 1773, this ambitious project was supposed to run from Mawgan Porth, via St. Columb Major, Colan, St. Columb Minor to Trevelgue Head and its purpose was to transport sand and seaweed for use as manure. It was named after its creator, John Edyvean, who apparently was blind and spent all of his money and some of his sister's on the canal. After his death the project was abandoned and much of what had been excavated was filled in. There are several ruins which could have been associated with this, or with the plentiful evidence of mining activity. The drive rises through the woods, now a bridleway, to reach Colan church. But not before passing the substantial ruins of the last house of the Hoblyns – The Fir Hill.

Fir Hill

There are few records of this house, commissioned in 1855 by William Paget Hoblyn, but he was known for his liking of gothic architecture. Fir Hill was described as a 'pleasant villa residence', with gardens and plantations and when newly completed, was considered one of the show places of Cornwall. There was also a farm house and cottage

Fir Hill in 1936 from a press cutting (Western Morning News 13.02.07)

to complete the new estate. William Hoblyn and his wife, Jane, had four daughters and one son, William Ernest. The 1871 census lists the household which included two governesses and four servants, three females aged between 20 and 23, and one boy aged 11. William served as a JP and would have been a respected member of society, but the loss of income from the Nanswhydden lands had its effect. By 1879 the daughters were attending a private school in Truro. In that year an agent was appointed; William was beginning to be concerned – his son's education had to be funded, and his wife and daughters given a secure future. But under the terms of his father's entail, he could not sell any part of the estate unless he could show it was not for his own gain, and that his heir agreed. Hoblyn took advice from a local solicitor, Mr. Whitfield, who prepared a disentailing deed, dated 3rd March, 1879, which was duly signed by father and son – William Ernest was then aged 12. This was followed by a 'Family Settlement' in their joint names, the subject of much criticism when matters finally came to court.

William Ernest was to receive £300 whilst at University and thereafter £50 per annum during his father's lifetime. The daughters were to receive £500 each with annuities of £75 after his death. The clause that caused the most problems, and one which, in 1899, the son challenged, allowed William Paget to set up trusts for raising 'any sums not exceeding £2,000 to be payable as William Paget Hoblyn should appoint'.

The flow of life at Fir Hill was considerably disrupted in 1882 when Rosalind, then 22, eloped with the groom, John Jones, living in the farmhouse with his pregnant wife and three small boys. The couple took the pony and trap, drew the servants' wages and boarded the London train. It is believed they travelled to South Africa, but young Rosalind soon returned to England without him. There are varying accounts of her marriage – one is that on the voyage home she became involved with one of the crew; another is that her future husband was a prize fighter, and a third that he was the son of a tea merchant. All agree that Rosalind married Thomas Figg – in March 1884, in Islington; her father would have none of her in Cornwall, and paid for them to emigrate to Canada, where he agreed to pay them an allowance as long as they stayed away. It is from her that the current owner is descended.

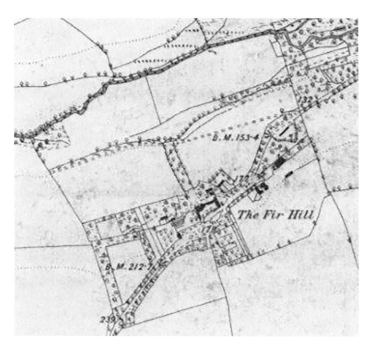

1888 map showing the extent of The Fir Hill

Hoblyn v Hoblyn 1889. William Ernest had sat by for ten years whilst his father mortgaged more and more of the Fir Hill estate, availing himself of the £2,000 clause in the family settlement whilst his son managed on £50 per annum. With increasing concern he watched his future inheritance dwindle alarmingly and he decided to act. The decision of the High Court was that this clause should be removed from the 'Family Settlement' and the case was dismissed. Not surprisingly, family life became somewhat strained, and William Ernest sought refuge in alcohol. He was described as a Captain of the 4th Royal Fusiliers, a City of London militia regiment of part-time volunteers, where perhaps he lived, away from the repressive atmosphere of his father's house.

The 1891 Census makes sad reading. Resident at Fir Hill were William Hoblyn, aged 76, his wife Jane (70), William Ernest (33), Wilhelmina (34), Zoe (29) and Laura (27). Why were those three daughters dwindling into old maids? The estate was impoverished, but there had still been money when Rosalind ran away. Was their father an autocratic tyrant who would not let them go? Was he terrified of a repetition of Rosalind's behaviour? What a dreary life they must have led, with each birthday not a cause for celebration, rather a marker in their status as 'old maids'. William Paget Hoblyn died in 1899 – and a year later Zoe was married to Capt. Allen, RN. William Ernest, a confirmed alcoholic who had been housed in an annexe, died just four year later, and father and son are buried in the churchyard of Colan church, closer in death than they had been in life.

The estate passed in trust to the four daughters, the two married ones being required to adopt the name and arms of Hoblyn. Not until all four sisters had died could Rosalind's children, now the Figg-Hoblyns, inherit. But Rosalind's dream of one day

114

returning to her childhood home with her son, Francis (b. 1886), never materialized as she died in 1925, the first of the four sisters.

At Fir Hill, Wilhelmina and Laura lived on – and on. Under the terms of the trust, the income was shared between the four sisters, and all four had to agree before any money was spent. Not surprisingly, this meant little or nothing was done to any of the properties as they had little interest in a property that would ultimately pass to Rosalind's children. Year by year Wilhelmina and Laura must have watched as the house and farms became more and more dilapidated. Their status would have required they kept a servant, but by 1930 they were reduced to one gardener. Life must have been monotonous and the prospects bleak. Latterly they spent much of their time in a bungalow at Porth, on the coast, perhaps more economical to run. Wilhelmina died in 1937, and Laura moved to a nursing home in Perranporth, where she died in 1943. The furnishings of Fir Hill were sold in 1939, and the house became a boarding school until the end of the war.

That the estate survived at all would seem to be largely due to Mr. Ernest Hewish who became trustee in 1926 – a responsibility he struggled with for 46 years. There was no spare capital, no money for upkeep and consequently the rents were low. Once the school had moved out, the house was more or less abandoned. The lead from the roof disappeared, followed bit by bit by the fabric of the house until little was left but the foundations. Building supplies were rationed and in very short supply for many years after the end of the War and here was a ready supply just waiting to be claimed. It must have been something of a shock to Francis Figg-Hoblyn when he first visited Fir Hill in 1943. He is reported to have fallen out with his surviving aunt, Zoe, who was in sole control, but never visited and was completely uninterested. He had expected to take over his mother's portion, but was told he could have no part until all four sisters had died – a ruling he never fully accepted. Somehow he managed to mortgage 1000 acres of the estate – and disappeared back to America with £4,000. On his next visit, three years later, he borrowed £1,000.

Zoe Allen-Hoblyn died in 1951, aged 80, and at last the estate was freed. Mr. Hewish contacted Francis Figg-Hoblyn requesting he complete the formalities to take up his inheritance, which would have involved proving his title as he was not British, and signing the necessary papers. Mr. Hewish must have looked forward to being relieved of his responsibilities at last, and the tenants must have looked forward to a landlord who might take an interest in the estate. In vain. Francis Figg-Hoblyn never signed. Perhaps he had realised there was virtually nothing left of any worth; perhaps he just wasn't interested in a rundown Cornish estate without even a habitable house. And he would have had to pay Death Duties, although these would not have been high, given the condition of the property. He died in 1965, without visiting Cornwall again. Neither his wife, nor his son, John Paget Figg-Hoblyn, showed any intention of completing the legal formalities, and another huge problem was caused by Mr. Thomas who had parted with the £4,000 back in 1943, and had not received a penny since. Mr Thomas could either seize the land, or take action to recover the money, which is what he decided upon. A receiver was appointed to collect the rents from the estate until such time as Mr. Thomas was repaid. This was the final straw for the trustee, Mr. Hewish. The estate was deprived of most of its slender income, and he applied to the High Court to appoint a Judicial Trustee. Despite opposition from the Figg-Hoblyns, this was how the matter rested.

To clear debts and pay for modernisation, the local agents for the High Court had to sell several of the farms, including Colan Barton. All that is left of the once large Hoblyn estate is now around one thousand acres. Whilst John Figg-Hoblyn showed no interest in becoming the legal owner and could not be contacted, a cousin, John Westropp Figg-Hoblyn, also descended from Rosalind, visited the estate, and the Official Solicitor, in an attempt to sort matters out. But he, too, failed to contact John Paget Figg-Hoblyn, and so the impasse continued until his death in June, 2011.

For over eighty years the last house of the Hoblyns had been abandoned, the once immaculate grounds disappearing under brambles and scrub and only the shell of the house left. The estate had become the victim of family feuding, from which no-one gained. The Official Solicitor stated that the rent roll, which in 1973 stood at little over £2,000 per annum, had risen to over £100,000 by 2008, making the estate once again viable. Two years later the Court of Protection decreed the estate should go to John Paget's two elderly sisters, with a smaller sum going to John Westropp.

As a result, the estate was quietly divided and sold off, most to the existing tenants. With one exception, the site of Fir Hill and its grounds have been purchased by Mr. Charles Hoblyn, a descendant of the original Hoblyns.

It is a truly incredible story.

Sources

'Thomas Edwards of Greenwich – Country House Architect', Pamela Dodds. University of Bath, 2000.
'Natural History of Cornwall', Wm. Borlase 1758.
Hoblyn Archive – Charles Hoblyn.

Carclew, seat of Sir William Lemon (F W Stockdale, 1824)

Carclew, Mylor

If only Carclew had survived! Even as a ruin, the building has a quality that speaks of a grandeur departed, and of a deep history. Its very position is one of dominance, orientated east-west on a height commanding views over Restronguet Creek and towards Carrick Roads. Today, the trees have grown up around the ruins so that they have become invisible until you are almost upon them, but in its heyday, Carclew would have stood out clearly on its hilltop. Described as one of the finest Palladian houses in the county, with fine interiors, set in beautiful parkland with a superb collection of trees and rhododendrons, Carclew would have been a wonderful attraction, to rival anything else on offer in the county. But it was not to be. All destroyed by fire in 1934. And what was left was first pillaged, and then left to moulder. But the ruined Carclew still stands, thanks to an enlightened owner who, having bought the bungalow built in 1963 next door to the shell, decided to buy what was left and hopefully preserve it.

The estate had been sold only once before that disastrous night in April, when fire caught hold and could not be put out. For almost 200 years, Carclew had been owned by the Lemon family, passing down three generations before the only son and heir died untimely, and the estate passed through the female line to the Tremaynes, who might have been there still if the house had not gone.

Carclew was the last of the Thomas Edwards' houses, but here he was constrained by the unfinished skeleton of an earlier house. This had been begun by Samuel Kemp, who had married Jane, the heiress of the last of the Bonythons of Carclew, who died out in 1697. The estate had passed from the Daunger family to the Bonythons some time in the 15th century, but when Kemp took possession, the old manor house of the

Bonythons was not good enough for him. He set about building for himself, with his wife's money, a house described by Tonkins in Carew's *Survey of Cornwall*, 1730;

> *A noble house with plans for avenues, gardens etc., which when brought to perfection would have made it one of the pleasantest seats in the county.*

Tonkin also stated that Kemp had sold off some of the 'ancient lands' and describes Jane as a lady 'who for her many virtues, bounty and other accomplishments deserveth a much better fortune in every respect than she has had the luck to meet with.'

But Samuel Kemp did not live to see his grand new house completed. He died in 1728, aged 59, and his widow immediately stopped all work. She continued to live in the old manor house which was about 60 yards distant, quite content to stay put in what had been her childhood home, and not spend any more of her money on a grand new house. For the next 21 years, her husband's dream was an abandoned, decaying neighbour; no records survive of how much had been built, or who had designed it. And nothing remains of the Bonython house. On Jane Kemp's death, Carclew passed to her nephew James Bonython, who immediately sold it to William Lemon. It was said that Bonython was indebted to Lemon, who paid £3,300 for the whole estate, with 230 acres of parkland, including a deer park with 150 fallow deer. The grounds at that time were described as being a remarkable combination of natural and artificial beauties – though what these were is left in doubt.

It was William Lemon who completed Carclew and laid out the grounds, much of which survives to this day. By 1749, Lemon was in his 50s, and had amassed a large fortune from his mining activities. By any standards he must have been a remarkable man. Born in 1696 at Breage, into a family of whom not much is known, he is thought to have been well educated, and appeared astute from an early age. His career began at the Chyandour Smelting Works as a clerk, but he rose rapidly to become manager. His marriage to Isabel Vibert in 1724 brought to him his wife's fortune, left to her by her godmother. It was not long before he had his own mining interests, mainly at Gwennap, and became a major owner of the Cornish Smelting Works. He was keenly interested in modern methods; he had already commissioned Thomas Newcomen to provide a pumping engine, and in 1733 he took the bold step of taking a 30 year lease from the Duchy of all minerals other than tin on Duchy lands. This would give him sole rights to copper – the new gold.

It would seem that William was also an astute merchant, dealing in mining supplies to other owners throughout the county, and also in building materials. By 1739 he was sufficiently well established to commission a new townhouse in Truro – and the architect he chose was Thomas Edwards. The house, Princes House, still stands, largely unaltered. When it was built it was considered the grandest house in Truro, with fine interiors, ornate plaster ceilings – the best of everything. This was the family's principal residence, close to William's business interests. Known as 'the Great' Mr. Lemon, he was by now firmly established. He had twice been Mayor of Truro, a dignity associated with commerce, and in 1724 he became Sheriff – the ceremonial position usually filled by members of the gentry. He and Isabel had only one child – William the second –

'The Great' William Lemon

who married Ann Williams, and the first grandchild was born in 1748 – William the third.

By this time, William Lemon had 'arrived'. His mining interests and expertise would have brought him into close contact with the great landowners – the Bassets, the Pendarves and the Hoblyns. But unlike these, William had not been born a gentleman, and he had not inherited ancestral acres, some of which just happened to contain large mineral deposits. He was 'nouveaux rich' without a drop of noble blood to boast of. It was necessary that William Lemon should acquire a country estate and that he should build himself a new house in keeping with those of his contemporaries. In 1749, ten years after moving to Truro, Carclew became William's country seat. Thomas Edwards would seem the obvious choice as architect – not only had he designed the Truro house, but also Tehidy Park for the Bassets, and Nanswhydden for the Hoblyns. He was instructed to 'alter, enlarge and fit up with colonnades, and face the carcase'.

The design of Carclew was given the familiar Edwards look, with a central pediment and rusticated basement level, and windows surmounted by an arch with central keystone. The drawing by Dr. Borlase shows a plain exterior, with the grand portico measuring some 25 feet, and two small pavilions linked to the main house by colonnaded loggias. Behind the left hand pavilion is the roof of a clock tower of what would appear to be a quite separate building. One account states that the new work concealed the original masonry piers, scroll reliefs and corbels at ground level – the only mention of the Kemp building.

Although, in common with Edward's other houses, no architect's drawings have survived, an inventory taken in 1760 at the time of William Lemon's death lists the principal rooms. On the main floor were the 'lobby, saloon, India paper room, Tapestry room, the common parlour, study'. On the upper floor were 'the best room, green room, china room, Mr. Lemon's room, Garland room, Mst. Ricky Lemon's room, Master Lemon's room'. On the ground floor – the semi-basement – were the domestic quarters – the housekeeper's room, kitchen, steward's room, butler's pantry, laundry, scullery, wash house and brewhouse, maids chamber and shepherds chamber. Outside was the Yard, wainhouse and coach house. Reference was made to the brick-built stables – which still exist almost intact, together with the coach house.

Carclew, from this description, was a compact house, not overly large, and with the

Wm Borlase, Natural History of Cornwall, 1758

domestic offices contained within the main building. Old William must have been well satisfied – the local lad had become a mining magnate with a country seat, and a son and grandson to continue the line. How proud he would have been to see his grandson created a baronet in 1774, and his descendants marrying into the established county families. But tragedy struck in 1757 when his son died, aged only 33, leaving two sons and a daughter. Old William died three years later. He was 63 and had not lived long to enjoy his new home. Young William was only 12, and the management of the estate and mining interests must have rested with his mother and grandmother.

The inventory taken at the time of William's death also includes details of Princes House in Truro. This was no constrained terraced property, but a superior residence with grounds running down to the Kenwyn river, with its own stables, bowling green, gardens and dairy. The house had a servants' hall, not mentioned at Carclew, a men's room, a breakfast room and library, as well as the usual saloons and bedchambers. The contents run to 20 pages and list quantities of plate, silver, bone china – still a rarity – glass ware, much mahogany furniture and a grand staircase of the same wood, which had only recently been introduced to this country. Carclew, it would appear, was the 'second home' to which the family would retreat. William did not like to be too far away from his business concerns; at the time of his death he was recorded as having interests in 49 separate mines, and stock valued at £26,000. The same document also lists various people who had borrowed from him, ranging from £7,000 lent to Lord Edgecumbe, £9,300 to Sir John Prideaux, £6,000 to Sir William Courtenay, down to a debt of £35. These were called mortgages; bonds of £1,100 were due from Sir John St.Aubyn, and £2,000 from John Molesworth. It would appear that this is how the gentry financed themselves. One estimate put his estate at £300,000.

In stark contrast to his grandfather's early life, young William received the very best education, possibly at Harrow where later generations went, followed by Christ Church, Oxford. Then came the finishing touch to a gentleman's education – William made the Grand Tour. Not only had his father died young, his mother lived only four years longer, and his grandmother another four. Within the space of only eight years, young William had lost his grandparents and parents; he was just 20. Fortunately he appeared to be a sensible and responsible man, for instead of squandering his grandfather's hard won fortune, as many in his position did, he entered Parliament in his 21st year, as Member for Penryn, supporting the Whig government. His younger brother, Lt. Col. John, who never married, joined him in 1786 as Member for Saltash, and later for Truro, ending his career as a Lord of the Admiralty.

William and his sister Ann cemented the family's position by marrying John and Jane Buller of Morval, an old Cornish family of considerable standing. The Lemons were now good enough for anyone. 1774 was an important year for William. His first child, William the fourth, was born; he was returned as Member for the county, a seat he was to hold until his death 50 years later, and he was created a baronet. Over the next ten years, another nine children were born to the couple, the tenth being Charles, born in 1784, who became the 2nd baronet.

Carclew must have been a wonderful family home and a great place in which to grow up. Not surprisingly, the house began to feel somewhat small. Sir William embarked on a series of alterations and enlargements. Accounts dated 1768 show that William Wood, the Truro architect much used by the Lemons, was overseeing repairs and alterations; these included taking down and rebuilding the parapet wall to the north front of the mansion, repairs to the parapet over the nursery wing, and repairing the moorstone cornices. This is the first mention of a nursery wing, but with all those children, it would have been essential.

Country Life magazine, which seems to have a habit of recording houses that later suffer disastrous fires, twice featured Carclew. The first article appeared in May, 1916,

The entrance hall with its fine plasterwork   (Country Life)

and a subsequent one in April, 1934 shortly after the fire, largely repeating the earlier version. This is the best record of the glorious interiors of Carclew. The work appears to have been to the highest standard and it is frustrating that no records have come to light of the craftsmen employed, or the amounts they were paid, or even of the date.

In the last years of the 18th century Sir William turned his attention to the grounds. Detailed accounts survive for these years and are full of references to work carried out and purchases of seeds, trees, flower pots etc. By 1791 there was a dogs' house, pigeon house, a smiths shop and a thatched icehouse, and bathhouse. Much tree planting was carried out and beech trees are specified. The 'new road' was built at this time and one item records the 'removal of the old coach road into the round pond'. Hedges were levelled, railings provided to the deer park, and several barge loads of dung arrived at the quay. The winter of 1793 would appear to have been severe as there is reference to clearing snow, and repairs to the roof of the house after a storm, and rails for the 'haha ditch'. In 1794 reference is made to bricks for the garden walls.

The accounts for 1797 refer to fencing the sunk fence that had been made the previous year – an early reference to a ha-ha. Also in this year, the round pond was walled, the garden wall rebuilt, and the terrace paved.

At a time when a gardener was paid 20 guineas a year, Sir William was paying £7 8s 7d land tax, £29 2s window tax, and 15s house tax (1787). Household spending for 1792/3 was listed; 'sundry payments while the family were at Carclew from June until 19th January when the family went to London' included 'beer for the young ladies', oats, dog food, sadler, surgeons and taylor, brandy and shoes totalling £602 17s 11d.

By the end of the century, the original Carclew was bursting at the seams. Children required nannies, then governesses and maids. The decision was taken to considerably enlarge the house and local architect William Wood was again called in. Between 1800 and 1802, the flanking pavilions which could only have served as summerhouses, were replaced with much larger wings over a new basement storey, and masking extensive domestic offices behind. The scale of the operations is noted in the accounts of Mr. Wood. Stone had to be 'raised from the quarries between March and July – £51.8s. This was for 62 ft of stone plinth, 104 ft of string course, 22ft for the arches, and 61 ft for the window sills. Another entry lists 333 ft of stone for the east front, slate for the roof, 2000 bricks, cornice cutting, and 404 yds of plastering. There was work to the dining room, and the window cills to the east front were raised. For the cellar there were 4 large pair sashes and frame, 2 smaller, and 2 blank.

In 1802 work was carried out on the west wing which included taking out old beams and girders, making window frames and sashes, glazing windows on the west and north fronts, and large quantities of white paint. The central portico, measuring 25ft. was

Carclew 1764, Crow & Marsh   (Trefusis Estate)

not altered, and the original steps were still there in a photograph taken in 1841. Later these were replaced with a double flight projecting forward.

The alterations were sensitively done, so that the balance of the original design was preserved. From the tithe map, the north front, which was much the plainer of the two, appeared to have two projecting wings and to be regular in outline; from this front there would have been good views down to the creek, and it was on this side that in 1797 the ha-ha had been created and the ornamental gardens laid out. Still surviving is the delightful little gothic structure later referred to as a chapel, but more likely to have

The north front

123

The summer house

been a summerhouse. This is now in separate ownership and a thick hedge screens the building from the ruins.

A detailed tax bill survives for 1803 which gives an interesting insight into how the government raised money in the 19th century; Sir William paid £30 4s 6d for 128 windows; £1 10s for the house; £15 1s for seven male servants; £11 for two 4-wheel carriages; £2 12s 6d for one 2-wheeled carriage; £20 10s for ten saddle horses; £1 for his armorial bearings; £1 10s for six dogs; £2 7s 6d for 13 windows in the town house and £2 16s 3d for nine farm houses, totalling £88 11s 9d – and five guineas for hair powder for one year!

Of Sir William's 12 children, three are of importance to Carclew's history; Caroline, who married John Hearle Tremayne of Heligan, whose son, Arthur, was to inherit from his uncle; Charles who became the 2nd baronet, and Harriet, who married, as his second wife, Francis Bassett, Lord de Dunstanville, of Tehidy Park. The two families were close, Sir William's wife, Jane, and Lady de Dunstanville being great friends, and dying within days of each other. Young Harriet's marriage, a year later, perhaps would not have been approved of, but being one of such a large family, a daughter risked being left at home, dwindling into an old maid – the fate that befell three of her sisters.

The eldest son, William the fourth, who died in 1799, aged 25, is strangely absent from the family records. All that is known is that he was a major in the Coldstream Guards – and that he shot himself in his lodgings at Princes Street, Hanover Square, London on 28th February, 1799, and was buried at South Audley Street Chapel. There are no records of a coming of age celebration, or of his education. Following his death, an entry in the *Gentleman's Magazine* casts some light on the black sheep of the family. The entry begins by stating that

The death of Major Lemon ought to be an example to all young men. Heir to a baronetcy worth £6,000 per annum, blest with the affections of a beautiful woman to whom he was about to be married, but devoted to the gaming table …

It would seem that his father had previously paid off his considerable debts only when his son promised never to gamble again, and Miss K. also stated that their union was dependant upon him weaning himself from the vice – but

In an evil hour he returned to the gaming table, lost a large sum, stung on reflection of the forfeiture of his promise, shot himself through the head.

A tragic story – and it would seem that William was no longer mentioned by the Lemons and expunged from the family records. His only brother, Charles, was ten years younger, born in 1784 when his father was 36.

Sir William died in December, 1824, aged 76. His will named John, his brother, and James Buller of Downes, his brother-in-law, as Trustees. To his wife he left the lease on the house at Whitehall, Westminster and an annuity of £1,000; to his son Charles, 'all leasehold properties, wines and other liquors, bottles and casks, deer and stock of cattle, grain, hay, husbandry implements and the house in Truro in which his grandfather lived called Mount Fuddle (Princes House). He refers to the Family Settlement made by his grandfather when 'his late son William lived' which placed Carclew 'intail male'. Reference is made to the £11,000 he took out of Trust funds at the resettlement of the Family Estate to make provision for his daughters, which he then repaid £7,000 and £4,000 when Lady Lemon died. All his mines were left to Charles for his lifetime; and 'thereafter shall go along with the reversion and inheritance of Carclew.'

And also all books, plate, pictures and all furniture at Carclew shall be Heir Looms to be enjoyed by the person or persons entitled to the said capital mansion at Carclew.

Then a sum of £4000 was set aside to provide for the younger children and the three unmarried daughters on a 'share and share alike basis', after 100 guineas had been give to the married daughters, and the £4,000 to be made up to £6,000 to provide an annuity of £100. The last clause requests that Sir William

Should be interred in as private a manner as decency will permit.

In 1795, when he was still under 50, Sir William had safeguarded the family fortunes for future generations. He set up a Trust which placed £38,352 12s 3d in Consolidated Bank Annuities, and a further sum of £13,000 17s 1d in Reduced Annuities. These enormous sums were to be used to purchase lands and properties which it would seem Sir Charles considered a safer bet than annuities. And the Trust survived until a Deed of Release was drawn up in 1868 after the death of Sir Charles, by which time most of the funds had been invested in a considerable property portfolio.

The Lemon men were staunch supporters of the Whig party, and although the first William decided against a parliamentary career, he was complimented by Sir Robert

Walpole on the manner in which he negotiated from the government a drawback on the duty on coal used in mining operations. His grandson served all his adult life as a Whig member, and Charles joined him in 1807, representing Penryn for the next 23 years. He had married Lady Charlotte Fox Strangeways in 1810. She was the daughter of the Earl of Ilchester, and Charles had waited until he was 42 before securing his aristocratic bride. And here the history of the Lemon family enters a tragic phase. The first child died an infant, but a son, Charles William, was born in 1813, and a daughter, Charlotte, two years later. Whilst abroad in Switzerland with her mother, possibly because of her health, Charlotte was taken ill, and died. She was buried in Geneva in 1825, aged just ten. The following year, on 18th April, Charles also died, shortly after returning to Harrow School for his second term there – 'as a result of a fit whilst bathing in the Duck Puddle'. This is the official version from Harrow School– the Ducker is the name for the school's lake. The poor mother died later the following year. Her memorial in Mylor church records her suffering:

> *Her Christian fortitude and resignation never failed her, but her health broken by attendance at the death bed of her daughter, sunk under the sudden stroke which deprived her of her son, and in a period scarce exceeding a year, the mother and both her children were numbered among the dead.*
> *Born February 1774 died May 1826*

It must have been a truly dreadful time for Sir Charles. In the space of just sixteen years he had seen his hopes of marriage and a family materialize, only to be cruelly destroyed. Perhaps mercifully, his father had died before the loss of young Charles

and was spared the knowledge that it would not be a Lemon who would benefit from his careful management of the estate.

Sir Charles never remarried and lived for another 42 years. How empty Carclew must have seemed in contrast to his childhood there. He became involved in several enterprises, founding the School of Mines in 1834 in Truro, and was a founder member of the Royal Statistical Society, of which he was

Sir Charles Lemon

the second president in 1836. In 1822 he was elected a Fellow of the Royal Society and served as High Sheriff in 1827. When he wasn't away in London, he found solace in his gardening activities He had a perfect site, and a perfect climate. His father had begun the gardens, planting large numbers of fine trees, building the greenhouses and laying out the terraces. Sir Charles, who would have grown up with all this going on around him, continued where his father left off. He lived at an exciting time, with voyages of discovery taking botanists and plant hunters all over the world. He was also fortunate in that the two sons of James Lobb, who was employed on the estate as a carpenter, were to become famous plant hunters – and they began their careers in the gardens of Carclew. The brothers regularly sent quantities of seed back to Carclew, including previously unknown conifers, many of which still thrive on the estate. He was also one of the first to receive seed from India sent by Joseph Hooker, which included the earliest rhododendrons. The head gardener and steward was William Beattie Booth, an acknowledged expert on camellias, and the two men transformed the grounds with, in addition to the camellias, rhododendrons, azaleas, magnolias and many trees.

Along with many of the Cornish gentry, Sir Charles was a founder member of the Cornwall Horticultural Society which was formed in 1832. One of its aims was 'improving the condition of the poor by the distribution of prizes to cottagers', not so much for the size of their vegetables, as the quality and quantity. Sir Charles was himself awarded the Society's silver medal for 'the largest number of new and hitherto undescribed plants which have flowered in the possession of the competitor.'

A description of the gardens written in 1870, by then one of the foremost in the county, refers to the 'fine old Scotch firs, fine firs many of them collector's items, many of great height, and a proper pinetum'. There were hot houses for ferns, orchids, palms as well as houses for grapes, peaches and pears. In fact, everything that was deemed necessary to the running of a gentleman's estate of the time.

But Sir Charles had died two years previously, and with his passing the tenure of the Lemons came to an end. The Great William had bought the shell of an uncompleted house, albeit set in a fine deer park and in a pleasant position. He finished the house, and the two succeeding owners made alterations and adaptations to it, and spent hugely on the grounds. Their reign had lasted just over 150 years.

In his will, Sir Charles left £100 to the Royal Institution of Truro, £200 to the Royal Polytechnic Society, and £300 to the Royal Geological Society of Cornwall. His five nieces and nephews received £1,000 each and there were bequests to his servants – two year's wages for those who had served him for six years or more, and one year's for the rest. Apart from these sums, his entire estate, real and personal, was left to his nephew Arthur Tremayne. Like his father, he desired his funeral to be plain and simple and to be buried near to his late wife, and that his name should be inscribed on the vacant tablet in Mylor church – and that 'the inscription on the tablet erected to the memory to our two children should be corrected according to the dates in the small Bible in my bedroom which formerly belonged to my wife.' Sir Charles' personal estate totalled £51,200 – which did not include the mining interests and Trust funds set up by Sir William.

Col. Arthur Tremayne was 41 when he inherited Carclew from his uncle. His

The altered south front

mother, Caroline Lemon, had married John Hearle Tremayne of Heligan, and Arthur was their fifth child, born in 1827, a year after the death of Sir Charles' only son and his wife. It is likely that Tremaynes were frequent visitors, and one wonders if little Arthur knew that his uncle's palatial home would one day be his. It would have been some comfort to Sir Charles to instruct his nephew in the ways of the estate, and pass on its history to him. Arthur initially pursued a military career, fighting in the Crimean war and surviving the Charge of the Light Brigade. However, on his uncle's death in 1868, Arthur returned and took up his inheritance. One of the first things he did was to gain control of the estate by getting the Trustees to sign a Deed of Release terminating Sir William's Trust Fund. This required him to buy out the six surviving beneficiaries under the terms of Sir William's Will, one of whom was Frances Lemon, the sole surviving unmarried sister of Sir Charles. In April of that year, a deed was drawn up whereby Frances Lemon, would surrender her eighth share (as one of eight sisters) of the estate in return for an annuity of £1,000. Frances, whose address was given as Upper Brook St, Grosvenor Square, London, died later that same year, and Arthur Tremayne was in command of the entire Lemon fortune.

At some stage Carclew was considerably enlarged, it is thought by Henry Harrison, who had worked on several other Cornish houses. The left wing was extended, destroying the symmetry, and as part of increasing the servants' quarters, the clock tower was rebuilt.

Col. Tremayne carried on the Lemon tradition, serving as Sheriff in 1871 and MP for Truro 1878-80. His bride, in 1858, was Lady Frances Margaret Hutchinson, daughter of the Earl of Donoughmore, and Sir Charles must have wondered if history was going to repeat itself when their first born, another Arthur, died in 1862, barely one year old. Lady Frances died in 1866, having had three further children, the youngest of whom, Charles, also died young.

Interior views
(private collection)

129

Col. Tremayne died in 1903, and his Will named the Earl of Donoughmore and William Salusbury Trelawney as Trustees, and states that his heir was 'Tenant for Life'. He left £12,000 to each of his children by his first marriage, and £10,000 to each child from his second marriage (to Emma Philpotts in 1870) – also two. The will gave the Trustees permission to 'lease any part of the estate except Carclew and its park, for terms of 21 or 40 years dependant upon the terms, but excepting any mining rights. One intriguing clause refers to the 'Sultan's Diamonds'. These were part of Lady Frances' marriage portion and passed to her children on her death. However, young Charles' share passed to his father on his early death, and Col. Tremayne proposed to dispose of them. The diamonds should be offered to the Earl of Donoughmore at a price agreed by the Trustees, but if not sold then they would revert, together with all furniture, jewellery, plate, books, pictures etc. to the settled estates.

His obituary in the Royal Cornwall Gazette states that 'few men were better known in county circles and better loved than Col. Tremayne. He was a man at times with a brusque manner savouring of the old military man that he was but at heart he was the kindest and gentlest of men.' It goes on that 'he was much loved of all in the parish of Mylor...for he lived amongst his people, loved the old demesne and took the greatest pride in the beautiful grounds of Carclew.' Among his many interests listed were Truro Cathedral committee, Royal Cornwall Infirmary of which he was a liberal financial supporter, Royal Cornwall Agricultural Society, Cornwall Home for destitute girls and the county asylum. He was a magistrate and county councillor. His must have been one of the last traditional funerals, with his coffin born in state along the four mile route

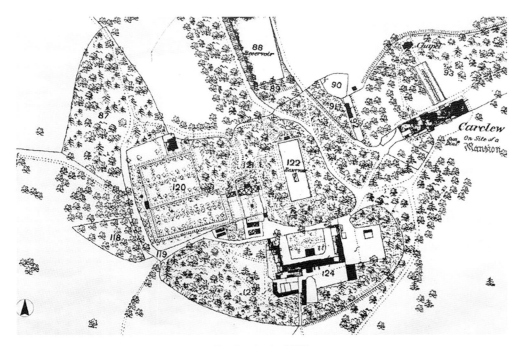

Carclew in the 1900s

from Carclew to Mylor church, followed by family and tenants. The route was lined with mourners, flags at half mast and the shops shuttered. He joined his forebears in the family vault, followed by his wife in 1915.

Capt. William Tremayne succeeded to the estates on the death of his father in 1903. He had married Zoe de Roback in 1890 and there was one son, named Charles. Apparently they were somewhat reluctant to move to Cornwall, but once there he entered into county life, serving as a JP and County Councillor, and as President of the Royal Agricultural Society. He served as a Recruiting Officer during the lst World War, and died in 1930. He was the last of the owners of Carclew to be buried in the family vault at Mylor church.

William did not alter the house, but he made the decision to break up the estate. In June, 1920 a sale lasting three days was held at the Concert Hall, Truro, when 2,637 acres of lands from St.Columb Major, Kenwyn, Kea, Feock and St. Gluvias were auctioned off – but without the mining rights. The value was given as £2006 13s. Land around St. Columb Major, totalling 872 acres, had been sold a few days earlier, value £904. All those holdings so carefully built up by the Lemons – gone, leaving just the house and park and around 900 acres. Rentals were low, and mining returns had all but ceased. The farmhouses and cottages would all have been in need of updating for which there was little money – a familiar story. And it may be he thought the day of the land gentry was coming to an end and no longer wanted the responsibility.

The final blow came in the night of 14th April, 1934 when fire took hold. Capt. Tremayne was woken by the fire, by which time the central block was well alight, and he and his wife and two small children escaped down the back stairs. The household consisted of five housemaids, the cook, footman and two nursery maids, all of whom escaped. Next morning, the pride of the Lemons was a smouldering, burnt out ruin.

No attempt was made to rebuild Carclew. The Tremaynes departed, and in 1937 put the whole estate on the market.

The house and 100 acres passed to the Society of Friends through the efforts of one of their members, Arthur Jenkins, who ran it as a rest home for refugees until 1940. Some restoration was carried out to make the ruin habitable – new floors and doors, and the rooms that remained, redecorated. The semi-basement kitchen areas, which would have been the least damaged, were brought back into use. Later, those fleeing Nazi Germany found a home. Carclew and the Home Farm were requisitioned by the War Department and at one period the grounds were occupied by American troops who, in 1944, were preparing for the disastrous Operation Tiger at Slapton Sands, where many of them lost their lives.

The ownership of Carclew between 1937 and a date after the end of the war when the estate, with 890 acres with an annual income of £1,200, and the remains of the historic mansion were offered for sale at £250,000, is very muddled. Arthur Jenkins, who had been the land agent at Lanhydrock, was unable to complete the original purchase. He was elderly and in ill health and died in 1940. In 1942 Frederick Knight Wynne from the Midlands and his aunts became the owners, and Carclew might have begun a new chapter if he had not been killed fighting in Greece in 1945. The next owners were messrs. Sims, Lamb & Dingle; it was Dingle who dismantled the east wing of the house as it was unsafe, and at some stage he sold out to Jack Siley who planned to develop the estate. Had it not been for the intervention of Jack Neale few traces of Carclew would have remained. He was from Porthgwidden, a house with associations with both the Lemons and the Tremaynes, and after wartime service he returned there. In the 1950s he purchased an old gamekeeper's cottage on the Carclew estate, with sitting tenants who remained for a further ten years. Hence, requiring a home, he built a bungalow on a plot adjacent to the ruin, about 40 feet from the original east wall. When Siley proposed building houses on the land in front of the old house, Jack Neale was so incensed that he negotiated to buy the land and the ruin from Siley. He later bought more of the estate land to save it from the same fate. Mrs Neale and her family are now the owners of the ruin and are currently beginning the long process of attracting funding to enable them to stabilise what is left of Carclew – a very long-term project which would safeguard its future. The rest of the surrounding estate land has over the years been developed into farmland and other private dwellings, and consequently, as with the ruin itself, there is no public access to any of the estate.

There is little trace left of the Lemons in the city of Truro where for two centuries they had so much influence. There is no statue of the 'Great' William, or of the 1st baronet. Even their memorials in the parish church of St. Mary disappeared when it was rebuilt as Truro cathedral. Lemon Quay is filled in and now a shopping precinct. Lemon Street and their town house are the only memorials – and a haunting, ruined country house.

The ruin prior to any demolition (courtesy Mrs R Maclagan)

Sources

Notes on the Parish of Mylor, Hugh Pengelly Olivey, 1907.
The Book of Mylor, Mylor Local History Group, 2004.
Country Life, May 13th, 1916 and April 14th, 1934.

Cornwall Record Office	BRA 1118/303
X 897/45	BRA 1118/184
WH/1780	WH/1911/2
BRA/1118/150/165	WH/1/1671/1677/1756

Wm. Borlase, Natural History of Cornwall 1758

Clowance – Crowan

Clowance has not 'vanished' for there is still a substantial house to be seen, and enough of the grounds to give some idea of what once existed there. But the house dates from 1843 following a fire that largely destroyed the original building. And the grounds are interspersed with holiday lodges and caravans. The whole is run as a holiday complex with the house serving as the administrative centre and the delightful eighteenth century orangery as an office.

Little is known about the original Clowance, ancestral home of the St. Aubyns. They are first recorded in the days of Henry IV when Geoffrey St. Aubyn married Elizabeth Kemyell around 1380. She was the heiress of Clowance, so there must have been a dwelling of some substance from earliest times. The Hearth Tax returns of 1664 record 'John Sayntaubyn' as having 21 hearths in the parish of Crowan, making it one of the largest properties in Cornwall at that time. The family remained there until 1921 – a long tenure, but not without difficulties.

The earliest image is given by Dr. Borlase in his *Natural History of Cornwall* of 1758. He depicts a most unusual building which appears to consist of a range of first floor rooms over an unimportant ground floor, with two projecting oriel windows supported on columns, possibly overlooking the bowling green. Unusually for Dr. Borlase, he has not shown the principal entrance front, but from the roof line and number of chimneys, Clowance at this time appears a large house. It would seem to be surrounded by grass.

The engraving was carried out at Sir John's expense so it must have been his choice to feature the west front.

An early view of Clowance dated 1766   (courtesy of the Molesworth St. Aubyn family)

Another view, dated 1766, does show the main front with a large, rambling house behind it with what looks like a chapel, and the Borlase wing to the left. The stables and the orangery are shown, all in the same style. As these are usually attributed to the 5th baronet in the mid to early nineteenth century, the unsigned drawing is something of a conundrum. Is the date wrong? Or were these buildings the work of the 4th baronet? Two slightly later views show the central portion with trees obscuring the rest of the house.

Very little reference is to be found concerning its building or decoration, though a new south front is mentioned, and it escaped the wholesale rebuilding that was so common in the eighteenth and nineteenth centuries.

The St. Aubyns are one of Cornwall's oldest families, and have been prominent figures in the history of the county, with six St. Aubyns serving as High Sheriffs, and many of them taking a seat in Parliament.

John St. Aubyn (1610–84), was a leading Parliamentarian, and in 1659 purchased St. Michael's Mount which had previously been owned by Francis Basset of Tehidy, a staunch Royalist. St. Aubyn married Catherine Godolphin, heiress of her father Francis, and from this marriage came considerable neighbouring property. It was his son, also John, who was created a baronet in 1671.

The third Sir John – they were all called John – served as MP for Cornwall from 1722 until his death in 1744. He had a reputation as an outspoken politician, but refused office as he wished to maintain his independence. Back in Cornwall in 1727 he managed to keep the peace when trouble broke out with the miners threatening to riot. Pay and conditions were far from good but it was a shortage of corn at affordable prices that sparked an outbreak. Sir John 'advanced a considerable sum of money to the tinners, by which they were saved from starving and plundering their neighbours.'

Undated sketches   (courtesy of the Molesworth St. Aubyn family)

With his marriage to Catherine Morice in 1725 came a sizeable injection of money. She and her sister, who married Sir John Molesworth of Pencarrow, (the first of several unions between the two families), were co-heiresses of their father's large estate at Werrington and she is reputed to have brought with her £10,000 in cash, plus the manor of Stoke Damerel at Devonport. But they don't appear to have embarked on a spending spree and much of their time would have been spent in London. Sir John appeared more interested in the grounds than the house, where he planted many trees,

135

some rare, and the first known plane trees in Cornwall. Both died young, in their 40s. Catherine is said to have gone into a decline as a result of threatening letters from a criminal convicted by her husband, a JP, and Sir John in 1744 as a result of a fever. The couple had four daughters and John, the 18 year old heir.

The will of Sir John, written in 1740, contains an interesting clause. Despite having a son, he states that if there were no male heirs, then the estate passes first to his eldest daughter, Catherine, and her heirs, then to Mary, then to Margaret, then to Barbara. The heir was to take the name of St. Aubyn and to use Clowance as his chief residence; the men who his daughters married to take the name of St. Aubyn, or be disinherited; after his daughters the estates to pass to Godolphin Arundel St. Aubyn. £500 was left to each daughter living at his death with income settled on them by marriage settlements.

Apart from Catherine, who remained a spinster, the daughters made good marriages. Margaret married Francis Basset of Tehidy, Mary married John Buller of Morval, and Barbara married her first cousin, Sir John Molesworth of Pencarrow.

The 4th Sir John followed the family pattern of Oxford and Parliament, and again died young, aged 46, in 1772, leaving an heir of 14, the 5th Sir John. And here something went wrong. His mother, Elizabeth Wingfield, remarried and some accounts state she let her son be badly influenced by his tutors. He was born in London and went to Westminster School so would not have spent much time at Clowance. He then spent three years in France where it is said he fathered a child with an Italian woman. He must have known about the entail, but instead of choosing a bride from amongst the county families, in 1783 at the age of 25, he fathered a son with Martha Nicholls, the daughter of a Cornish landscape gardener who was employed on the grounds at Clowance. The couple had a further four children before she was supplanted in his affections by Juliana Vinnicombe – who bore him nine children and finally married him in 1822. Poor Martha was pensioned off to a house at Ludgvan opposite St. Michael's Mount of which she may well have had fond memories. Apart from the fact that Sir John spent a great deal of time in London, he would have had no incentive to improve the entailed Clowance estates as no son of his would inherit. And entertaining with such a household would not have been without its problems.

Despite this, some work was undertaken on the house, and to make certain of his mark, two stone coats of arms were incorporated into the west front, dated 1813, one with a crossed shield, and one with a chough surmounting a helmet. These have survived.

In the diaries of Robert Mylne (a leading architect of the day), there is reference to a meeting with Lady St. Aubyn in 1775, and of a survey carried out on the front of Clowance House, and the possibility of securing it with iron straps. The next year he records that the front is to be taken down and rebuilt. It would seem that Sir John's mother was still involved with the estate, though she surely cannot have approved of her son's lifestyle. Mylne designed a house for her on Richmond Hill, still known as The Wick. She died in 1796.

In the early days Sir John spent much of his energy – and money – improving the grounds, employing John Nicholls, father of Martha. Nicholls had a good reputation, and the park was laid out with avenues, plantations, a Great Pond, a circular lawn

*The 5th baronet's memorial –
coat of arms dated 1813*

in front of the house, and a serpentine haha, to the open ground. The whole was enclosed in a five mile stone wall and this, and much of the original planting, survives. Sir John was also believed responsible for the elegant stable block and the orangery close to the house, and had he been minded to replace the somewhat antiquated house, it would presumably have been in the same style and to the same good standard. From this period dates the gazebo, or folly, overlooking the walled garden, a boiler house, probably the garden itself, and a temple by the lily pond. The temple has been destroyed, but although the gazebo is roofless and floorless, sufficient of this elegant two storey building survives to demonstrate its high quality. The same applies to the boiler house, built to heat the glass houses. Described in its Grade II listing as a 'rare purpose built boiler house', it is of classical design with two floors, sash windows and dome-headed niches surmounted by eagles. Was Sir John his own architect? No records have come to light of architects or building materials. The attention to detail and the high quality of these outbuildings makes them a fine example of the period.

Sir John fulfilled his responsibilities being High Sheriff when he was 23, and serving in Parliament. The estates at this time were considerable and from the late eighteenth century onwards a large number of mining setts were negotiated. In Clowance Wood, close to the house, a grant was made for 21 years of all minerals with the requirement that a good engine of 63 inches cylinder should be built, and mentions the 'new wall lately built by Sir John.'

The Dictionary of National Biography describes him as an educated man – he went to Oxford – a lover of science and the arts. He became a member of the Linnean Society, the Society of Antiquaries and in 1797, a Fellow of the Royal Society. As with many of his fellow Cornishmen, he had a keen interest in minerals and bought an important collection, with which he decorated the temple in the grounds. A Whig supporter, he served as an MP from 1807 to 1812.

Apart from not marrying their mother, Sir John appears to have cared for his children, providing them with a good education, and with generous marriage portions. When he died it was found that the Devonport property was encumbered with debts of £130,000 as a result.

Sir John had been a generous benefactor to Devonport, and when his body was brought back from London, where he died in 1839 aged 81, the municipal dignatories accompanied the carriage through Devonport. It was estimated that around 30,000 people lined the streets to see the cortege pass, which had left London six days previously. The coffin then lay in state in St. Austell for three days before being finally laid to rest in the family vault at Clowance 'with great Masonic ceremony'. Part of the inscription on his memorial states that he was 'a person whose estimable qualities none who knew him could fail to admire. Generous without ostentation, charitable without display, courteous with perfect sincerity …' etc.

The 5th baronet   (courtesy of the Molesworth St. Aubyn family)

Not surprisingly, his will was long and complicated – and contained some surprises. His eldest son, James, was named as his principal heir, but he had only daughters. Sir John then by-passed his next two sons (by Martha Nicholls) and his eldest son (by Juliana Vinnicombe)- William, rector of Stoke Damerel – and named Edward, their second son. Edward ultimately inherited in 1862 on the death of his half-brother James, and was created a baronet; his son became the first Lord St. Levan of St. Michael's Mount, where the family still live. (The Devonport lands, St. Michael's Mount and other Cornish lands were not included in the entail – only Clowance). He left Juliana the remainder of the lease on Shortgrove Hall in Essex, which would appear to have been their home for some time, and he instructed that 'all letters, private papers and books not relating to the estate at Clowance, St. Michael's Mount and Shortgrove be destroyed.' He also left her an annuity of £2,000.

The will appears to have caused much upset in the two families; did any of them ever visit Clowance again – or was it a closed chapter?

The entailed estates passed to the son of Catherine St. Aubyn, the Revd. John Molesworth, a grandson of the 4th Baronet and a nephew of the 5th, who was Vicar of Crowan and Rector of Redruth. In 1839, by Royal Licence he added St. Aubyn to his name. He was unmarried and preferred to stay in his Rectory rather than move to Clowance, and on his death in 1844 the estate passed to his brother, the Revd. Hender Molesworth St. Aubyn, who was also Rector of Redruth.

But the will he made encumbered the estate, leaving bequests totalling £17,000, and this generosity must have contributed to the declining fortunes of the family.

Clowance suffered two fires in less than ten years. An account of the first that broke out on 10th November, 1836 in the time of the 5th baronet, describes Clowance as square around a courtyard. The fire began in a beam over the brewery and most of the rear of the house was destroyed. The newspaper account recalls that miners on their way to work rushed to fight the fire. Two servants barely escaped with their lives, one male being forced to jump from a window in a 'state of almost nudity'. Many pictures and valuables were saved and stored in the riding house – where they were guarded by 20 special constables, hastily sworn in for the task. Sir John also distributed rewards totalling several hundred pounds to those who had helped.

There are no records of how much was rebuilt but when fire again broke out in 1843, the newspaper report stated that it started in the dining room at the front and that the rebuilt back portion survived. The library was entirely destroyed. A document drawn up in May 1847 created a Declaration of Trust concerning the Marriage Settlement of 1828 between Helen Napleton and Hender Molesworth St. Aubyn as 'with numerous other papers and writings and other valuable property had been accidentally destroyed by the fire which took place in the mansion house of Clowance'.

Plans for a new house were drawn up by Piers St. Aubyn, a relative and established architect, and the building went ahead providing a grand new front with spacious receptions rooms overlooking the grounds.

The brothers, both clergymen and sons of a clergyman, had no estates of their own. They brought no new wealth to the St. Aubyn inheritance which consisted only of those lands that the 5th Baronet could not dispose of among his own family. In view of the later history of Clowance it may be that they over-reached themselves in the building of the new house, as well as a substantial Home Farm. Had they turned a blind eye to the state of the family finances? Or were they eternally optimistic that things would improve? They didn't.

The Revd. Hender Moleswoth St. Aubyn died in 1867, aged 69, and was buried in the family vault leaving three sons, Hender John, St. Aubyn Hender, vicar of Collingham in Yorkshire, and Walter, MA of Christchurch, Oxford and a barrister. His will left an annuity of £300 to his wife, Helen, and £6,000 'to be raised from the estate for the use of his younger sons, St. Aubyn Hender and Walter'; household goods and furniture to his wife, and the residue of his estate to the trustees for investment. It would seem that the clerical Molesworths were somewhat unworldly.

'Mr. Hender's case is one full of difficulties.' This was the dismal conclusion reached by the agent, Mr. Grylls, in a statement presented to the Trustees on the afternoon of the funeral on 23rd December. Presumably such a statement had been asked for some time previously as considerable details as to income and outgoings were given. The total estimated income, based on the previous 20 years, was given as £3,350, allowing the continuing fall in mining yields from around £1,300 to, say, £500. Incumbrances including his mother's annuity of £300, totalled £2,040 of which the largest sums involved the mortgage to Hogg – £450 – and insurances on his life as collateral – £2,500.

Balance left – £1,310.

But

> *… this balance is subject to still further deductions and at this stage of the calculations the question may be asked – will Clowance House be the residence of its owner? If it will not, then the expense of keeping up the house, gardens, grounds and plantations in repair, involving tradesmen's bills, coal, servants wages and keep, all horses and carriages, must be deducted and what these are likely to be is best ascertained by a reference to what they were during the last Sir John's non-residence there.*

These were calculated over the years 1834-39 when the house was not occupied, total £810 –

> *House, garden and lands £287, smiths bill £22, servants board and wages £250, tradesmens bills and coal £251.*

This, said Mr. Grylls, reduces the income to £500 which is only £200 beyond Mr. Hender's present annuity. As if all this were not daunting enough, the agent continues;

> *I cannot conclude these observations without asking how is Mr. Hender's mortgage debt to his father of £5,000, and which now becomes part of the younger sons fortune, to be raised? Two ways, one by insuring Mr. Hender's life, if his state of health render it possible, if affected for seven years at £105 would reduce his income to £500. The second would be to raise money by selling leases with only one or two lives remaining but that would be attended by great sacrifice being in the nature of a forced sale without competition and would, in fact, be ripping up the Goose that lays the Golden Egg.*
>
> *In conclusion, I consider Mr. Hender's case is one full of difficulties.*

Mr. Grylls went on to suggest a possible way out.

> *Application be made to the Trustees of Hoggs mortage and of the late Mr. St. Aubyn's will to permit Mr. Hender to raise a definite sum by the power of leasing, a list of the principal estates capable of reversion be made, and that whatever be done should be done under the advice of counsel so that the Trustees be saved from blame in any course of action they may adopt.*
>
> *Since the Funeral, the question of whether Clowance mansion could be let it would seem new in its history, but there may not be any legal objection. However, Trengwainton, Trevayler and Bosahun after repeated advertisements, remain unlet and were obliged to be kept in hand.*

It must have been a truly depressing gathering at Clowance. It is interesting that Hender John, the heir, was not present whilst his future was being discussed, a further document mentioning that he would 'shortly remove from Leamington to his mother in Plymouth on his way to Clowance where he would spend three months.'

A telling phrase states that 'Mr. St. Aubyn's life is uninsurable and his state of health unsatisfactory.' Things got so bad that in May 1868, a Memorandum to the Trustees suggests that 'Mr. Molesworth St. Aubyn leave the country as the only means of preventing proceedings against him.'

In June, 1868 Mr. Grylls drew up a Mortgage agreement;

> *Hender John Molesworth St. Aubyn, as tenant for life of the estate was heavily charged with legacies under the will of his uncle, and a jointure to his mother under his father's will, has mortgaged his life estate for £10,000 on security of life insurance policies and also mortgages by his father on which, by his will, £5,000 is due.*

It goes on to mention debts owing to tradesmen and others amounting to £900 'which must be paid immediately to avoid litigation. The two brothers have suggested that the maintenance of the estate be vested in trustees who would allow him £700 per annum, with power to let Clowance mansion on a 3-5 year lease. His brother, St. Aubyn Hender Molesworth, paid the £900 out of money due to him.'

It would appear that for some reason, Hender John was not considered capable of running the estate, and in June the Trustees stepped in and took over – but not for long. Hender died later that year at Clowance. His will was pathetically brief; he left his signet ring given to him by his father to his brother, and the rest of his personal estate to his dear wife Kythe Catherine, and his address was given as Kiltylan Villa, Leamington, Warwick. The will was proved at under £3,000 and there was no mention of the estate.

Quoting from a journal kept by their mother, a diary kept by St. Aubyn Hender, gives an insight into Hender's life.

> *5/2 HJ (&St.AH) ill in the organ room – v.bad with chicken pox.*
> *1839 10/2 Parents and HJ to Exmouth where HJ had a dangerous illness at*
>   *Mrs. Whickams.*
> *1843 21/12 HJ returned from school to Illogan.*
>   *22/12 HJ poorly all night (mince pies).*
> *1844 26/2 HJ started for Rugby.*

In June, 1846, the whole family and a large party left for a visit to Switzerland, returning in September the following year. It was a fairly hectic itinerary with a stay of almost a year at Lausanne. Was this for health reasons – no clue is given? In September the family returned to Clowance and:

> *1850 Hender was now at Oxford.*
> *1851 21/12 HJ came of age.*
> *1856 1/1 Hender's wedding to Kythe Popham at Sithney. Ball at Clowance*
> *1863 11/5 HJ at Malvern with his mother.*
>   *4/7 HJ visited by St.A at Malvern.*
>   *30/7 HJ celebrated his birthday with St.A at Leamington*

Hender John on his wedding day   (courtesy of the Molesworth St. Aubyn family)

The Dining room   (courtesy of the Molesworth St. Aubyn family)

1866 18-28/2 H*J* and Kythe stayed with St.A at Swindon.
1867 13/12 H*J*'s father (Rev HenderMolesworth StA) died at Clowance, buried at
        Crowan 23.12.
1868 26/6 H*J* died at Clowance
        2/7 H*J* buried at Crowan.

St. Aubyn Hender duly inherited, and in 1913, a year before his death, he also succeeded to the Molesworth estates, which had passed in quick succession since 1855 through three baronets. The last, Sir Lewis, had preferred to live at his mother's home, Trewarthenic, and virtually closed Pencarrow. He also removed some of the contents which caused considerable wrangling later. Now the 12th baronet, Sir St. Aubyn Hender Moleswoth St. Aubyn was in possession not only of Clowance, but also of the Pencarrow estate, which included the Tetcott estate on the North Devon borders. All this passed to his son Hugh, b 1865, who had married Sybil Wake, a grand-daughter of Sir Edward St. Aubyn, son of the 5th St. Aubyn baronet.

Pencarrow is an attractive estate, some 40 miles from Clowance with a beautiful late eighteenth century house set amidst well-planted grounds. The great house at Tetcott had been demolished in 1831 and replaced with a sizeable 'hunting lodge' which subsequently burnt down, but there still remained the stabling and a large farmhouse. The upkeep of all these properties, plus death duties resulting from the deaths of the previous two baronets within a year of each other, would have placed a considerable strain on the estates, and in 1919 the decision was made to sell the impoverished Clowance estate.

Firstly, a five day sale was held 27-31 October with 323 lots; many tenants bought their holdings in advance of the auction. Then in November the remainder of the estate went, divided into two sections. First was 1962 acres around Redruth, Gwennap and St. Agnes. Lots ranged from whole farms to single fields – all excluding the mining rights – and oddities such as the old lime kiln and boat station and refreshment hut at St. Agnes beach and Trevaunance Coombe. The second section was 5521 acres around Camborne, Crowan, Gwinear, Perran, Breage, Germoe and St. Kevern, the manors of Penponds and Barriper, Leedstown and Praze. This included HM Coastguard station at Prussia Cove and the Lifeboat House at Porthoustock. Reserved from the sale were the reservoirs of Clowance House between the house and the railway line, with a clause that no building or house was to be erected on this land without the consent of the owner.

Clowance House and grounds were not included in the sale; perhaps Sir Hugh did not think it a good time to sell, or was hoping to find some use for the ancestral home, where he and his family were living, as Pencarrow was occupied by the sister of the 8th baronet, who had died in 1910. He finally moved to Pencarrow in 1921, and on 5th and 6th June, 1923, Clowance itself was offered for sale with 1,300 acres.

The sale particulars for the house were unusual in that they began on the first floor with the main bedrooms – situated at the front of the house – and continued with the Servants' Hall (20ft 6 inches x 18ft with bay window), servants' bathroom and bedrooms, before proceeding down the Main Staircase to the ground floor. The principal rooms were in the new south front, but facing west were the dining room with bay window and the smoking room with double doors giving access to the billiard room. The domestic offices were 'suitably separate from the main building.' The house had central heating and electric light. As well as stabling, garaging for three cars, loose boxes and accommodation, there was a granite-built riding school 119ft x 40ft and 25ft high.

The gardens and grounds were described in some detail and must have been very fine, laid out in the best fashion of the time. The rose garden had a circular fountain and there was a stalagmite grotto with pigmy ornamentations to the east of the house. To the west were 'parterres with eight exceptionally fine yew trees, a tennis lawn, and forest trees of great girth abound in the beautiful park.' The Kings Pond was listed and an ornamental water of about four acres with a boat house. The kitchen gardens were enclosed with a soundly built brick wall, and contained four glass houses, two of which were 54ft in length, and heated. There were growing frames, fruit trees and an

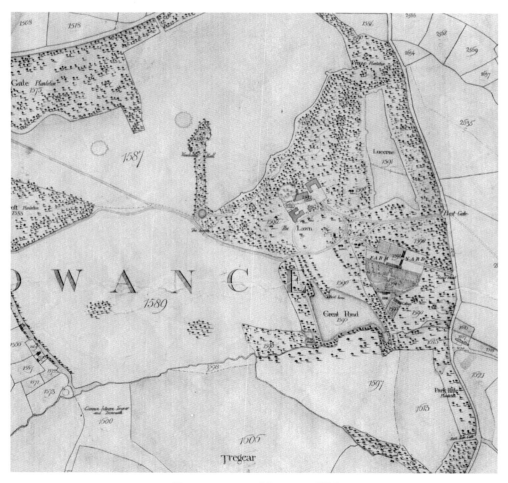

Clowance estate – tithe map, c 1836

144

orchard, woodland and excellent shooting. The estimated annual income was £350 for the mansion, park and woodland, and £8 for the kitchen gardens.

However, it seems to have been a dispiriting sale, the bidding being very slow. No-one bid for the principal lot of Clowance House, the Barton Farm, two other farms and six cottages, nor was anyone interested when Clowance was offered separately. The two day sale raised just £2,500 with many lots withdrawn, failing to make their reserve.

The estate was finally sold in 1923, and fortunately it escaped the fate of many large houses, bought by timber companies who so often wrought wholesale destruction, so that the beautiful parkland of Clowance survives. The walled garden also survives, albeit with several new dwellings augmenting those already converted to domestic use.

The St. Aubyn presence is still to be felt, particularly in the parish church of Crowan where so many of them were buried. There are several fine monuments, but sadly the set of six brasses, the earliest dated around 1400 of Geffry St. Aubyn and Elizabeth Kemyell, have disappeared. They were removed some time after 1878 when they were said to be in a poor state of repair to a 'place of safe-keeping.'

Sources

The St. Aubyns of Cornwall, Diana Hartley, 1977

Dr. David Donaldson and the archive at Pencarrow House, Washaway, by kind permission of the Molesworth St. Aubyn family

Coldrenick in 1820

Coldrenick, St. Germans

Coldrenick is unique among these lost houses in that its owners, descendants of the original builders, took the decision to demolish the family home. In 1966, possibly with rejoicing, but certainly with great relief, the unwieldy, decaying and over-large Victorian mansion came crashing down, thus ending four centuries of history. All that remains are a few parts of the earlier house, the fine stable block converted into a replacement dwelling, and the grounds.

The house that the descendants of the Trelawnys demolished was the third known structure on the same site, and possibly incorporated portions of the two earlier houses. In the sixteenth century the estate was the property of the Drenycke family but at the turn of the century passed to Jonathan Trelawny of Pool, in Menheniot. There must have been some financial dealings between Drenycke and Trelawny whereby Coldrenick was mortgaged to Trelawny in 1590. It would appear Drenycke could not meet his obligations, for a document was drawn up whereby the 'mansion and tenement' passed to Jonathan Trelawny with a clause that Drenycke could recover the property if he paid £300 by 1st January, 1569. This he failed to do and in 1598 a 'final concord' was drawn up citing John Drenycke as the 'deforciant' and Jonathan Trelawny as plaintiff for the 'mansion house and tenements of Coldrenick alias South Coldrenick' for the consideration of £100. It would seem that Drenycke continued at Coldrenick for a Quitclaim exists dated 1614 between him, styled as 'gentleman of Coldrenick', and Edward Trelawny of Lamellion, whereby he released his right to South Coldrenick to Trelawny, and in that year he was named as tenant for life of South Coldrenick This was the last time the property changed hands. Jonathan Trelawny left Coldrenick to his second son, Edward, and the main branch of the family later moved to Pelynt on the south coast.

Edward Trelawny does not appear to have lived at Coldrenick, preferring his own estate of Lamellion – to the Trelawnys it was just another acquisition. Records survive showing that in 1622 the estate was let to H. Price, and in 1676 to Edward Harris for a consideration of £53, renewed in 1678 for £90.

The memorial in Menheniot church to Edward's son, another Jonathan, styles him as 'of Coldrenick' so it may be he chose to live there. His heir, Edward (d. 1726) became Dean of Exeter, with a handsome Deanery at his disposal. His wife was Elizabeth Darrell, whose family had inherited the Trewornan estate, and it is from the Darrells that all the subsequent owners of Coldrenick descended when the Trelawny blood ran out in the next generation. The couple had two sons, neither of whom married. The elder, Darrell, died in 1727 aged 30, when his brother, Charles, inherited. The brothers must have planned to make a proper estate of Coldrenick for a large and rather graceless house was built on the site of, and incorporating parts of, the earlier house.

The only clue to the interior comes from an inventory taken in May, 1727, possibly following the death of Darrell. The house was newly completed, which might explain why so little furniture is recorded, but it does give some kind of description of the house. No indication is given as to the whereabouts of the various rooms, nor whether they were entered in the order in which they were viewed. Three bedchambers come first – Green, Wrought, My Son's, and then a Parlour. Next a staircase containing a clock, screen and cane chairs. Miss Haney's bedchamber had a canopy bed, as did the Middle and Bell Chambers. Next is Mr Jetow's chamber, and Patience's, which had a curtain bed. Then comes a maids' chamber with three beds, and a corner garret with two beds. Were these all in the new house, because next comes the new long garret with three beds, another with two, and the men's chamber with three, and the Bell chamber with one?

The Long Old Gallery had four Turkish wool carpets hung upon the beams, and then come the main rooms of the house. The Great Parlour had a large table and 12 cane chairs, two 'ovill' tables and cane chairs. In the Little Parlour were a clock, card table, three other tables and cane chairs. As yet the Drawing Room contained no furniture, only cups and saucers etc. The Passage Hall had a cupboard with a large quantity of plates etc., and pewter. No mention is made of the kitchens or servants' quarters , but there was a Brewhouse, Malt Chamber and Cellar 'which was full when I went'; strong and bitter beer, hogshead on tap, Syder – full 4 pipes and 'about the house, 6 pipes, 15 hogsheads, 5 ale barrels, 5 little barrels'.

It was noted that a quantity of plate was left with Mrs. Peto, and plate in the butler's room is listed.

Charles, like his brother, never married and for almost 40 years lived the life of a country squire. On his death in 1764, Coldrenick passed to Henry St. George Darrell, his mother's nephew, who was the first to add Trelawny to his name.

There would appear to have been some antagonism between the Coldrenick Trelawnys and the main branch. Darrell insisted that his brother should not leave anything to their aunt, Mary Trelawny, because of the way in which the Trelawnys looked down on the Darrell relations 'since they have behaved towards me and my family in such a manner as if they thought us no part of theirs and as if we were beneath them'. Consequently Henry St. George's inheritance of Coldrenick was disputed by the Trelawnys, and he had to prove his right to the estate. Henry was the third bachelor in a row to succeed. The family had a strange characteristic – a reluctance to marry; six times *dsp* appears after the name of an heir to the estate, which makes its descent difficult to disentangle. Henry's heir was Darrell Crabbe, yet another bachelor, who also took the name Trelawny.

Very little is known of the early medieval house which disappeared somewhere amongst the vast new pile. The earliest plan of the new Coldrenick is shown on the map produced by Daniel Gumb in 1756. This shows a rectangular block with a courtyard in the centre, possibly incorporating the earlier house. The map shows the house surrounded by a pattern of small enclosures including a bowling green, typical of a house of an earlier period. To the west was the 'best garden' which may have been a formal, symmetrically laid out, pattern of paths and squares. By the 1795, when a later map was drawn, these had been swept away and replaced with a more open layout with lawns coming right up to the house, and shrubbery replacing the bowling green. At some stage a ha-ha was constructed. The 1795 map, by G. Bentley, depicts two elevations; the North West was the entrance from with a simple central door – no portico or colonnades – flanked by four bays on either side. There is no basement level and no steps. It is depicted as brick built, devoid of any ornamentation except for balustrading on the roof with four urns. The South West front is even plainer. Both maps give the house the same outline with the central courtyard. The stable block was much closer to the main house than was the norm, and a range of demestic offices were shown to the south. These survive and could predate the 1726 house.

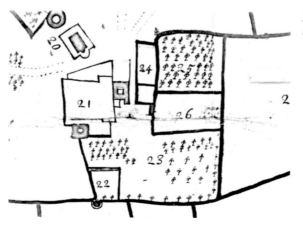

Detail from map by Daniel Gumb, 1756

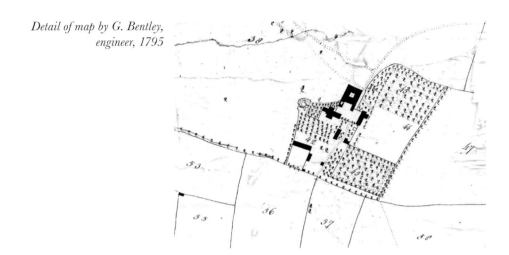

Detail of map by G. Bentley, engineer, 1795

The map shows the house surrounded by a pattern of small enclosures including a bowling green typical of a house of an earlier period. To the west was the 'best garden' which may have been a formal, symmetrically laid out, pattern of paths and squares. By 1795 when a later map was drawn, these had been swept away and replaced with a more open layout with lawns coming right up to the house, and a shrubbery replacing the bowling green. At some stage a ha-ha was constructed. Both maps give the house the same outline with the central courtyard. The stable block was much closer to the main house than was the norm, and a range of domestic offices was shown to the south. These survive and could predate the 1726 house.

In 1795 Coldrenick passed to Captain Edward Stephens, a descendant of another brother of Elizabeth, wife of the Dean. He had four children, Charles (1799–1883), Anne (d 1868), Edward and Eleanor. Edward, who also took the name of Trelawny, died in 1807, so Charles was only eight when he inherited. He served as High Sheriff in 1822 – the only member of the family to hold this position. But according to the Census

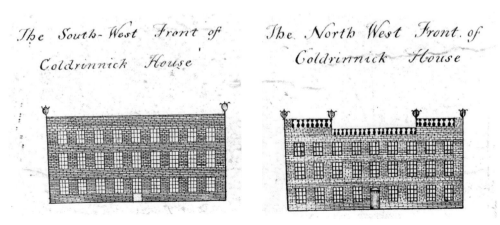

The South-West Front of Coldrinnick House

The North West Front of Coldrinnick House

Drawing of the house dated 1795   (G. Bentley 1795)

returns, he was not living at Coldrenick. In 1851 it housed James Sowden, farmer, six servants and two charwomen. William Barley, farm bailiff, and his family were in the Mansion in 1861 and in 1871. There is no record of Trelawnys living on the estate.

Charles Trelawny lived in prosperous times and, in common, with many of his neighbours, was benefiting hugely from the mines developed on his land. The house, however, was not his main interest – horses were. He hunted, but his main obsession was racing. Across the drive from the house was a sizeable stable block with loose boxes and grooms' accommodation above. A short distance away was the stallions' stable. Charles was a successful breeder – of horses – entering all the prominent races all over the country. The main door into the stables remains unaltered from Charles' time, covered with the horse shoes of his winners, with a record of their successes and the prize money won. In 1842 he owned the Derby favourite – named 'Coldrenick' – but, so it was said, gave up the turf in disgust when the horse was 'nobbled' the night before the race. A photo of the billiard room shows the walls covered with pictures of his horses. He was a keen hunter with the Dartmoor Fox Hounds and took over the hounds on the death of his friend John Bulteel in 1843. For the next thirty years he ran the hunt at his own expense, housing the hounds at Woodlands, Ivybridge and only retiring through old age, when he was living in Bedford Street, Plymouth.

So, with no wife and no children, and living most of his time away, why did he decide to do away with much of the old house and embark on an ambitious new project? The

Billiard Room complete with pictures of horses

150

north wing of the house was to be replaced, and the west wing demolished entirely, opening up the original courtyard.

An intriguing account of the house, built around 1865, is given in *The Architect* magazine of 11th February, 1871.

Unfortunately the writer does not given any indication where he got his information from – a temporary substitute for a mansion of more durable character? No reference to such a project has come to light, and nowhere is there any indication of the cost of this innovative new building except to say it 'was remarkably inexpensive.' By now the old house was over a hundred years old, and was out of fashion. With a succession of childless and absent owners, it is likely that little had been spent on it by way of maintenance – and if *The Architect* is to be believed, was poorly built in the first place. Was a grand new mansion really being considered?

The Jago family

Although Charles did not marry, his sister, Anne, did. Her husband was her cousin, Edward Jago, son of Captain Stephens' sister, Lucretia who married the Revd. John Jago, vicar of Milton Abbott. Anne and Edward had a prolific family – the eldest son John was born in 1826 followed by two more sons and a daughter in as many years, a daughter and another son – six children in ten years. When Anne died in 1868 (aged 71) she was buried in Menheniot church, and it may be that the new house was home to this numerous family. It may even have been John Jago who was instrumental in the demolition of parts of the old Coldrenick and the erection of the then fashionable new dwelling. It is sad that in all its long history, unless the Jagos lived there, no owner was brought up there, and until the present, no family made it their main home.

ILLUSTRATIONS.

COLDRENNICK, CORNWALL.

THE building which we illustrate to-day is a recent work of framed timber construction, erected as a temporary substitute for a mansion of a more durable character.

The remains of a late fifteenth-century house, with a small internal courtyard, enclosed by an arcade, carried on rough granite columns, existed at Coldrennick (near Menheniot, in Cornwall, on the edge of Dartmoor), amidst a large mass of eighteenth-century work, piled up on the ancient walls, without reference to their power of endurance, and so as to transform the original building into one of those very square-set and ugly edifices of that period. Long rows of square-headed windows, with heavy sash frames (some of them blank), tall parapets, with panels of balustrading in wood, vases at the angles, and such like, were the characteristics of this building. Almost the only parts which showed any original taste were the rain-water heads of lead, elaborate productions wrought into such forms as the plumber was able to compass, and bearing the date of their formation.

Better work was to be found in the interior, consisting chiefly of fine oak panelling, with well-worked pilasters, architraves, friezes, and cornices of the Corinthian order.

The want of constructive skill, however, caused such threatening appearances that it was found necessary to take down one part after another till, at last, what now remains is but a fourth or less of the original structure.

The new building is constructed chiefly of old ship timbers, once forming part of Her Majesty's Navy. The walls are bricknogged between the framing, and covered on the exterior with plaster, while on the interior they are lined with boarding and finished with the old panelling, adapted to its new position as far as it could be. A fine old staircase of oak is refixed.

The building, though of considerable size, as will be seen by the Plan, and connected with the remains of the old house, was remarkably inexpensive. But it had also this special advantage—that it required but little time to prepare it for habitation, the walls being ready for finishing as soon as completed. They are also remarkably warm in winter and cool in summer, and prove more effective against driving rains than ordinary 3-feet stone walls, which have frequently to be slated externally to make them watertight when in exposed situations. The works were carried out by Mr. Trevena, of Plymouth, very satisfactorily, under the direct superintendence of the architect, Mr. C. F. Hayward, of Montague Street, Russell Square.

NORTH EAST VIEW.

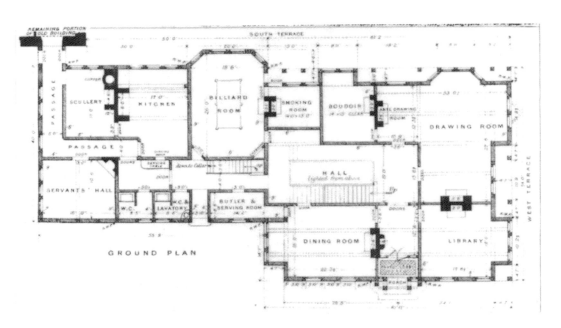

'Old Coldrenick' dining room

'New Coldrenick' dining room

'New Coldrenick' drawing room

'New Coldrenick' hall

Around the middle of the century, Charles Trelawny turned his attention to the grounds and began transforming them into what was to become a famous and noted garden and parkland. In this he was helped by his gardener, William Nanscawen, who was living at Little Coldrenick in 1861. The conifer collection was extensive , including many rarities and was recorded in the Horticultural Directory from 1907 – 1908, and was worthy of inclusion in *The Gardener* in 1876. William Nanscawen was still there in 1901 when he was photographed outside the walled garden. He would, no doubt, have been annoyed by the actions of the new owner, Major General Jago Trelawny, who threw away all the labels with the name, date of planting and country of origin, that had been provided for every tree and shrub.

A handsome granite cross in Menheniot churchyard records the death of Charles Trelawny in August 1883, and of several of the Jagos. The eldest, John, served in the army, retiring as Major General. The census of 1891 lists as living at Coldrenick John, (64) his sister Jane(63), brother Edward (62) a retired solicitor, Charles (61) a naval officer, Lucretia (58) and Robert (54) an army officer. There were also a butler, valet, groom, bootboy, lady's maid, nurse, cook, housemaid and two kitchen maids – which would indicate that the family lived in some style. A gardener and gamekeeper were at Little Coldrenick and a coachman and groom at Higher Coldrenick.

Only one of the Jago children married — poor Anne, their mother, must have despaired. But the youngest, Ellen, escaped, marrying the Revd. Francis Rooke, canon of Salisbury cathedral and rector of Rampisham in Dorset. She produced a large family

Lucretia Jago

of five sons and five daughters, (to add to the nine children by the rector's first wife). It is their descendants who still live at Coldrenick.

Lucretia, to whom the property had been left for her lifetime, lived on until 1914. Apparently she didn't think much of the Frederick Rookes, who were not frequent visitors, and she left most of the furniture and what money she could to Anne Ainslie, Frank's eldest sister.

A second inventory dated March, 1937, following the death of Frank Rooke Trelawny, describes the dilapidated state of the house. Written in pencil, on small, loose sheets of paper, it is a sad little document, recording the decay of Coldrenick. Headed 'Mansion House', it records that the old portion is of stone and slates, and the addition is half timbered with brick and stone noggins; lath and plaster internally; slate roof. 'Latter portion needs much expenditure on windows and woodwork, sawdust between walls and boarded rooms.'

Beginning with the Open Portico on the Ground Floor, the rooms are then listed; Outer Lobby, Hall, Staircase, Panelled Library, Drawing room (formerly two rooms) communicating with Small Room, Billiard room with overhead lights, Green room, panelled dining room. Then came the Domestic Offices beginning with the Butler's Pantry, back stairs, stone steps to cellar, side entrance, WC for principal rooms, WC for staff, old bells, the kitchen had an Aga stove and the scullery a small range. The staff sitting room had a wood floor, then came a large lobby, and the servants' hall – not used. The back staircase, presumably in the old part of the house, was formerly a main staircase with a fire hydrant in the lobby. The former dining room was a lumber room, and the old conservatory was not used. A store room had been the kitchen and there was a boot hall and box room; stoke hole with White Rose boiler for central heating and baths. The old servants' staircase was only used to access the clock tower. It all sounds very dispiriting.

Upstairs was a 'good landing with roof lights' and fewer bedrooms listed than would be expected; two bedrooms with dressing rooms, bathroom, a bedroom with dressing room and steps down to bathroom, a passage with hydrant, two bedrooms and housemaids' cupboard. There were four staff bedrooms and a WC and bathroom, plus a schoolroom. In the attic were four bedrooms, and a room with a clock – the clock tower?

Outside was the usual long list associated with a house of this size – apple chamber, coke, petrol and oil – garage for two, pump house with a well under, piggery, old brewhouse, leanto lobby with staircase to sitting rooms – not used, poultry house, woodhouse, carpenters shop – all of stone and slate, granary on posts of wood and slate – not used; old barn, roof derelict, not used. The water came from its own reservoir, and there was electric lighting.

The total acreage was recorded as 587.833 acres.

Francis Edward Rooke (1863–1937), eldest surviving son of Ellen Jago, married Gertrude Fellowes and their only son, Henry, was killed at the Somme two weeks before his 21st birthday and just before the Armistice. The tenants had commissioned a portrait of him in uniform as a gift – instead it served as a memorial. Another memorial to him is in the church – his face looks down from the stained glass window as the

Coldrenick in decay

head of St. George. His sister Marjory married Robin Sneyd (d 1950), a tea planter in Kenya. Gertie lived on until 1953. She moved to Liskeard the year after Frank's death. She had come from a wealthy family, and Frank struggled to maintain the standards she expected. He sold off many of the Menheniot farms and most of the lands in Devon and Cornwall that had provided the profitable mining returns. The trustees tried to let Coldrenick -but the war years had taken their toll, and the estate was not an attractive proposition, so Gertie moved back. During the war years, much of the house was shut up with Gertie struggling to cope in just two or three rooms.

Marjory and Robin never lived at Coldrenick and their two sons Henry (b 1918) and Richard were born on the family plantations. When the family returned in 1932, living at Coldrenick was not an option, so Robin set up a tea merchant's business in Somerset. When Gertie finally died in 1953, moving into a crumbling mausoleum of a house was not an attractive proposition to Henry and his wife, Jean, who were living in London. The house was shut up and left to crumble. On his retirement, Henry decided to convert the stable block into a home, across the way from the decaying house. And then, in 1966 they made the decision to demolish it. All that now remains is a portion of the old Coldrenick and part of the loggia that was possibly part of the medieval house – and nothing at all of the 'temporary' new house.

All illustrations are courtesy of Robert Sneyd, MD MA MB BChir, FRCA, SFHEA

Sources

Coldrenick Revisited Alison Newton, Cornwall Gardens Trust, 2007.

Professor J. Robert Sneyd, owner of the current house at Coldrenick, descendant of Charles Trelawny's uncle.

Richard Sneyd.

Cornwall Record Office	SN/35
SN/369/2 – Inventory 1727	SN/36/1
BY 455 – Valuation 1937	SN/37/39/40/41/42/43/44
DS/50	SN/369/2
SN/34/40	SN/396
BY/447/448	1907 map
DS/50	

Thanckes in 1846 from 'Mansions of England', Twycross

Thanckes House, Torpoint

Today, Thanckes Park is run by Torpoint Town Council as a recreational facility, a use which was formalised in 1972. Its neighbours are a housing estate, allotments and an extensive gas storage depot. The park slopes down to the Hamoaze, across which are the naval dockyards and the urban sprawl of Plymouth.

But it was not always so. In the eighteenth century, Torpoint was a maritime village, as was Devonport on the opposite bank. The naval dockyard came into existence in 1691, and although it brought great change to the area, it was tiny in comparison to today's huge complex. His Majesty's Men of War riding at anchor were of timber powered by sail; no bridge crossed the estuary and the only way across was by boat. And in the midst of the park stood Thanckes House, surrounded by ornamental gardens and plantations.

The Thanckes estate had become the property of William Warne around 1690. He had naval connections and so the property was ideally situated when Mr. Warne became the Master of the naval brewery established at Millbrook in 1729. The name came from the family of Tonkes who owned the manor of Pengelly in the fourteenth century. Few records survive from this period, and it is not known whether Pengelly Manor, now buried amidst the gas depot, was the main dwelling, but William Warne built the first house to be known as Thanckes in 1713, which went with his only child, Mary, when she married Captain Thomas Graves, RN, in 1714. She died childless only three years later – and the Thanckes estate remained with the Graves family until 1903.

The Graves are an ancient family, originating in France and coming over with the Conqueror, settling in the north, where they have been traced to parts of Derbyshire and south Yorkshire. The family seat of Mickleton Manor in. Gloucestershire, purchased by Richard Graves in 1656, was still lived in by the Graves family until recently.

Col. William Graves, as a commander in the Parliamentary army, was sent to Ireland in 1649, and was granted land there. He returned to England, but left two of his sons, Henry and James, behind. James, (1654–1689), married Marie Herdman, daughter and co-heir of Sir John Herdman of Stannington in the West Riding, and their youngest child was Thomas Graves, (b 1680) who married Mary Warne. The navy benefited greatly from the Graves – Thomas, one son of his brother Samuel, and four of his grandsons all became Admirals and it was estimated that at one time there were ten serving Graves.

The family were newcomers to Cornwall, with no relatives or connections. It was Thomas Graves, the elder, pursuing his naval career, who found his way to Plymouth and put down roots with his marriage. Despite the elevation of his son to the peerage, the family do not seem to have mixed with the gentry – there were no brides from the old-established families and succeeding generations seem to have spent much of their time elsewhere.

> *A most pleasant residence at the side of the Hamoaze though the trees surrounding it tend to throw an air of gloom over it, so contrary to the busy scenes with which it is surrounded. The grass slopes away from the house which was charmingly laid out. There is a promenade along the southern side of the hill which leads through a wicker gate to a quarry which is overgrown with luxurious vines, the tendrils of which entwine with the overhanging trees. The leafage which surrounds this spot was pleasantly intermixed with that of the vines, suspending in Autumn its clusters of fruit has an indescribable effect.*
>
> *The grounds slope down to the water's edge and are laid out with great taste and the gardens are particularly fine. At the northern side is a plantation of Norway firs and through it is a delightful walk of upwards of a mile in length from which the harbour and adjoining scenery have a most pleasing effect.*

This is an early description of the house, quoted by Twycross who states it was erected in 1713; there is no mention of an earlier property on the site. Twycross goes on to say that 'there had been many important additions since. The salon and ante room are very splendid apartments, and in them and other principal rooms are several good pictures, including large marine paintings and pictures of naval engagements in which many of this noble family conducted themselves with such distinguished bravery.'

Thomas Graves continued his naval career, becoming a Rear Admiral. His second wife was Elizabeth Budgell, who he married in 1723; she was just 20 and he was 43. Their eldest son, William decided upon law as his career and became a Master in Chancery, and it was their second son, another Thomas, (b. 1725) whose distinguished naval career brought him a peerage and a pension of one thousand pounds per annum. The Rear Admiral died in 1755.

From 1761–64 Thomas Graves (the son) had been Commodore Governor of Newfoundland with the duty of convoying the seasonal fishing fleet from England, and in 1762 he retook St. John's, Newfoundland from the French. It was a period of great naval activity and as a Rear Admiral he saw action against the French in the American Wars of Independence in 1781, but was unsuccessful, ultimately leading to Lord Cornwallis' surrender at Yorktown. Later under his command his fleet was caught in a violent storm off Newfoundland in which two captured French ships and two English ships sank with considerable loss of life. Then followed a spell at home, as Commander in Chief of Plymouth, until the outbreak of war with the French when, as an Admiral of the Blue, now aged almost 70, he took part in the famous victory under Howe in 1794, in which he was severely wounded. As a reward for his service, he became Lord Graves of Gravesend in the Irish peerage.

His bride in 1771, when he was 46, was Elizabeth Peere Williams, of Cadhay in Devon, of which she was the heiress. The year before he married her, a document was drawn up making provision for Sarah Davey with whom 'he had cohabited for many years' and their three surviving children. She was awarded an annuity of £40 per annum on their agreement to separate. It was something of a family trait for his father, in his will, had left provision for one Jane Hervey of Antony and their three children, David, George and Mary Graves.

Lord Graves died in 1802, so he did not have long to enjoy his retirement and pension, and he cannot have spent much time at Thanckes.

Detail from Thomas Smart's map of 1765   (BL K Top 11.78.2)

The original house seems to have undergone considerable changes. The earliest known house, depicted on Thomas Smart's map dated 1765, shows an irregular outline facing the Hamoaze with an almost separate block to the south, a somewhat rambling house with several projecting wings. In front are formal gardens with two avenues of trees leading towards Torpoint with plantations to the north; some kind of causeway is shown crossing the basin. By 1784, Gardner's map shows the house as more of a solid block with a regular front and a projecting bay. The formal gardens to the front have disappeared and a new walled garden is shown to the north west of the house. A belt of trees line the water's edge. The causeway is not shown on the 1784 map, but reappears on the 1859 Ordnance Survey map. Perhaps it was a temporary brushwood affair. The quarry appears in 1784, by which time many of the trees have gone.

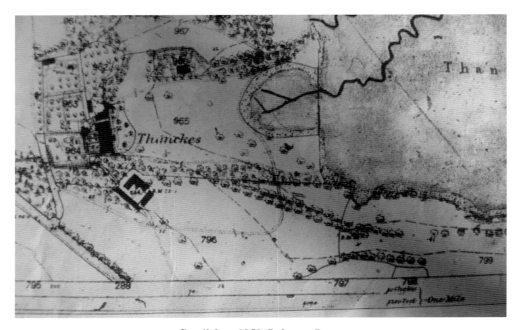

Detail from 1859 Ordnance Survey

The illustration in Gilbert's *History of Cornwall*, of 1820, shows a neat symmetrical front of four bays each side of a central projection with a pediment. An oil painting in the possession of the family shows no pediment, and a range to the north hidden by trees. An unfinished, undated sketch shows an asymmetrical front with a small projection, and a doorway to the right, more clearly shown in the illustration in Twycross, which includes a double flight of steps to the central bay, and a rusticated basement level. Trees obscure the northern end of the building. All these show the east-facing garden front of Thanckes, a long, simple facade, unbroken by any ornamentation – simple windows, simple roof, nothing grand, no pediment or balustrading or terraces. No drawings of the other elevations have come to light, one of which would have been the entrance front. There are no records of building work, but one possibility is that a new front was built to the older house, presenting the regular appearance common to all the drawings.

Featured on all the maps is Gravesend, a house situated on the promontory to the

162

Thanckes in 1820   (C.S. Gilbert, *Survey of Cornwall* 1820)

Unfinished sketch by W.Dawson   (CRO)

163

east of Thanckes. In 1722 Thomas Graves sold the site to Admiral Harrison who built Gravesend House. Lord Thomas North (2nd Baron) bought back the property as a dower house for his mother, and until its sale in 1903,the family would seem to have preferred it to Thanckes.

Thomas North Graves was born in 1775, when his father was 50. He broke with family tradition and instead of the navy, he entered politics, becoming the conservative MP for Okehampton, 1812–18, Windsor 1819-20 and Milborne Port, 1820–27. He had been educated at Eton and Oxford, and the Inner Temple. In 1803 he married Lady Mary Paget, daughter of the Earl of Uxbridge, and between 1804 and 1826 the couple had three sons and six daughters. Milborne Port was a Paget constituency, held by her brother, later the 1st Marquess of Anglesey, and it may have been the influence of her family that secured the 2nd baron his court appointments; in 1813 he was appointed Lord of the Bedchamber to George IV and became Comptroller of the household of the Duke of Sussex. In 1827, Lord Graves semi-retired from public duty by becoming a Commissioner of Revenue and Excise. But such a distinguished career was to end in tragedy. On 7th February, 1830, Lord Graves shot himself at his lodgings in Hanover Street. For some time he and his wife had been living apart – she was established in a grace-and-favour apartment at Hampton Court, the mistress of the Duke of Cumberland, and that evening Lord Graves had been due to have a meeting with the Marquess of Anglesey, his wife's brother, to discuss the situation.

In December, 1829, Lord Graves wrote a Will in which he wrote:

> *all my personal estate to my only son Thomas William Graves … reflecting with every confidence that he will act with every kindness to his Mother and Brothers and Sisters … and I do hereby give devise and commit the care guardianship or tuition and education of such of my children as shall at the time of my death be under the age of twenty one years unto my said son Thomas William Graves and to my good friend the Rt. Hon. Sir Edward Paget who I trust will cooperate with my said son for the welfare and interest of all my children …*

Two months later he was dead. Thomas William, aged 26, became the 3rd Baron Graves, who, far from attending to the welfare of his siblings, 'proved the will in the month of November last having departed this Kingdom and being now resident out of the jurisdiction of His Majesty's Court of Law and Equity', and administration was granted on behalf of Sparks Bank in Exeter, being creditors of the deceased. In other words, young Thomas had done a runner. Apparently he returned to France, where the previous year he had married a French widow. She died in 1833 and he almost immediately remarried, remaining in France until 1847 when the couple returned to Gravesend, which his father had bought back, and where their younger son, Clarence, was born that year. Tragedy struck again when their eldest son, another Thomas, died in a boating accident on 24th August, 1849.

The family seemed to have little love for Thanckes itself. Census returns for 1841 show the house was let to Sir George Lisle, his family and nine servants. In 1844 it was advertised to let:

Beautiful marine seat on the banks of the Tamar; To be LET for a term with immediate possession, the spacious MANSION HOUSE called Thanckes formerly the residence of Admiral Lord Graves and lately the Lady Graves deceased; consisting of entrance hall, dining room, break-fast parlour and lobby, best bedroom and dressing room, on the ground floor, drawing room and dressing room adjoining; 5 bedrooms and 2 dressing rooms; and housekeeper's room, on the first floor, study and bedroom adjoining; and 6 servant's rooms on the upper storey; servants hall, kitchen, laundry, larder, pantry, dairy, scullery, 2 cellars etc. under the ground floor; coach houses, extensive stables and other outhouses: 2 excellent walled gardens stocked with the choicest fruit trees, in the highest order; a greenhouse filled with the finest lemon and orange trees; also about 30 acres or less quantity of rich pasture land (including the lawn) adjoining the house. Thanckes is universally admitted to be one of the most beautiful seats in the west of England; nothing can exceed the views from the house and grounds, in richness and variety. The lawn extends in declivity to the harbour of the Hamoaze, in which are floating a considerable portion of the British navy, many of the largest class men-of-war are seen, and are objects of peculiar beauty from the house. The town of Devonport (so celebrated for the abundance of all kinds of fish, meat, etc. and for its cheapness) is within a mile, and Plymouth about 2 miles distant, and the mail coach passes within 50 yards of the house twice daily.

The third baron died in 1870 and it was that year that saw land he owned in Antony parish and Devon 'sold by the Trustees'.

And now the history of Thanckes entered its last, somewhat bizarre, phase. His father had been a military man, but Clarence, the heir joined the navy and served as a lieutenant for just two years. He was 23 when his father died in 1870, the same year he married Katherine Murdoch, daughter of Sir Thomas Murdoch, KCMG. Whether it was her influence, or some desire for a more up-to-date house, despite the family's financial problems, Clarence decided to rebuild Thanckes. Alfred Norman, a leading Plymouth architect, drew up the plans, and work commenced in 1871 with Lady Graves laying the foundation stone. It was to be in the Tudor gothic style, and having laid the stone, the company, according to a newspaper report, then proceeded to the old house to witness the demolition of the 35 foot high chimney wall.

The new Thanckes was built on a higher site and faced towards Torpoint and the sea, rather than the Hamoaze. It was substantial, with a castellated tower – and it would appear that Lord Graves could not afford it. As early as 1876, the property was advertised to let;

To be let by the year or for a short term of years, this fine Mansion in complete repair having been beautifully furnished throughout only three years ago, contains dining room, 23ft by 22ft, drawing room, 35ft by 27ft, morning room, conservatory, entrance-hall, large inner hall and corridor, billiard room (with table by Thurston), gun room, study, 18 bedrooms and dressing rooms (including 3 men-servants rooms) dairy and large offices, together with stabling for 4 horses, large coach house, cow houses. etc. The house is lighted throughout with gas and is supplied to the top with hot and cold water and the drainage is perfect.

165

The new Thanckes – the old house was at the bottom level   (Torpoint Archive)

Sale particulars
(Torpoint Archive)

Whitsand Bay Hotel – Thankes in its new position

The gardens and pleasure grounds, vineries and greenhouse are all described – a desirable modern mansion yet one which the Graves seemed unwilling, or unable to live in. Bankruptcy hearings were posted in the London Gazette in August and September, 1876, and the family must have decided to live economically elsewhere as they are not listed at either Thanckes or Gravesend in the 1881 census. Their grand new mansion ended up as a college for boys destined for Sandhurst or Woolwich. They had departed by the turn of the century and only a gardener is listed in the 1901 census.

Then in 1903 came the final blow – the estate was to be auctioned by Order of the High Court of Justice, in an action Graves v Heneage. Lot 1 was the house and grounds, Gravesend House and grounds and eleven acres of land 'ripe for immediate development'. Lot 2 was three houses in Torpoint. If not sold, then Thanckes, Gravesend and the land would be split into three lots.

The house as it existed then is described in the sale catalogue. The conservatory with span roof was 31ft by 14ft 6in, there was a suite of noble reception rooms with marble mantle pieces and enriched ceilings – morning room, library, drawing room, dining room; billiard room with smoking room and lavatory. The 'domestic arrangements' included a wine cellar with iron doors, large coal cellar. The staircase had a magnificent stained glass window and there were five principal bedrooms, two dressing room and a bathroom, with five servant's bedrooms; separate stabling. Gravesend, on a smaller scale, had a drawing room, dining room and breakfast room, five bedrooms and dressing room and three servant's bedrooms and stabling for four horses.

But although Thanckes no longer exists on the banks of the Tamar, it underwent a metamorphosis. The estate had been bought by Sir Reginald Carew Pole of Antony, who sold the house to a consortium. They proceeded to demolish it brick by numbered brick, and reassemble it a few miles away at Whitsand, where it still stands as Whitsand Bay Hotel. The only difference was the repositioning of the tower, and the English Heritage Listing (Grade 2) states that 'this is an unusually complete interior for a house of this date, with fine period detail. The principal rooms are panelled, and over the Jacobean-style staircase presides the 12 light fine stained glass window showing galleons in full sail.'

Clarence, 4th Lord Graves, died a year after the sale, aged just 57, and was buried in Co. Cork. His widow moved to Marlow in Buckinghamshire where she died in 1926, and was buried, at her request, with him. The title went to a nephew and eventually to Tasmania to a descendant of a brother of the 5th Baron. There is no heir.

Thanckes Park is very pleasant – a grassy valley sloping to the water with remnants of the avenues and walks laid out by the Graves; the site of the first house now occupied by tennis courts and that of the second by a bowling green. One of the walled gardens survives – but nowhere is there any mention of the Graves family.

Sources

Torpoint Archive
Dictionary of National Biography
Thankes, Torpoint, Conservation Assessment 2012, Cynthia Gaskell Brown

Cornwall Record Office   BRA 833/4/5/6
EN/2476/1   CF/2/610/618/620/641

Saunders Hill from the grounds of Prideaux Place
(C S Gilbert, *History of Cornwall* 1820)

Saunders Hill, Padstow

'The town of Padstow, consisting of schist and slate ... is now flourishing as a mercantile town, chiefly through the influence of Thomas Rawlings, esq. His newly erected house, substantial in its materials, and compact in its construction, seems to promise durability to the town it adorns.'

History of Cornwall, Richard Polwhele 1803

Described as an 'elegant modern structure with two superior fronts formed of Portland stone and the remainder of slate', Saunders Hill was built by Thomas Rawlings, a merchant of the town in 1803. He chose a prominent position overlooking the town and harbour for his new house.

Contemporary prints show a neat house, with an Ionic portico opening to a vestibule, tall rather than large, as if his intention was to demonstrate his wealth. Mr. Rawlings was not short of land for the same description by Gilbert in 1820, extols the 'plantations and walks which are raised over the adjoining eminences' which were laid out with 'considerable taste', as were the gardens and shrubberies. Gilbert comments that despite its 'infant state' the whole is 'a striking point to the town and its environs.' If he had been writing a few months later he could have described its sad demise, for the property was never to fulfil this role; it was extremely short lived. Rawlings died on 31st July, 1820, leaving his property to his children, but such were his debts that almost everything had to be sold, including Saunders Hill and its contents, which included a library and mineral collection. And here is a twist; the purchasers were the Prideaux family, lords of the manor and owners of Prideaux Place which had long been the premier property of the town. They lost no time in knocking down Mr Rawlings' attempt to upstage them, and sold off the materials at auction. The site is now the recreation ground and car park in the centre of Padstow.

The story of Saunders Hill takes some unravelling. It would seem that there was rivalry between Thomas Rawlings and the Revd. Charles Prideaux, owner of Prideaux Place and much of Padstow. Thomas Rawlings is described as a merchant, and from the inventory taken after his death, he was also a considerable property owner in the town and surrounding area. But it seems doubtful that the two men were on good terms; was Thomas Rawlings being deliberately provocative when he chose to build his new home directly in front of the Prideaux' ancestral home – and to ensure the height was sufficient to be clearly visible to them, and the rest of the town?

On 4th August, 1820, the *West Briton* carried a notice inserted by Messrs. Rashliegh Coode & Sons, solicitors of St. Austell;

> The Creditors of Thos. Rawlings, late of Padstow, and also of the firm of Thos. Rawlings & Son, are desired to send accounts of their respective demands, calculated interest up to the 29th September next to Messrs Rashleigh Coode & Sons …
>
> And all persons indebted at the time of his death (particularly for arrears of rent) are requested to pay amounts of their respective debts immediately.

This was followed by a Notice of Sale to be held on 19th August at the Red Lion, St. Columb Major, of 'freehold and leasehold land scattered over several parishes, and Clawton and Pyworthy in Devon, and including the Manor of St. Columb Major.' These were to be sold in separate lots, unless disposed of by private treaty. There was no mention of Saunders Hill.

Thomas Rawlings married Margery Price of St. Wenn in 1783, and the marriage settlement dated 29th May awarded her the sum of £30 per annum if he should die before her. They were married at Padstow, and she was said to be an heiress. Very little is known of him – except that he was a merchant and was of sufficient standing to serve as High Sheriff in 1803. The parish church contains several substantial monuments to the family, so it would seem that, for a brief period at any rate, he was a person of some worth. His brother was the Rector for nearly 50 years, until his death in 1836, aged 76, and there are memorials to three Revd. Rawlings – James, Charles and William, of local parishes, who died in 1870 and 1871. His will was lengthy, and was not made until lst July, 1820, barely a month before his death. His address was given as Saunders Hill, and various manors in the parish of Padstow were listed. The will leaves one fifth part of the estate –once sold – to his son William and his daughter Ann

Saunders Hill showing the church and Prideaux Placce

Paynter, and the rest to be divided equally between his remaining children – who are not named.

The Will was proved at Canterbury at under £45,000. The *'Particulars of the Estate of the late Thomas Rawlings'* runs to 20 pages. The members of the Rawlings family are listed, but it is not certain if all 12 of them were Thomas Rawlings' children. William heads the list, then aged 31, his sister Anne Paynter, aged 30, the Revd. Wm. Rawlings, (brother), Padgey, Kitty, Edward, George, Emma, Jane, Price, Fanny and Harriet .

This list of properties is long and diverse – the Ship Inn and the Kings Arms, the Methodist Chapel, a large number of houses, and several manors; tin stream works at Goss Moor, sail lofts, gardens, orchards, malt houses and lime kilns – Thomas Rawlings had a finger in many pies. He also owned the entirety of Ninnis Park and part of Saundry's Close – which was let to Mrs Peggy Hoblyn for 14 years, along with several other properties let to her for life.

The rents vary from 1d to £60 per annum, and brought in an annual income of £3,485.

The involvement between the Prideaux family and the Rawlings went back at least to 1785. In July of that year, Humphrey Prideaux leased to William Rawlings and his son, Thomas, the North and South Quays at Padstow for a term of 21 years with all the tolls, duties on all goods that may be landed, except salt. The rent was £30 per annum. This was later the subject of a dispute when Charles Prideaux Brune declared it to be void following Humphrey's death.

Then in 1807 the 'Padstow Settlement' was drawn up between the Revd. Charles Prideaux Brune, and Thos. Rawlings in which they agreed

To purchase the Estates of the late Hooper Martyn, to the children of Martha Parnell and Richard Elliott on the best terms in their power on their joint account and not to oppose each other in said purchase either at this time or hereafter.

The document ends with an agreement to go to arbitration if they could not agree on the said value of their respective holdings. The Revd. acquired part of Saundry's Close and field, about 5 acres, and various other estates and holdings. Thomas Rawlings gained 3 acres of Saundry's Close, and other holdings.

Among the long list of documents in the Record Office is an Indenture dated 1804 for an apprentice mariner – his father had been a mariner at Looe – and in 1792 his name appears amongst a long list of 'Adventurers' concerned in Hornblower's Engines at Wheal Pool. There are numerous deeds relating to mortgages, leases etc. and all are part of the Prideaux Brune archive. But there appears to be no record of the house and its fate amongst their papers. Saunders Hill just disappeared as if it had never been.

Sources

Prideaux Brune Family
Cornwall Record Office
CF/1/2696
   /4262
PB 1/510
  5/151

AD 134/24/3
   /7/4
CF 3428/1 – particulars of the estate of
Thomas Rawlings

The south front of Trehane; the portico survives

Trehane, Probus

Trehane is that rare thing in Cornwall – a romantic ruin. After the disastrous fire of 1946, the house was left to gently decay. Rebuilding would have been out of the question; the Second World War was just ending and building materials were rationed and in very short supply. The severity of the fire had left little except the walls and charred timbers. The owners abandoned the shell, and converted the coach house.

And what had been one of Cornwall's foremost gardens, the result of two centuries of careful cultivation, continued to decline until the whole thing resembled a Sleeping Beauty stage set.

Rescue came in 1962 when David Trehane and his wife heard it was up for sale and went to view. He describes what he found:

> By 1945 longevity and the wars had destroyed the garden and in a few short hours of September 26th 1946 a neglected blowlamp started the fire which left the house a burnt-out shell at the centre of what was to become a wilderness of woodrushes, sycamores, giant polygonums, brambles, bamboos and laurel. Two great chimneys were blown up to provide bricks to heighten the walls of the coach house which became the dwelling of the new owner.

173

The Trehanes bought the property, with which his family had never had any connection, and set about rescuing the garden. It must have been a monumental task, which he recorded in an article in the *Journal of the Cornwall Garden Society* of 1986. He was obviously a knowledgeable and dedicated horticulturist and the garden was gradually brought back to life

The history of Trehane stretches back to the thirteenth century and trickled down through the days of Elizabeth I when Sir John Trehane appears on the muster roll for the militia in the event of the Armada landing. He lived until 1640, leaving four daughters, the eldest of whom married John Scawn of Molenick, St. Germans and Trehane passed down through Trehane Scawn, his son Richard, to his daughter, Honor. She married William Courtenay of Trehane Vean, a neighbouring farm, but in 1696 the estate was sold. According to David Trehane, it would appear that there was insufficient money to pay the jointures of Honor and her mother, and the family became indebted to John Williams of Carvean, to whom the estate was sold.

But all was not lost for in that year John Williams married Catherine Courtenay, Honor's daughter, so it may be that he 'acquired' the property on his marriage. Theirs, it would appear, was a love match and in 1700 John set about building a new house for his wife and family. Two children were born and all seemed set for a long and prosperous interlude, but it was not to be. In 1703, just as the house was completed, Catherine died in childbirth. Her husband, broken-hearted, followed about a year later leaving a beautiful house as their memorial.

What happened to the original house is not known, but the new Trehane was unusual in Cornwall, the county of plain granite facades. It was built of brick and it is possible that these were made at Trewithen, also owned by the Williams family at that time. The newly introduced sash windows broke the plain front, three on either side of the entrance and four enormous brick chimney stacks rose from the roof. There was a central courtyard and a 60ft well. David Trehane describes it;

> *The craftsmanship was of the best – bricklaying (look at the main garden wall), panelling, a fine oak Adam staircase with plastered ceilings above, ornamented by an Italian who died before the completion of the house leaving as his memorial the signs of the Zodiac beautifully moulded on ceiling plaster for the first time in England. The house had its private road of 1½ miles through the woods and pastures of Trehane and the Tregeagles, with their fishpond and decoy pond, to Tresillian.*

The three daughters of Catherine and John, orphaned at so young an age, were brought up by their grandfather, John Courtenay, a widower, who moved into Trehane.

In 1738, Catherine, the eldest, married the Revd. William Stackhouse, of St. Erme. He was 56 and she must have been over thirty. For an heiress of a considerable property this was unusually old. They had four children, the eldest of whom, another William, inherited Trehane on his father's death aged 89. The second son, John Stackhouse, inherited the Pendarves estate in 1764 and later married Susanna Acton, of Acton Scott in Shropshre, a considerable heiress.

Trehane passed quietly down through William to his son and grandson, both

William, and also long lived dying at 90 and 88 respectively. The last William had five daughters, the eldest of whom married Revd. James Pinwill of Oxfordshire. However, on his father-in-law's death he declined to move to Cornwall and passed Trehane over to his son, Captain William Stackhouse Church Pinwill, in 1861.

There are no surviving records of the family through those years – whether any alterations were made, whether they began developing the garden, planting trees etc. Gilbert dismissively described the house as 'a hundred years out of date,' so perhaps it survived unaltered.

For the first time since the death of John Williams, Trehane had a young man at the helm. But Captain Pinwill was a serving officer in the Indian Army and did not return home until 1868. As a young man, he was keenly interested in natural history and spent much of his time in India collecting birds and butterflies, which were sent home to the British Museum. And once he had returned to Cornwall, his brother-in-law, who was Archdeacon of Bombay, sent a steady stream of plants which found a home in Trehane's garden. Captain Pinwill married Anne Snell in 1872, and they had four daughters.

The name of William Pinwill has been largely forgotten, but in his day he was considered one of the county's foremost gardeners. He was influenced by John Boscawen, responsible for much of the planting at Tregothnan, and year by year the glories of Trehane expanded. The index that he compiled listed 4,500 plants, and in 1914, he was awarded the Victoria Medal of Honour by the Royal Horticultural Society. Trehane was famed for its rarities, many sent from abroad and many grown for the first time in this country - for its great trees, its peaches trained against the brick walls, for sheets of spring bulbs - and for its hard-working owner who was usually up and about before six in the morning.

Capt. William Pinwill with his grand daughter c. 1911

The *Gardeners' Chronicle* of 1926 carried an obituary in which the garden is described for its

> *unequalled cultivation of rare hardy plants and fruits. His observation, judgement and wisdom enabled him to form a collection of plants that was unique not only for the good forms of ordinary plants and the host of rarities but especially for their quite amazing cultivation. Those of us who were fortunate enough to visit Trehane between 1880 and the war were indeed favoured. We can certainly never see the like again.*

The obituary mentions his generosity and that 'no plant was too rare or too small to be shared with a fellow gardener.'

The Captain was succeeded by his son, William Richard, b 1873, of whom little is known. At some stage he sold Trehane and moved to Surrey where he died in 1963, aged 90.

When David Trehane bought the property, though there was nothing he could do with the ruin, he set about rescuing what he could in the garden. A surprising number of trees survived, including the *Davidia* which had flowered for the first time just days before the Captain died, pines and magnolias - and many of the spring bulbs.

When the Trehanes left, once again the gardens began a slow decline. In Cornwall's mild, moist climate it doesn't take long for the native plants to take over and the whole to become overrun with brambles and nettles.

But in recent years new owners have begun, once again, the formidable task of reclamation, and even of stabilising the ruin.

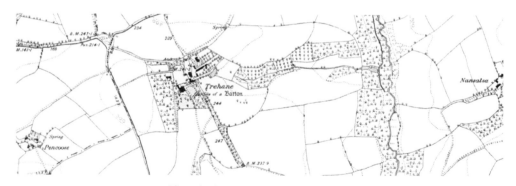

The ruin from the 1998 sales particulars

There is no public access to either Trehane or the gardens; the ruins are unstable and highly dangerous.

Sources

The Journal of the Cornwall Garden Society, 1986

Undated painting of Stowe   (Courtesy of Peter Prideaux Brune)

Stowe, Kilkhampton

Stowe House, which had been the residence of the Grenvilles for at least 600 years, was taken down soon after the Restoration by order of John, Earl of Bath, and a most magnificent edifice erected on the site, which after having flourished in unusual splendour for more than half a century, was demolished and has not since been rebuilt.

(*Survey of the County of Cornwall* – C S Gilbert 1820)

Few houses were as short-lived as Stowe. Built in the 1670's as a very visible sign of the success and newfound status of its owner, with his death some thirty years later, it was all over. The house lingered, unwanted and rarely visited, until one of the earliest recorded demolition sales of a large house occurred in 1739. The builder was John Grenville, head of the famous west country family. He was created Earl of Bath in 1661 by a grateful Charles II in recognition of the prominent part played by Grenville in his Restoration, and of the family's part in the Civil War.

Stowe House was built close to the site of the earlier manor house, on a bleak, exposed plateau high on the cliffs of North Cornwall, facing the rough Atlantic ocean. Most of the neighbouring manor houses were tucked away in the valleys, sheltered from the gales, huddled into ranges of outbuildings. Not so Stowe. Proud and tall, with two floors of fine rooms, a basement and an attic storey, it would have been visible for miles around. Built of brick, instead of the local stone, with plenty of large windows, it must have looked completely out of place. At the time there was no other house like it in Cornwall.

For its origins we have to look away from Cornwall, to the grand houses that were being built at this time by other Royalist supporters, being similarly rewarded. The role model was Clarendon House, in Piccadilly, built by the Earl of Clarendon to designs by Roger Pratt, in 1664. Grenville sought to emulate this, but Clarendon house was a town house, and other such houses sat in gentle parkland. As Daniel Defoe noted in his *Western Tour*, 1742;

> *The situation of this stately Palace renders it a disagreeable habitation for which reason the owners have disposed of the materials and it is now pulling to Pieces.*

The building of such an imposing mansion was the culmination of long years of Grenville dominance. In common with many another illustrious Cornish family, they have died out in name and no longer have any connection with the county of their origin. But they were once the most powerful family in the west country. Today their descendants, through the female line, live on as the Marquis of Bath at Longleat, and the Duke of Sutherland, and there are branches surviving under the name of Granville.

The lineage of the Grenvilles links them to William the Conqueror, and, according to the Revd. Roger Granville of Bideford writing in 1895, the Grenville lands in Devon and Cornwall were bestowed upon Richard de Granville by his cousin William Rufus. This was probably as a reward for military service, and Richard de Granville, like his father, became a crusader and went with a great gathering to the Holy Land:

> *Of all these holy wars none had been announced with greater ostentation; of none had it been more boldly averred that it was of divine inspiration, the work of God; of none had the hopes, the prophecies of success been more confident; none had been conducted with so much preparation and pomp; none had as yet been headed by kings; none ended in such total and deplorable disaster. At least thirty thousand lives were sacrificed, and there was not even the consolation of one glorious deed achieved. Amongst those that perished was Richard de Granville, 1147.*

His eldest son, also Richard, held the manor of Bideford, and lands in Devon and Cornwall. He was knighted by King John in 1204 and styled Lord of Bideford and Kilkhampton.

A very early mention of Stowe comes in the sixteenth century when 'Sir Roger Granville resided chiefly at Stowe, and for his princely liberality was called "the Great Housekeeper." He was at this time High Sheriff of Cornwall.

Richard Grenville succeeded his father, who died at Stowe in 1524. He was MP for Cornwall, High Sheriff of Devon, and later of Cornwall, and was knighted by Henry VIII. His 'martial employments' endeared him to the king, who made him Marshal of Calais.

The family seems to have been involved in what appears to have been a life of piracy sanctioned, or at least not condemned, by the government. Small fleets of some twenty or thirty vessels from the harbours of Devon and Cornwall, patrolled the English Channel, pillaging rich cargo ships from Spain and France; this was in retaliation to similar treatment from France and it would seem that an unofficial state of war existed. Granville quotes from a letter sent by the Lord High Admiral of England in 1548, Lord Seymour, to Sir Richard Grenville, Sir Peter Carew, Sir Thomas Denys, Sir William Godolphin, Sir Hugh Trevanyon and John Grenville giving them authority to commission privateers to take French ships and goods.

Sir Richard died at Stowe in 1550 and is buried in Kilkhampton church. His will lists his manors;

> *His mansion and lands called Buckland, his mansion house in the town of Bideford, and all the residue of his town and borough of Bideford, his mansion place of Stowe, together with all gardens, orchards, and ponds therewith, Stowe Park in Cornwall; his house and borough of Kilkhampton and his mansion of Woodford in the same county, together with all his other lands in Devon and Cornwall.*

Life in those days was a risky thing, and it was not granted to many to die of a peaceful old age. Richard's eldest son, Roger, was among those who drowned when the *Mary Rose* sank off Spithead in 1545. He left behind one son, Richard, forever associated with his ship, the *Revenge*.

The golden age of (official) piracy continued under Queen Elizabeth, and Sir Richard Grenville was one of a number of 'adventurers' who regularly harried the ships of both France and Spain with the blessing of their sovereign. Sir Richard's colourful life is well documented, including attempts at colonization in Ireland, and the new found lands of America. He enriched both himself and his queen by the many prize ships he captured and became one of her must trusted advisors, as one of the nine members of the Council of War called to plan resistance to any possible invasion. To Sir Richard was given the responsibility of the defence of the west, to which end he embarked on a survey of maritime defences and the training of an able-bodied force of men. He took no part in the defeat of the Armada at sea, and one can only imagine the feelings of this hardy, fearless sailor with his many previous encounters with the Spanish confined to shore away from all the action.

How much, or how little, time Sir Richard spent at Stowe is not known. Few letters or manuscripts survive from this period, but there is one letter written by him 'from Stowe in Cornwall' on one of his brief returns from Ireland, where the Queen had sent him in an attempt to colonise the country. But in 1590 she had need once more of his sea-faring skills and recalled him, appointing him Lord High Admiral of England. The Spanish were planning a second Armada, and to equip this, a heavily laden treasure ship was being prepared in the Azores. The English fleet of six men-of-war, including the *Revenge* under the command of Sir Richard Grenville, were surprised by the Spanish fleet sent to protect the treasure ship. Most of the fleet managed to slip away, but not so the *Revenge*. The glorious, if somewhat futile, battle fought by Sir Richard has been told many times, and the inevitable loss of the ship, and of his life, made him a hero of naval battles for all time.

Sir Richard had married Mary St. Leger from Annery, near Bideford and their eldest son, Bernard, inherited his father's estates. He had completed his education at Oxford and appears to have been more interested in his estates than in the sea or affairs of State. He compiled a family pedigree, which included all the armorial bearings, including those of his wife, Elizabeth, heiress of the ancient and wealthy Cornish family of Bevill, whom he married in 1592. It would seem they were content to make their life at Stowe, apart from a spell of service in Ireland, and Sir Bernard took a keen interest in the welfare of his Bideford estates, procuring a new charter in 1610 for the port which enabled it to trade profitably with Newfoundland.

In all the many letters and documents that are quoted in Roger Granville's history, there is little or no mention of Stowe, except as an occasional address. A wildly romantic description of the old house is given by Charles Kingsley in his novel *Westward Ho!* where he describes it as a ruined castle with 'machicolated turrets, loopholes and downward crannies for dropping stones and fire on the besiegers' and that the old Norman keep had been ruined in the Wars of the Roses, 'and been replaced by the rich and stately architecture of the Tudors.' There is no mention of such a building in any of the county histories, and there is no evidence or documentation that such a castle ever existed in this remote spot, or that the Wars of the Roses ever came anywhere near Kilkhampton. Kingsley, it must be remembered, was writing a novel.

It is strange that so little is known of the original Stowe, except that it was granted a licence for a chapel in 1386. Echoes of the houses of the other great Cornish and Devon families have come down to us, mentioned in old deeds and parish records, or in family paintings, but of Stowe there is no trace. One conclusion is that the earlier Grenvilles were too busy at sea, or abroad, and rarely at home, to spend much time or expenditure on a remote Cornish house. They had several other properties, including a manor house at Bideford, and one in Kilkhampton, both more accessible than Stowe, reached down three miles of narrow, muddy lanes, and sat high on its windy, exposed headland. But Bevill, the eldest son of Sir Bernard, appears to have spent his boyhood there, following his father to Oxford, and then on to the fashionable London scene in the early years of the seventeenth century. In 1617 Bevill married Grace Smith, whose half sister had married Sir Thomas Monk of Potheridge, near Torrington. Their second son, George, who was later to play such a prominent part in the Civil War and the Restoration, was brought up with Grace.

From 1621–25, Bevill represented Cornwall in parliament, and some of his letters home to Grace have survived. In one there is a rare mention of Stowe, where he refers to the 'moorstone windows' he has ordered and 'I would have the masons to goe on as fast as they can, about the stable, that if possible the walls may be up and finished against my coming downe.' He continues with instructions about the timber to be used, and to make shift with what he can at home, and some work was to be carried out to the 'Parler – as plain and cheap as possible.' Here, at last, is a little information about the house, and that Bevill and Grace were treating it as their main home. Unfortunately, that is the only mention in a copious correspondence between husband and wife, which largely deals with their health and family.

Bevill and Grace had five sons and three daughters, and they made Stowe a central hub for many of the young men of the county. Correspondence reveals that he was fond of field sports and kept a pack of hounds. By 1638, their eldest son, Richard, had followed the family tradition and gone up to Oxford, and it would appear from letters from his father that his conduct was anything but satisfactory, with continual exhortations to work harder and pursue his studies.

Had it not been for the bitter years of the Civil War, Grace and Bevill would probably have lived out their lives at Stowe, surrounded by numerous children, grandchildren, aunts and cousins. The house they occupied would have been enlarged, and altered to bring it more into fashion with the times, and might even have survived today. The parishes of Morwenstowe and Kilkhampton are dotted with ancient manors and farmhouses of great antiquity, some at least as old as the original Stowe of Bevill's day. But the long interlude of peace that had lasted from the beginning of the Tudor era was over. The country divided between Charles I and the Divine Right of Kings, and the forces of Parliament. It was unthinkable that a Grenville should stay at home and take no part in the fighting. Each generation had faithfully served their monarch, and accordingly, Bevill Grenville stood for the king. He was required to raise a small force by voluntary enlistment; he was also required to pay them, and to do this Sir Bevill mortgaged his estates and sold some of his plate and valuables. He was not alone among the gentry in doing this.

Few major battles have been fought on west country soil. Cornishmen, in particular, tended to regard the rest of England as a foreign country whose affairs were no concern of theirs. Had it not been for the local gentry taking sides, the Civil War might well have passed them by, unscathed. As it was, skirmishes raged up and down the countryside as first one side and then the other gained supremacy. One of the most important battles was fought in 1643 at Stamford Hill, within a few miles of Stowe, and not surprisingly, Sir Bevill was in charge of the Royalist attack on the vastly superior Parliamentary troops. The determination of the Cornish men won the day, routing the Earl of Stamford's troops. The victory was seen as a turning point in the battle for the west, with the Parliamentary troops retreating. Later that year, the Cornish troops formed part of the force that moved upcountry hoping to join the King at Oxford, but the Parliamentarians blocked their way near Bristol. The battle of Lansdowne, near Bath, was one of the great Royalist victories, but it cost the lives of 1400 men, among them Sir Bevill Grenville. Such was his standing, that both sides lamented his death and his body was conveyed, unmolested, from the battle field, to his home. He was 48, and was buried at Kilkhampton, with full honours.

He was indeed an excellent person, whose activity, interest and reputation were ye foundation of what had been done in Cornwall, and his temper and affections so publick, that no accident which happened could make any impression on him and his example kept others from taking anything ill, or at least seeming to do so. In a word, a brighter courage and a gentler disposition were never marryed together to mek ye most cheerfull and innocent conversation.

(From his epitaph in Kilkhampton church, erected 1714)

An account of the church by a visitor (Mrs Bray) in 1845 states that his helmet and gauntlets were on display. She mentions that the backs of the seats near the altar were 'composed of old carvings nailed together, and one long piece running along the top must either have been taken from the altar or come from Stowe – it was of oak and forms one of the most exquisitely bold and raised pieces of carving that I have ever seen. I could put my fingers in between and take hold of some of the stems and stalks of the flowers, and the wood is as hard as if but just cut.' Neither the helmet nor the carving are visible today.

Lady Grace died in 1647 'broken-hearted and sorrowful at the overthrow of the Royal cause in the West to which so much life and treasure had been sacrificed'. John Grenville, their eldest son, was appointed Governor of the Isles of Scilly in 1648, the last Royalist stronghold, where he proclaimed Charles II, King. Sir George Carteret was Governor of Jersey and between them they raised a small fleet of privateers to harry the English trade and carry on a kind of robber warfare – nothing new for the Grenville family. However, Parliamentary forces overcame the island strongholds in 1651, and about 1659 Sir John and his family returned to Stowe after a long absence; the war had taken a heavy toll on the family fortunes and they seem to have been short of money. But all this was to change with the Restoration, in which Sir John played such an important part.

Sir John was one of those charged with the task of communicating with Charles in exile in Brussels, and of beginning negotiations for his return.

> *'The King received Sir John with open arms, and there and then, 2ⁿᵈ April, signed a Warrant bestowing on him the place of Groom of the Stole and 1st Gentleman of the Bedchamber together with the dignity of an Earl of England. He also engaged to repay all the debts incurred in the service of Charles I'.*

The new king was not slow in rewarding the family that had been so prominent in his own reversal of fortune. Sir John was appointed Warden of the Stannaries, High Steward of the Duchy of Cornwall, Master of Dartmoor Forest. A few months later he was made Lord Lieutenant of Cornwall and his appointments as Groom of the Stole and first Gentleman of the Bedchamber confirmed. Bernard was similarly rewarded with the post of Gentleman of the Horse and of the Bedchamber. Three days before the Coronation the final honour was granted and Sir John became Baron Grenville of Kilkhampton and Bideford, Viscount Grenville of Lansdowne, and Earl of Bath. As was the custom of the time, lucrative agencies could be obtained; Grenville gained the agency to issue wine licences, and a lease for ten years of duties on the coinage of tin; this latter was later changed to £3,000 annually – awarded to him and his heirs, for ever.

The Grenville star was firmly in the ascendancy, and Lord Bath a favoured member of the inner court circle. Peace and prosperity seemed assured, and a wave of building swept the countryside. Many of Charles II's circle had spent long years on the continent and become familiar with the Renaissance style of architecture; the homes of their ancestors to which they returned must have seemed unbearably old-fashioned – low

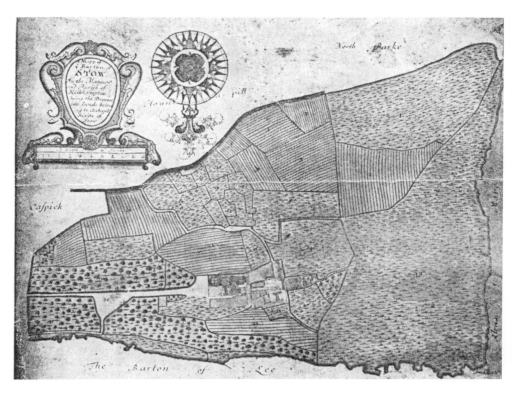

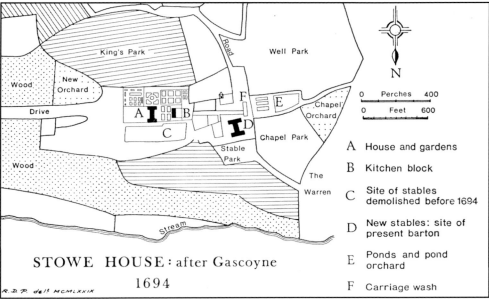

STOWE HOUSE: after Gascoyne
1694

A House and gardens

B Kitchen block

C Site of stables
   demolished before 1694

D New stables: site of
   present barton

E Ponds and pond
   orchard

F Carriage wash

R.D.P. del! MCMLXXIX

Joel Gascoyne's map, dated 1694   (CRO FS/2/80)

and rambling with small rooms and few windows, and a simple front porch as the main entrance. Grand houses were being built in the capital, and nearly all of the court favourites decided to rebuild or remodel their country houses. John Grenville, Earl of Bath, decided to demonstrate his new found status with a grand gesture – in 1679 he set about building a grand new mansion, on a new site slightly higher than the old house, which was pulled down, leaving the stable block. Two illustrations and some contemporary descriptions survive of 'by far the noblest house in the West of England' so that the magnificence of the new Stowe is not in doubt. Which is as well, because standing on the windswept site it is hard to imagine that such a house ever existed there. The most reliable evidence of Stowe and its surrounds is found in the survey commissioned in 1694 from Joel Gascoyne. Here is a contemporary account including the gardens and outbuildings – but not the site of the original house.

Edmund Prideaux of Prideaux Place, near Padstow, included two sketches in his 1716 tour, the only certain contemporary images. One of them admirably illustrates the dramatic impact of the house from the drive rising through the woods, and the other shows more of the house and its service wing and gardens.

Edmund Prideaux drawings, 1716
(Courtesy Peter Prideaux Brune)

The 1762 copy painting

Neither he, nor Gascoyne, show any building to the north of the house and drive, which features in the two paintings known to have existed of Stowe, both done some considerable time after the house was demolished.

The earlier painting was originally at Tonacombe, home of Dennys Waddon, agent to the estate, and was undated, a copy of which hangs there to this day. But in his letter book of 1762, after Stowe had been abandoned, Waddon wrote to Thomas Coombe of London 'the enclosed is a draught of Stowe House which I beg you will get copied

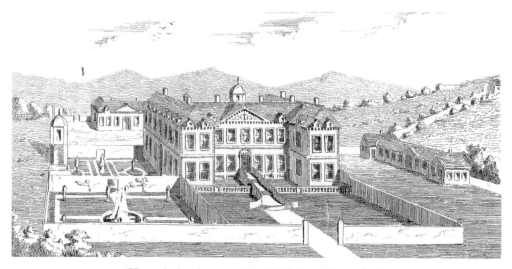

The early drawing owned by the Waddon Martyn family

by one of the best hands you can meet with.' This 'draught' was not a painting but a drawing, later in the possession of the Revd. William Waddon Martyn, (1832–1900) of Lifton and was reproduced in Roger Granville's *History of the Granvilles (1895)* and does show a range of outbuildings. It is possible that this drawing was the basis of the two later paintings, although it, too, was undated.

Stowe's heyday was very short-lived, for Lord Bath died in 1701, and thereafter the house was only occasionally occupied.

> *… large Square pile projecting 2 wings which are not longer than to contain one Window on a side, but they each have two in front, which added to the others make the whole number of Windows in the front to be twelve. Tis a Brick House.*

This was John Lovelace, writing in 1736, when he was touring the west country, and he makes no mention of the elaborate formal walled gardens that surrounded the house, except to describe them as 'in decay', nor of that very grand flight of steps leading to the front door. He thinks it worth mentioning that Stowe was built of brick, which was an unusual and expensive choice for the area. He does give descriptions of the interior;

> *Fret-work ceilings to some of the rooms elegantly performed, and very good carving in Wood to adorn the chimney-pieces of fruit, flowers, fowls, etc. The Chapel is wainscoted and fitted up with Cedar, the pavement of black and white marble. The grand staircase is adorned on the three broadsides with Views of this house, etc. Plymouth and Biddiford.*

Loveday also mentions the bed in which Charles II died, which came to Lord Bath as Groom of the Stole. And, almost as a throw-away line, 'The house is very dark because the Panes of Glass are remarkably small.'

This gives a tantalising insight into a house already in decay. What happened to those paintings on the staircase? They would be of huge significance if they came to light; Stowe because it would give a rounder picture, Bideford because it would have depicted it in the days when the Grenville's had a townhouse on the quay, and Plymouth because Lord Bath as Governor in 1666 built the Citadel, which still dominates the city and the harbour, and where in 1688 he welcomed William of Orange. The Fitch brothers, John and Thomas, London master builders, were employed both at the Citadel and at Stowe and were responsible for the brickwork at Kingston Lacey, another Renaissance house designed by Roger Pratt.

Dr. Borlase, writing three years later, viewed 'the remains of Stow' from the churchyard. He neatly sums up the problems of such a house in such a situation;

> *But it was too large for a situation so distant from London & so bleak & naked in itself (exposed as it is to the North Sea without the shelter or beauty of one tree) that people who wanted the bias of birth, & nature, & family regard could want no excuse for not living in it.*

He lists the costs of maintaining such a property – the mason, the carpenter, the hellier, the painter – who 'took their money and neglected the house,' so that it 'suffered in every part' and the decision was made to take it down 'and an Undertaker, as I am informed purchased all the materials as they stood for about £2000.'

The fate of Stowe was bound up with that of the family. With the death of the lst Earl in 1701, aged 73, the estates passed to his eldest son and the tragic end began. Whether it was accidental or not has been disputed, but the 2nd earl died when his pistol went off as he was polishing it, prior to journeying down to Kilkhampton for his father's funeral. The two were buried together, leaving the 3rd earl, a boy of nine, to inherit. William was the only child and the Stowe of his father's day must have seemed a distant memory. The first earl had a large family – five sons and eleven daughters, though not all survived childhood – so that the house would have been full of life and laughter, with the bustle of servants and the coming and going of visitors. How gloomy the vast rooms must have seemed to a small boy of nine.

He was brought up by his maternal grandmother, and showed early promise of becoming a true Grenville, engaging in campaigns in Flanders, and becoming Lord Lieutenant of Cornwall in 1711, on which occasion his cousin George wrote to him;

> *You are placed at the head of a body of gentry entirely disposed in affection to you and your family. You are born possessed of all those amiable qualities which cannot fail of fixing their hearts. You have no example to follow but to tread in the steps of your ancestors. Tis all that is hoped or desired from you. You are upon an uncommon foundation in that part of the world, your ancestors for at least 500 years never made any alliance, male or female but of the Western counties. Thus there is hardly a gentleman either in Cornwall or Devon but has some of your blood, or you some of theirs….From the Conquest to the Restoration your Ancestors constantly resided amongst their country men, except when public service called upon them to sacrifice their lives for it. Stowe in my grandfather's time till the Civil Wars broke out was a kind of academy for all the young men of family in the county."*

Within eight months of this letter the young earl died of small pox, aged 19 and unmarried. And with him died the senior branch, his father's two brothers both having died without issue.

The possession of the Grenville estates was disputed between a cousin, George, Lord Lansdowne, (d. 1735), who moved into Stowe, and the two surviving daughters of the first earl, Lady Jane Leveson Gower and Lady Grace Carteret. After a lengthy lawsuit, and a large sum paid to the cousin, the two sisters were successful, Lady Jane taking the Devon lands, and Lady Grace the Cornish, including Stowe. Both were already possessed of large estates and it is easy to understand how large, remote, neglected Stowe would have been of no interest to them.

It is fascinating to speculate about the end of the great house of Stowe – it is known where whole rooms ended up, and some of the principal features. A century later would have seen a grand demolition sale, well advertised, with a catalogue detailing the numerous lots, from the slates on the roof to the flagstone flooring. But all that has come down to us is the one remark that it had been bought for £2,000 and was in course of being pulled to pieces. Was the purchaser a local builder? Did he advertise in the west country newspapers? There can be little doubt that building material

187

from Stowe ended up in many of the farms and cottages within quite a wide radius of Kilkhampton. One account, kept by Dennys Waddon of nearby Tonacombe, who acted as agent to the Grenvilles, states that 36 feet of coping stone and 24 seams of slate flooring at 6d per foot went to the parish church in 1739; the wall around the churchyard is indeed topped by good quality coping stone, and the granite in the lych gate is also suggestive. The church accounts also state that a year later they bought 80 foot of stone, 550 bricks, timber and 10 foot of steps. Waddon also mentions an undated plan showing bricks sold at Stowe arranged in 57 heaps – 450,000 bricks. This could be contemporary with records of 1789 when lead piping and sheeting were sent to Bristol; over 1,000 feet of lead piping were recorded on site.

Because of the way in which it was sold, more survives of Stowe than is the case of many lost houses. As nothing else could do, an idea is gained of the sheer opulence and craftsmanship that characterised this extraordinary house from these remains. Lord Bath's chapel travelled the furthest to the grand house in Buckinghamshire, also called Stowe, which was being built in the 1740s by Viscount Cobham, who was very distantly connected to the Grenvilles. Unfortunately, it did not survive in its entirety when the estate was sold up in the 1920s, but some of it was built into the new chapel in 1929. The original chapel rose through two stories and contained much of Michael Chuke's ornate panelling, the octagonal pulpit dated 1707, and an elaborate reredos reaching almost the full height, with Corinthian columns flanking the altar above which was

The chapel, reconstructed at Stowe in Buckinghamshire (J. Mudd, Stowe School Photographic Archive)

a richly carved Royal coat of arms. Photographs show an ornately carved room, with swags of fruit and flowers, and cherubims.

Cherubim and flowers are also to be found in the great staircase at Cross, a property outside the nearby town of Torrington, which was being greatly extended and improved in 1740. As well as the staircase, Henry Stevens, the owner, incorporated an entire panelled room, with ornate swags above the fireplace, and six-panelled doors

Cross – the staircase – once painted white – and hall
(Courtesy Mrs R. Cotton)

Detail showing a female putti doing a handstand
(Courtesy Mrs R. Cotton)

Detail showing the 3D effect from the hall side
(Courtesy Mrs R. Cotton)

The panelled room before its sale   (Courtesy Mrs. R. Cotton)

and moulded panels which are found in the other examples of rooms from Stowe. This room, in its entirety, was sold in the 1920s and shipped to America.

A smaller room, containing much carved panelling, remains at Cross. The tall window with its elegant pilasters which lights the staircase is also said to have come from Stowe. Here, at Cross, sufficient remains to demonstrate the quality of craftsmanship employed by the Earl of Bath. He had brought Stephen Chuke, a notable carver, down from London, who settled in Kilkhampton. Stephen sent his son, Michael, to be apprenticed to Grinling Gibbons, and between them the Chukes were responsible for the high quality of workmanship. Father and son were buried in Kilkhampton church.

Another complete room is to be found a few miles down the coast from Stowe, at Prideaux Place, above Padstow. The Prideaux were relations of the Grenvilles and Edmund Prideaux must have been all to aware of the deteriorating condition of the grand house he had sketched only a few years after the earl's death. He was engaged in extending his home, and to acquire one of the sumptuous rooms would have been too good an opportunity to miss. He would have known what the dining room looked like in situ – did it fit exactly or did it have to be altered, perhaps reduced in height? It is a very fine room with a wealth of ornate carving, and two handsome oak doors, with painted overdoor panels.

If guests at Prideaux Place were impressed by all this, what must have been the impression on visitors to Stowe itself, where all the main rooms would have been similarly decorated?

The foresight of the mayor and corporation of South Molton was to ensure that a large quantity of the old house survives in this north Devon market town. They sent one of their members to Stowe, and Joshua Bawden duly returned triumphant in early

August, having acquired a large amount of building materials and internal fittings. The accounts kept give a clear picture of how such transactions were carried out. Not only are the prices paid noted, but payments made for the carriage, first by oxen and horses to the little port of Bude, for the customs permit, to the Captain for shipping the goods up the coast to Barnstaple, and to the sailors for ale. The total for the purchase and transportation was £171 8s 3d, and the new Town Hall when complete, cost just over £1,000. Upstairs, the mayor's parlour and the council chamber survive – both largely fitted with items from Stowe – including the painting of the 'Triumph of King Charles II – £7 7s 0d'. Purchased complete was a 'Lady's Fine Bedchamber – £35 0s 0d, 3 architraves with pediments for doors and 27 yards of wainscotting in the lobby – £2 2s 0d, and ye casing and ornament for 3 windows'. Sash windows, window shutters, 172 rustic quoins, 4 Corinthian columns and pilasters and 2 eight-panel doors all made the journey from Stowe to South Molton.

The former Doctor's house in South Street, Molton House, also contains items from Stowe, perhaps purchased at the same time.

In 1988 the National Trust purchased the farmlands and site of Stowe. For many years, Stowe Barton was just another of the Trust's tenanted farms, and curious walkers climbing up from the woodland would have no clue of the origins of the mysterious humps and bumps the footpath passed through. Latterly more interest has been taken and leaflets and a signboard have appeared.

The site of Stowe

(Image used with permission of the Cornwall & Scilly Environment Record © Cornwall Council 2020)

Key in this was the survey carried out in 1993 for the Royal Commission on the Historical Monuments of England by W.R. Wilson-North. With the help of aerial photographs and excavations, the layout of the house and gardens was established. Prior to this, the only evidence was the Gascoyne map of 1694. Sufficient evidence was uncovered for the layout to be established, and although grass has once again grown over, it may be that in the future the foundations could be exposed and the site properly interpreted.

Fronting the parish road is a high wall, part brick, part stone which screens the farmyard and buildings. On the higher side is what is described as a 'carriage-wash' fed by a spring. On the seaward side of the lane is a series of ponds and gardens. Excavations here suggest that these belonged to the earlier house, but subsequent farming and gardening operations have obliterated much, including evidence of the early chapel recorded in the fifteenth century. The survey does state that the old house was here, to the west of the 1670s house, and was demolished making way for an access drive, but leaving the original stables.

A farmhouse had been created in the 1670s service block, which survived demolition, and memories of the grand house faded. By 1787 what was left was described as ruinous and was demolished. A contract was signed in March, 1787 to 'make a farmhouse out of part of the stables and put the rest into good repair for barns, stables and outhouses for Stowe Barton'. And this is what remains on site today. They are a fine group of buildings, seemingly much more at home in their surroundings than ever the 'great house of Stowe' could have been.

Sources

The History of the Granville Family Roger Granville MA, 1895

Stowe; the country house and garden of the Grenville Family; A survey by the RCHME 1993

Historical Survey of the County of Cornwall, C S Gilbert, 1820

The Great House of Stowe; Journal of the Royal Institution of Cornwall, Michael Trinick, 1979

The Granvilles and The Grenvilles, Their Portraits and Their Story , Richard Granville 2018